THE HIGH SCHOOL HANDBOOK

Junior and Senior High School at Home

by Mary Schofield

Published by

Christian Home Educators Press
P.O. Box 2009
Norwalk, California 90651-2009
800/564-CHEA

All Scripture quotations are from the King James Version of the Bible, unless otherwise noted.

Copyright 1989, 1990, 1992, 1994, 1997, 2004

Christian Home Educators Press

First Edition	—	1989
Second Edition	—	1990
Third Edition	—	1992
Fourth Edition	—	1994
Fifth Edition	—	1996
Sixth Edition	—	1997
Seventh Edition	—	2004

ISBN 0-9660937-7-1

Thank you to the many homeschoolers who have helped with the writing of this book through the sharing of their insights and tips, commenting and suggesting additions to the previous editions, and listening to workshops as the newer material was developed.

Thank you also to Philip and Evella Troutt for their years of encouragement and for their dedication to the Christian homeschooling community.

Thank you especially to Paul, Scott and Steven, who have borne the burden of this work through their patience during the writing process.

Wherefore seeing we also are compassed about with so great a cloud of witnesses, let us lay aside every weight, and the sin which doth so easily beset us, and let us run with patience the race that is set before us, looking unto Jesus the author and finisher of our faith.

Hebrews 12:1-2

❖ Table of Contents

❖ 3 Teaching Senior High 29

❖ 4 Setting Requirements & Planning Your Year 43

❖ 5 Course Descriptions 65

❖ 6 Designing Courses 91

❖ 9 Transcripts 161

❖ 10 Resources 171

❖ 11 After High School 185

❖ Special California Supplement 203

❖ Preface to the 2004 Edition

Homeschooling has, of course, grown in leaps and bounds during the past few years. It has been especially interesting to watch the growth of *ways* to homeschool. Besides the styles, like unit studies, classical education, living books, or Principle Approach, there are so many options used for individual subjects: co-op classes, independent study, family lessons, and work-study programs, all of which may be formal or low-key.

When I first wrote The High School Handbook, my husband and I had just finished homeschooling our niece, Robin, who had lived with us for a year. Robin moved in with our family right after Christmas break during her junior year of high school. While living with us, she completed 11th grade, including retaking three courses she had failed in public high school. She worked straight through the summer and graduated the following Christmas, several months ahead of schedule.

With Robin, we followed what I would call a "school at home" approach, laying out courses much like they would be in any institutional school, with the exception of being able to individualize materials and content to fit Robin's needs. We tried to keep pace with the public school, never knowing if she would be returning there. With our own boys, we have always followed a more "homeschool" approach, also individualizing materials and contents, but not following the same scope or structure of institutional school courses.

The original 1989 edition of The High School Handbook reflected our experience and research at the time. Most courses were laid out a lot like those in a typical public high school, records were developed to follow the public school model, and each course taught was in a neat semester-long package, with a clear beginning and ending date. We chose six to eight individual courses to be taken each semester.

With our own children, we laid out courses quite differently, overlapping school years, combining subjects and specializing in a few non-traditional areas according to their gifts and interests. We would begin a new study when we finished an old one, or when an opportunity or interest came up and we had the time to take advantage of it. Some studies took just a couple of months; others took several years. We still kept our records in a way that looks professional and would be easily understood by others, but we were not so concerned with making it look like our children went to an institutional school.

At this writing, we are finished with homeschooling. Our older son, Scott, completed his high school education at home, including taking many college level courses, and passing CLEP and AP exams. He continued his education by taking a few courses at several local colleges and universities, while also working through a distance-education program, and earned his Masters of Business Administration from Edinburgh Business School, Heriot-Watt University. Scott is now married and a father of two.

Our younger son, Steven, also completed his high school education at home. He took a class or two at the local community college "just to get his feet wet" during 12th grade, then enrolled full-time after high school graduation. He obtained his AA in criminal justice and now works as a sheriff's deputy.

I consider my kids to be "homeschool success stories" not so much because they graduated and went on to do well in post-secondary education and now have good jobs, but because they turned out to be great people. This was not due to homeschooling, it was due to God's grace. But homeschooling gave us the opportunity to focus on God and His grace in a way that we could not have done if they attended school outside the home. Homeschooling allowed us to develop their individual gifts and talents, while focusing on each one's spiritual growth and attempting above all to follow God's unique plans for each of them, rather than following a standardized program designed for millions of students.

As homeschooling has grown, so have the options for those who are teaching their teens at home. When we began, not much was available for homeschooling teens. Now there are almost too many options, making it hard to choose and pressuring parents to do too much. This book addresses many options for homeschooling teens, but the underlying goal remains unchanged. It is my hope to encourage you, as both parents and teens reading this book, to seek God's will and direction for your education plan. He does have a plan, a special one, just for you. Rest in that knowledge, take time to seek His guidance and to listen, and He will provide the inspiration you need.

Mary Schofield
February 2004

❖ Legalities

Homeschooling, though becoming more and more popular, is not without its critics and controversy. I am personally supportive of all parents' God-given authority over their children and believe that the Constitution guarantees the right of parents to bring up their children according to their own beliefs. However, I am not an attorney. The information offered in this manual is given as a practical aid in teaching teenagers at home. It is not, nor is it intended to be, legal advice.

I strongly recommend membership in the Home School Legal Defense Association. HSLDA has full-time attorneys on staff who specialize in homeschooling. If you are ever in a position to need legal advice about your homeschool situation, membership will be invaluable. Even if you never personally need the legal representation provided by HSLDA to its member families, the annual membership fee is one of the best investments you can make in the future of education in America. More information about HSLDA and membership applications are available from

Home School Legal Defense Association, P.O. Box 3000, Purcellville, VA 20134.
(540) 338-8610, online: www.hslda.org.

In The High School Handbook, I assume the reader is familiar with basic information about what is needed to set up your homeschool to comply with your state's education laws. Whether your state allows you to operate as a private school, or whether it has a separate homeschool law, you will need to know what records, if any, are required of you as the parent/teachers, principals, or administrators of your homeschool programs. If you are new to homeschooling or if you have questions about your state's education laws, contact HSLDA to request information about the laws covering your state. Also contact your statewide homeschool association to request any materials they have prepared to help you start your homeschool legally.

I have found that most state departments of education are knowledgeable about *public* schools, but not about homeschooling. Seldom will you be able to get specialized information from a pro-homeschooling viewpoint through a public school agency. So start with HSLDA and your state homeschool association, which you can find by asking HSLDA for a referral.

❖ 1 Planning to Teach

There are some parts to planning your educational program that are the same for both junior and senior high. The graduation requirements for junior high will be different, of course, than the requirements for high school graduation, but the way in which those requirements are set is the same. Success in both junior high and high school will depend on many of the same factors, for example, the student's attitude, his readiness to learn, how well your course of study fits your ultimate goals, and how well your requirements and assignments are communicated.

The scope of this book is to help you set requirements and design studies and courses for your own school that meet the goals of your family. It would do no good for me to simply show you all my family's requirements and course outlines if you had no interest in studying the same things, or if your students are not at the same level of learning in each subject area as mine are. Your requirements will be different from mine because your family is different.

Occasionally a parent will say to me, "Can't I just go out and buy a pre-packaged program for each grade level and follow that without all this other planning?" To some degree, you could do that. However, even with the pre-packaged programs, you have to make some decisions at high school level about what to study. Not only will you need to decide which subjects to study, you will also need to decide which assignments and projects to use within each course.

You can't avoid doing *some* planning for junior high, and even more for high school. Choosing a pre-packaged program doesn't mean that no planning has been done; it simply means that you are letting the designer of that program do your planning for you. That may be fine if you like his plan, but even this will require you to do some thinking and assessing.

The easiest, most successful, and most fun way to make a decision about your school program is first to decide what *you* are looking for, and then find or design a program that fits *your* needs. Choosing a pre-packaged program is usually hit and miss. Some subjects work out fine; others turn out to be a waste of time.

The wisdom of the prudent is to understand his way. Proverbs 14:8

Some people become nervous about developing a plan for junior or senior high school, feeling that they aren't "experts" and might make mistakes that will seriously mar their children's future. There is no need for fear. There are plenty of high school plans adopted by "experts" that you can use as a guide. Plus, you have access to the most expert "expert" there is.

Seek the Lord and His strength: seek His face evermore.
Remember His marvelous works that He hath done. Psalm 105:4-5

Taking time to pray over your school plans is the single most valuable aid to setting up your program. The Lord promises that if we ask for His direction, He will provide. Can we honestly think that if we turn to Him, He will lead us wrong?

Ask and ye shall receive, that your joy may be full. John 16:24

If we trust the Lord to guide us, He will fill in any gaps that would cause crucial mistakes. It is naive to think there will be no gaps at all in your children's education, whether they attend your private homeschool, a campus-based private school, a public school, or even if you hire an expensive master tutor to move into your home and teach your children full time. Who among all the adults you know learned everything he ever needed to know in high school? Can it even be possible for us to ever learn all we need to know?

For we know in part, and we prophesy in part. But when that which is perfect is come,
then that which is in part shall be done away. I Corinthians 13:9-10

Think for a moment about what you do when you realize you need to know something that you haven't learned. For example, if you get a new alarm clock and don't know how to set it, or if you want to bake a new type of cake, or if you want to use a brand new type of building material, what do you do? Obviously, you look it up!

Rather than trying to teach our children everything they might ever be required to know, we need to consider that during their years under our authority, we should concentrate on covering the basic knowledge that will carry them through life, fostering a love for learning and teaching the basic tools of learning. We must trust the Lord to guide us as we make our plans, and trust that He will alter our courses if necessary.

A man's heart deviseth his way: but the Lord directeth his steps. Proverbs 16:9

So we begin by establishing educational goals that tell what is included in the basic foundational knowledge we want to cover. If you have not set educational goals for your family, this may seem like a lot of preliminary work. However, by not jumping ahead to the fun stuff you will save hours of time and many future arguments or misunderstandings. If you do nothing else with this book, I hope you will use it to help you set clear educational goals for your family.

Where there is no vision, the people perish. Proverbs 29:18

❖ Emergency Quick Start to Homeschooling Teens

If you have just begun homeschooling by pulling your child out of another school during the school year, you may feel like you don't have the time to plan carefully and set goals before you get started. In order to "buy time" for setting up your program or ordering materials, the following ideas for study can be followed as an emergency quick start. These ideas can supply a few days to a few weeks of study, giving the family time to establish their longer-term educational plan.

Each of these short-term studies may then be included in the full-length courses when they are set up later, so that what your student is doing now will count for school credit. How to include this type of individual unit of study is covered in Chapter 6: Designing Courses.

Bible:

- Choose a book of the Bible for the student to read.

- Have the student research "education" by underlining the main words in the <u>Webster's 1828 Dictionary</u> definition on page four, then looking up each of those words in a dictionary and writing a brief definition. Then have him look up the key words in a Concordance and do a word study from the Scripture, writing down the verses which shed light on God's view of education. (If your student is struggling with the idea of "keeping up" with public school, this is an excellent way to begin to "enlighten his understanding.")

- Have the student research the typical school subjects from the Bible in the same way described in the suggestion to research "education."

- Have the student research one or more character traits.

English:

- Assign a literary classic from the list on pages 179-180.

- Have the student write a letter each day to a relative or friend who would enjoy hearing from him.

Math:

- Have the student balance your checkbook, following the instructions on the back of the statement.

- Have the student research what it would cost to rent an apartment in your area. Using the newspaper, your household bills, or calling local utilities, have him create an itemized budget that includes rent, electricity, water, natural gas or propane (if used in your area), telephone, groceries, etc. Include start up costs like installation, and a monthly budget.

These basic subjects should be enough to give you a start. If you need to add a few other subjects to give you a little more time to get set up, the following ideas can be used:

- Select any area of interest and take a trip to the library to select several books or articles related to that subject. Have the student research, then write his findings. (subject will vary)

- Set an appointment with your local librarian to show how to use all the resources the library has available. (English or Study Skills)

- Make a menu plan for dinners for one or two weeks for your family. Have the student cook all the dinners. (Home Economics)

- Have the student prepare a shopping list and budget to follow for the cooking suggestion above. (Mathematics and Home Economics)

- Have the student repair or complete one of those home projects you haven't had time to do. (Home Economics or Vocational Skills)

❖ Setting Educational Goals

Begin to set your family's goals by defining what you think education ought to be, in other words, your philosophy of education. Consider the following definition of education, taken from the <u>American Dictionary of the English Language</u>, 1828 edition by Noah Webster, republished by Foundation for American Christian Education (address on page 171):

Education:

The bringing up, as of a child; instruction; formulation of manners. Education comprehends all that series of instruction and discipline which is intended to 1) enlighten the understanding, 2) correct the temper, and 3) form the manners and habits of youth, and 4) fit them for usefulness in their future stations.

To give children a good education in manners, arts and science, is important; to give them a religious education is indispensable; and an immense responsibility rests on parents and guardians who neglect these duties.

Take a couple of minutes to jot down the things you want to accomplish through homeschooling. They don't have to be neat and tidy at this point, just begin to put down on paper your ideas related to what kind of education you want to give your children. Of course, we all desire a "good" education, but what does that mean?

The following questions will help you get started:

- If my child grows up and is considered "well educated," what does that mean?

- Why am I homeschooling?

- What values do I desire my children to hold when they are grown?

- What kind of lifestyle would I like to see my children follow?

By answering these questions, you can see that you are heading quite a different direction than that taken by today's public school system. This is not to put down public schools, it's just that current laws actually prohibit them from teaching the very things which are most important to be taught! Certainly there are public school teachers who view their jobs as mission fields, and they are right. But they cannot teach as openly about the ways of the Lord as you can at home. Don't you want to take advantage of the freedom you have as a non-taxpayer-funded school to teach about Christ openly?

Especially for those of us who were, ourselves, educated in a school which did not teach the ways of the Lord, it will be vital to come to an understanding of what He desires in our schools. We may think we know this already, and probably we have some clear ideas about what kinds of education displease God, but when it comes to something as important as training up the children He has given into our care for a short while, we had better make sure we are following the right path.

Begin with the definition of education from the <u>Webster's 1828 Dictionary</u>, given on page four. Take time to read it carefully. Look up the main words of the definition in a dictionary to fully grasp the deeper meaning, and look up some of the main words in a concordance to find out what the Word says about teaching children. This task could be as lengthy or short as you make it.

If you are really getting interested in this, realizing that your own knowledge needs some enlightenment, order some of the materials on "The Principle Approach" from Foundation for American Christian Education (FACE), P.O. Box 27035, San Francisco, California, 94127. The Principle Approach will show you how to research subjects to find the relevant principles that govern them from God's Word. The "4-R"[1] process taught through the Principle Approach is invaluable as a learning tool, for both you and your students.

Spend some time looking in your concordance to find references to the key words from the Webster's definition, then look up some of the verses, pray and meditate. Just one afternoon spent in this way before you charge in will change the whole outlook of your program. (Isn't this what you are trying to teach your children—to gather all the needed facts and get wise counsel before making decisions that will affect the rest of their lives?)

Once you have finished the basic research, write down your thoughts and conclusions to keep in your school notebook. As this list grows and develops, it will become your own family's philosophy of education and your general goals of education.

You will notice that on your list of ideas about education, the items can be divided into two categories: those which refer to what education *is*, and those which describe what to *do* during the educational process.

Consider the items on your list which refer to what education is or which define general principles of education. These items are part of your "philosophy of education." Probably your philosophy will become more complete through the years. We learn and grow as we study and gain experience. Your written philosophy of education will be a valuable tool when you begin purchasing books and other materials for your student. Most Christian textbook publishers have their philosophy of education available, either in their catalogs, or by request. Comparing your own philosophy with that of a particular publisher will help you decide if their materials will be suitable in your home.

The items you have written which refer more to the end-product of education, or what you want to *do* during the educational process, will become part of your "educational goals." They set the path for each year of study and help you to focus on what is important. If you have goals written out, it will be much easier to plan each year according to where your student is in his progress toward each goal you have set.

As a sample, our family's "Philosophy of Education" and "General Goals" are on the following pages. Yours will be different; you may disagree with some of our goals, or you may want to include other items. Each family's program will necessarily be different from any other family's. After all, God has created a special and unique family by combining the special people who make up your family. He has a unique plan for each of you. How exciting it will be to begin to understand that plan and to follow it!

But seek ye first the kingdom of God, and his righteousness;
and all these things shall be added unto you. Matthew 6:33

---

[1] It isn't the scope of this book to present the Principle Approach. But, briefly, the "4-Rs" are: Research, Reason, Relate, and Record. *Research* a topic in the dictionary, the Bible, and other reference books, *Reason* through the information to find the underlying principles, *Relate* your topic and researched information to your own life, and *Record* your findings. This four-step process allows a student to uncover the principles of a subject, giving him a depth of understanding and knowledge that he will possess throughout his life. The Foundation for American Christian Education (address above) has a catalog of books that introduce and teach the Principle Approach.

Schofield Family
Philosophy of Education

- As a Christian family, our philosophy of education is based on Christian principles expressed in the Bible.

  All scripture is given by inspiration of God, and is profitable for doctrine, for reproof, for correction, for instruction in righteousness: That the man of God may be perfect, throughly furnished unto all good works. 2 Timothy 3:16-17

  Also see: Matthew 6:24-25; Psalm 119:1-5; Psalm 18:30-32; Matthew 6:33; Matthew 12:33; John 5:24; 2 Timothy 3:15

- The Bible, being the true and inerrant Word of the Almighty God, is the final authority in all areas of life and education.

  Every word of God is pure: He is a shield unto them that put their trust in him. Proverbs 30:5

  Also see: Proverbs 13:13; Luke 21:33; 1 John 4:1-3

- Any education based on principles opposed to those Christian principles set forth in the Word of God is an education which is against God.

  Either make the tree good, and his fruit good; or else make the tree corrupt, and his fruit corrupt: for the tree is known by his fruit. Matthew 12:33

  Also see: Psalm 119:11; Matthew 12:30; 2 Corinthians 13:8

- To be considered well-educated and thus suitable for service to God and country, a student must learn to deal with any situation or idea presented to him. He must be prepared to assess each idea or problem according to Biblical standards to determine a proper response or course of action. He must then possess the courage and wisdom to act upon his convictions. Without this strength of Christian character, a man may never be considered truly educated.

  Holding fast the faithful word as he hath been taught, that he may be able by sound doctrine both to exhort and to convince the gainsayers. Titus 1:9

  Also see: 1 Peter 3:15; Galatians 5:25; Acts 4:20; 2 Timothy 2:15

- God has given parents the responsibility of raising children. Parents are held accountable to God for the education of their children.

  And these words, which I command thee this day, shall be in thine heart: And thou shalt teach them diligently unto thy children, and shalt talk of them when thou sittest in thine house, and when thou walkest by the way, and when thou liest down, and when thou risest up. Deuteronomy 6:6-7

  Also see: Psalm 127:3-4; Proverbs 22:6; Proverbs 29:17; Titus 1:6; 1 Timothy 3:12

Schofield Family
General Goals of Education

- To raise Godly adults

  - Knowing Christ as Savior and Lord of their lives (John 3:16,17; 1 Corinthians 3:11; 2 Timothy 3:14,15; 1 John 5:1-5)

  - Knowing how to reason Biblically (1 Peter 3:15; Acts 17:2; Acts 24:25; 1 Thessalonians 5:21)

  - Possessing those qualities which identify a Christian character (Romans 8:2; 1 Corinthians 13; Galatians 5:22,23; Ephesians 4:32)

  - Able to handle the responsibilities that God gives: family, occupation, ministry, etc. (Ephesians 5:20,21,33; Colossians 3:23; Matthew 25)

- To set a standard in our homeschool where the children are not exposed to ungodliness masquerading as good

  - Our children should be trained by us, the parents, not by their peers or by strangers (Proverbs 13:20; Proverbs 19:27; Proverbs 20:11; Deuteronomy 6:6-9)

  - Ungodliness should be unmasked; God's will should be sought in all matters — justice, righteousness, and truth are not relative; they are constant (Proverbs 14:12; 1 Peter 5:8; 1 Kings 3:9; Ezekiel 44:23; Psalm 25:4,5)

- To work at individual levels and abilities, recognizing that God has given each of us special gifts, talents, and personalities

  - God made each of us a unique individual (Psalm 100:3; Psalm 119:73; Psalm 139:14; 1 Corinthians 12)

  - God would have us learn at the level we are at (1 Corinthians 13:11; Isaiah 28:9,10; Hebrews 5:14)

- To have a lifestyle that supports families as a God-designed unit

  - God created the family and sanctioned the establishment of families (Genesis 2:18,24; 1 Timothy 5:8; Ephesians 3:14-15; Hebrews 13:4; 1 Timothy 5:14)

  - A man is responsible first to God, then to his family and home, then to fellow Christians, then to the rest of mankind, in that order (1 Timothy 3:4-5; 1 Timothy 5:4; Titus 2:4; Galatians 6:10)

- To let our "light shine" so that all (our children, relatives, neighbors, etc.) can see the love of Jesus in our home

  - To treat others according to the "golden rule" (Matthew 7:12; 1 John 4:7-8; Mark 12:30-31)

  - To let others know about Jesus (Matthew 5:13-16; Matthew 28:19)

- To teach our children that a particular end does not justify the means by which we arrive at that end (process is more important than product)

  (Psalm 119:9; John 14:6; 2 Corinthians 13:8; 1 John 2:6; 1 John 1:6)

❖ Required Areas of Study

The laws in each state vary regarding requirements of subjects to be taught or numbers of courses in each subject area for homeschools. In most states, there may be general subject requirements, for example, English, math, science, etc., but there may be no laws telling *how much* English, math, science, etc. Before finalizing your high school graduation requirements, check with the Home School Legal Defense Association or your state's homeschool association to verify that you have not overlooked any specific requirements.

The following chart is adapted from <u>Homeschooling in the United States: A Statutory Analysis</u> by Christopher Klicka, and shows general subject requirements for each state. This information is not comprehensive; it is intended only for general guidance. For specific, up-to-date information, you should contact your state's homeschool association or the Home School Legal Defense Association.

✔ = state requirement is listed simply as the general subject shown at the top of the column.
If more specific wording is used in the state requirement, that wording is shown.
✧ = standardized testing required during junior or senior high.

	English	Math	Social Studies	Science	Physical Education	Foreign Language	Health	Other
Alabama	English, reading, spelling, writing	arithmetic	geography, U.S. history, state history	✔	✔		✔	
Alaska ✧	English, grammar, reading, spelling	✔						comparable to subjects offered in public schools
Arizona ✧	reading, grammar	✔	✔	✔				
Arkansas ✧	reading, language arts	✔	✔	✔				
California	✔	✔	✔	✔	✔	✔		fine arts, applied arts, vocational-technical ed, driver ed, parenting skills
Colorado ✧	reading, writing, speaking, literature	✔	U.S. Constitution, history, civics	✔				
Connecticut	English, reading, writing, spelling, grammar	arithmetic	geography, U.S. history & civics, including town, state, federal govt.					
Delaware								regular & thorough instruction

	English	Math	Social Studies	Science	Physical Education	Foreign Language	Health	Other
District of Columbia								substantially equivalent subjects
Florida	✔	✔	history, govt., U.S. Constitution	✔	✔			fine arts
Georgia ✧	reading, language arts	✔	✔	✔				
Hawaii ✧	✔*	✔*	✔*	✔*	✔*		✔*	guidance* * = "may" be included
Idaho								comparable to public schools
Illinois	language arts	✔	✔	biological & physical science	✔		✔	fine arts, honesty, justice, kindness, moral courage
Indiana	reading, writing	computa-tion skills	✔	✔	✔		health & safety	fine arts, practical arts
Iowa	reading, writing, grammar, spelling	arithmetic	geography, U.S. history, state history, government					
Kansas	reading, spelling, grammar, writing, composition	arithmetic	U.S. history, state history, govt., citizenship				health & hygiene	
Kentucky	reading, writing, spelling	✔						library research
Louisiana			Declaration of Independence & Federalist Papers					equal to public schools
Maine	reading, writing, spelling, grammar	✔	U.S. & state history & constitutions, citizenship	✔	✔		health, hygiene& safety	library instruction, music, art, drama
Maryland	✔	✔	✔	✔	✔		✔	art, music

	English	Math	Social Studies	Science	Physical Education	Foreign Language	Health	Other
Massachusetts	spelling, reading, writing, English, grammar	arithmetic	U.S. history & Constitution, geography, citizenship		✔		health, including CPR	drawing, music, good behavior
Michigan	reading, writing, literature, spelling, grammar	✔	history, civics	✔				comparable to public schools
Minnesota ✧	reading, writing, literature	✔	history, geography, government	✔	✔		✔	
Mississippi								none listed
Missouri	reading, language arts	✔	✔	✔				
Montana								same basic skills as public schools
Nebraska	language arts	✔	✔	✔			✔	
Nevada ✧			include U.S. & state constitutions					equivalent to public schools -- varies by district
New Hampshire	reading, writing, spelling, language	✔	history, govt., U.S. & state constitutions	✔			✔	appreciation of art & music
New Jersey			U.S. & state history, geography, civics					humanity -- equivalent to public schools
New Mexico ✧	reading, language arts	✔	✔	✔				
New York ✧	✔	✔	citizenship, patriotism, U.S. history, geography, govt., economics	✔	✔		health, fire safety, substance abuse, traffic safety	art or music, electives, (practical arts & library skills for grades 7-8)
North Carolina ✧	English grammar, reading, spelling	✔	citizenship, U.S. & state govt., free enterprise system				health, fire prevention, dangers of drugs	

	English	Math	Social Studies	Science	Physical Education	Foreign Language	Health	Other
North Dakota ✧	✔	✔	✔	✔		✔	✔	combination of business, economics, foreign language, industrial arts, or vocational ed
Ohio	language arts	✔	geography, U.S. & state history, govt.		✔		health, first aid	
Oklahoma	reading, writing	✔	citizenship, U.S. Constitution	✔	✔		health, safety	conservation
Oregon ✧			U.S. history & Constitution					courses usually taught in public schools
Pennsylvania ✧	English, reading, writing, spelling	✔	U.S. & state history, civics, geography	✔			health, safety	music, art, humane treatment of animals
Rhode Island	English, reading, writing	arithmetic	geography, U.S. & state history & constitutions, govt.		✔		✔	
South Carolina ✧	reading, writing, composition, literature	✔	✔	✔				
South Dakota ✧	mastery of English language, language arts	✔	U.S. & state constitutions, patriotism, free enterprise system					moral instruction
Tennessee ✧	spelling, reading, writing, grammar	arithmetic	geography; U.S. & state history, govt. & constitutions; free enterprise system		✔		hygiene & sanitation	vocal music, drawing, driver education
Texas	reading, spelling, grammar	✔	citizenship					
Utah			U.S. & state constitutions, free enterprise system				health, hygiene, disease prevention, alcohol abuse	branches prescribed by law, character ed

	English	Math	Social Studies	Science	Physical Education	Foreign Language	Health	Other
Vermont	English, reading, writing	✔	citizenship, history, U.S. & state govt.	✔	✔		✔	
Virginia	reading, writing, spelling	✔	history, govt., citizenship					
Washington	language, reading, writing, spelling	✔	social studies, history, U.S. & state constitutions	✔			✔	occupational ed., appreciation of art & music
West Virginia								not available
Wisconsin	reading, language arts	✔	✔	✔			✔	
Wyoming	reading, writing, literature	✔	civics, history	✔				

❖ What Subjects to Study

One of the hardest things about planning which subjects to study is deciding to trust one's own conscience as a parent seeking God. There is a temptation to unthinkingly follow the basic pattern of the public schools without checking the Word first. Often parents beginning homeschool will say, "I plan to do both... I want to teach the Bible, and I want to include all the subjects taught by the public school."

But as you have already found (if you worked through the preceding sections and wrote down your educational goals) there is much more to Christian education than merely adding the additional subject of Bible. As James Rose, author and "Principle Approach" teacher, has explained to many teachers and parents, a Christian education isn't just teaching a course on the Bible. Nor is it simply using Christian textbooks for all subjects. Even having Christian instructors and Christian students does not guarantee a Christian education. Christian education encompasses *all* these things, plus it requires that the *very method* of teaching be in harmony with God's Word:

> *Christian is used here as an adjective, not a noun, and literally means "of or pertaining to Christ; according to the Gospel, contained therein; relating to Christ, or to His doctrines, precepts and example."*

> *Christian education should comprehend a philosophy, curriculum and methodology which wholly "testify of me," Christ Jesus, and are properly reasoned from the Word of God.*[2]

---

[2]   Rose, James. A Guide to American Christian Education for the Home and School; The Principle Approach (Palo Cedro, California: American Christian History Institute, 1987) p 12.

Consider for a moment who it was that set up the current goals of the public school system. Is it run by men whose heart is seeking to please and glorify God? Or is it run by men who, however well-motivated and sincere, are "trusting in their own understanding?" Or worse, is it run by men who have made education their god? Again, I do not criticize individual public school teachers or administrators. I have many friends who are currently serving or who have served in the public school mission field. But the *system* as a whole has chosen to cast God out.

Can you follow both God's pattern *and* that of the public education system's? The answer is found in God's Word:

No one can serve two masters, for either he will hate the one and love the other,
or else he will be loyal to the one and despise the other.
You cannot serve God and mammon. Matthew 6:24

Happily, one of the blessings of our nation is that when institutional schools were first set up, most of those involved *were* Christians (or at least held Judeo-Christian values.) This means that while today's schools do not even pretend to serve God, the schools of our past history were set up to teach children the subjects of the Bible, namely those subjects that, as Webster described, would "enlighten children's understanding, correct their tempers, form desirable manners and habits, and fit them for usefulness in their future stations."

Many of our basic and historic school subjects were studied with Webster's purpose of education in mind. Imagine a boy who can't perform even the simplest arithmetic. Would he be "fit for usefulness?" How could he manage his future family's finances? Imagine a girl who can't read. How will her "understanding be enlightened" if she cannot comprehend God's written Word? Surely learning the basic three R's would not conflict with serving God, would it?

The problem is that once we cover these basic subjects, which are indeed, the tools used to learn other subjects, many Christians are not so sure what else should be covered. What about the subjects like art, drama, music, science, geography, etc.? What about the "new" subjects of AIDS awareness, psychology, self-awareness, etc.? At least two issues must be considered with each subject: is teaching the subject even biblical, and if so, what is the biblical way to teach it?

At first, considering each subject in this way can seem overwhelming to the parents who have the enormous responsibility of educating their children and bringing them up in the "nurture and admonition of the Lord." However, there are resources available to help provide direction and instruction to the parent who desires to serve God through the education of his children. Here are two excellent books which will help you learn how to teach all subjects from a biblical world view:

Encyclopedia of Bible Truth for School Subjects by Ruth C. Haycock, an excellent resource for finding out what the Bible says about the various school subjects. The book discusses each subject, outlining the basic biblical principles for each, and citing references in the Word for each principle. The book was republished in 1994 by the Association of Christian Schools International, P.O. Box 4097, Whittier, California, 90607.

A Guide to American Christian Education for the Home and School: The Principle Approach, by James B. Rose, covers the rudiments of American Christian education, including the Principle Approach methodology, and also gives thorough coverage of many school subjects, including full course outlines and sample lesson plans. This book is available from American Christian History Institute, P.O. Box 648, Palo Cedro, California 96073.

Our family has chosen to study subjects which we believe are in line with Scripture. We have listed each subject that we intend to study, along with a Scripture verse relating to that subject. Not that each verse listed implies a *command* to study the subject, but it does give an illustration of the subject's importance or Scriptural relevance to our lives.

We keep our list to show that we study these subjects not because they are required by state law (which was written by man and subject to change) but to show that we study subjects as directed by God. If our state's laws were to *require* that we present subjects which are offensive to us, we have established a history of our family's belief that we teach only what is in accordance with God's Word. Our list is written in the form of a school commitment and is part of our school's record file.

Putting together this kind of list can be an enlightening and enjoyable beginning project for you and your students to do together. The subjects you believe God directs you to teach will be the basis of both your junior and senior high school course of study. Once you have decided which subjects must be covered during the child's education, all that is left is to subdivide these subjects into courses, units, or bite-size chunks for each level.

Once the hurdle of deciding *what* to study has been passed, deciding *how* and *how much* and *when* becomes much more manageable. Again, the idea at this point is to make a decision about the general subject areas to be covered during the *entire* educational process. Turning these subject areas into clearly defined units of study (or courses) will be the focus of later chapters.

The following list includes many of the subjects taught in schools, with Scriptures related to each. This is not intended as a comprehensive list. Further study will reveal other subjects and will enlighten families with the knowledge that God truly belongs at the center of all aspects of education.

❖ Subjects in the Scripture

Bible:

And ye shall know the truth, and the truth shall make you free. John 8:32

Thy word have I hid in mine heart, that I might not sin against thee. Psalm 119:11

Show my Your ways, O Lord; teach me Your paths. Lead me in Thy truth, and teach me: for Thou art the God of my salvation; on Thee do I wait all the day. Psalm 25:4-5

All scripture is given by inspiration of God, and is profitable for doctrine, for reproof, for correction, for instruction in righteousness: That the man of God may be perfect, throughly furnished unto all good works. 2 Timothy 3:16-17

Character:

Though I speak with the tongues of men and of angels, and have not charity, I am become as sounding brass. 1 Corinthians 13:1

A good man out of the good treasure of his heart bringeth forth that which is good. Luke 6:45

Wherefore, brethren, look ye out among you seven men of honest report, full of the Holy Ghost and wisdom, whom we may appoint over this business. Acts 6:3

Giving all diligence, add to your faith virtue; to virtue, knowledge; and to knowledge, temperance; and to temperance, patience; and to patience, godliness; and to godliness, brotherly kindness; and to brotherly kindness, charity. For if these things be in you, and abound, they make you that ye shall neither be barren nor unfruitful in the knowledge of our Lord Jesus Christ. 2 Peter 1:5-8

Economics: *Now I pray to God that ye do no evil... that ye should do that which is honest.* 2 Corinthians 13:7

But if any provide not for his own, and specially for those of his own house, he hath denied the faith, and is worse than an infidel. 1 Timothy 5:8

Better is little with the fear of the Lord, than great treasure and trouble therewith. Proverbs 15:16

He that is faithful in that which is least is faithful also in much. Luke 16:10

The rich ruleth over the poor, and the borrower is servant to the lender. Proverbs 22:7

Fine Arts: *He hath made every thing beautiful in his time.* Ecclesiastes 3:11

So you shall speak to all who are gifted artisans, whom I have filled with the spirit of wisdom. Exodus 28:3 (NASB)

And thou shalt make holy garments for Aaron thy brother, for glory and for beauty. Exodus 28:2

Thou also, son of man, take thee a tile, and lay it before thee, and portray on it the city, even Jerusalem. Ezekiel 4:1

Foreign Language: *Go ye into all the world, and preach the gospel to every creature.* Mark 16:15

Except ye utter by the tongue words easy to be understood, how shall it be known what is spoken? 1 Corinthians 14:9

Geography: *In his hand are the deep places of the earth: the strength of the hills is his also. The sea is his, and he made it: and his hands formed the dry land.* Psalm 95:4-5

And God hath made of one blood all nations of men for to dwell on all the face of the earth, and hath determined the times before appointed, and the bounds of their habitation. Acts 17:26

Government & Citizenship: *Where the spirit of the Lord is, there is liberty.* 2 Corinthians 3:17

Behold, how good and how pleasant it is for brethren to dwell together in unity! Psalm 133:1

But if they had stood in my counsel, and had caused my people to hear my words, then they should have turned them from their evil way, and from the evil of their doings. Jeremiah 22:22

Let every soul be subject unto the higher powers. For there is no power but of God: the powers that be are ordained of God. Romans 13:1

Righteousness exalteth a nation: but sin is a reproach to any people. Proverbs 14:34

Be of good courage, and let us behave ourselves valiantly for our people, and for the cities of our God: and let the Lord do that which is good in his sight. 1 Chronicles 19:13

Moreover thou shalt provide out of all the people able men, such as fear God, men of truth, hating covetousness; and place such over them, to be rulers of thousands, and rulers of hundreds, rulers of fifties, and rulers of tens. Exodus 18:21

Then pleased it the apostles and elders, with the whole church, to send chosen men of their own company. Acts 15:22

Behold, how good and how pleasant it is for brethren to dwell together in unity! Psalm 133:1

Health:

I beseech you therefore, brethren, by the mercies of God, that ye present your bodies a living sacrifice, holy, acceptable unto God, which is your reasonable service. Romans 12:1

Know ye not that your body is the temple of the Holy Ghost? 1 Corinthians 6:19

This day is the fourteenth day that ye have tarried and continued fasting, having taken nothing. Wherefore I pray you to take some meat; for this is for your health. Acts 27:33-34

History:

I will remember the works of the Lord. Psalm 77:11

Only take heed to thyself, and keep thy soul diligently, lest thou forget the things which thine eyes have seen, and lest they depart from your heart all the days of thy life: but teach them thy sons and thy sons' sons. Deuteronomy 4:9

Now all these things happened unto them for ensamples: and they are written for our admonition, upon whom the ends of the world are come.
1 Corinthians 10:11

Home Economics:

For if a man know not how to rule his own house, how shall he take care of the church of God? 1 Timothy 3:5
That they may teach the young women to be sober, to love their husbands, to love their children, to be discreet, chaste, keepers at home, good, obedient to their own husbands, that the word of God be not blasphemed. Titus 2:4-5

She riseth also while it is yet night, and giveth meat to her household. Proverbs 31:15

She is not afraid of the snow for her household; for all her household are clothed with scarlet. Proverbs 31:21

Literacy:

(Reading, Writing, Spelling, Grammar, and Speech)

Now go, write it before them in a table, and note it in a book, that it may be for the time to come for ever and ever. Isaiah 30:8

So they read in the book of the law of God distinctly, and gave the sense, and caused them to understand the reading. Nehemiah 8:8

The Preacher sought out acceptable words: and that which was written was upright, even words of truth. Ecclesiastes 12:10

A word fitly spoken is like apples of gold in pictures of silver. Proverbs 25:11

Mathematics:

Let all things be done decently and in order. 1 Corinthians 14:40

And I will make thy seed as the dust of the earth: so that if a man can number the dust of the earth, then shall thy seed also be numbered. Genesis 13:16

Ye shall do no unrighteousness in meteyard, in weight, or in measure. Leviticus 19:35

And as soon as the commandment came abroad, the children of Israel brought in abundance the firstfruits of corn, wine, and oil, and honey, and of all the increase of the field; and the tithe of all things brought they in abundantly. 2 Chronicles 31:5

For which of you, intending to build a tower, sitteth not down first and counteth the cost, whether he have sufficient to finish it—lest haply, after he hath laid the foundation, and is not able to finish it, all that behold it begin to mock him, saying This man began to build and was not able to finish. Luke 14:28-30

Music:

Praise the Lord with harp: sing unto him with the psaltery and an instrument of ten strings. Sing unto him a new song; play skillfully with a loud noise. Psalm 33:2-3

Physical Training:

But I keep under my body, and bring it into subjection... 1 Corinthians 9:27

And let us not be weary in well doing. Galatians 6:9

She girdeth her loins with strength, and strengtheneth her arms. Proverbs 31:17

Science:

The heavens declare the glory of God; and the firmament sheweth his handiwork. Psalm 19:1

But ask now the beasts, and they shall teach thee; and the fowls of the air, and they shall tell thee: Or speak to the earth, and it shall teach thee: and the fishes of the sea shall declare unto thee. Who knoweth not in all these that the hand of the Lord hath wrought this? Job 12:7-9

For by him were all things created, that are in heaven, and that are in earth, visible and invisible, whether they be thrones, or dominions, or principalities, or powers: all things were created by him, and for him. Colossians 1:16

Vocational Skills:

Study to be quiet, and to do your own business, and to work with your own hands, as we commanded you; That ye may walk honestly toward them that are without, and that ye may have lack of nothing. 1 Thessalonians 4:11-12

This we commanded you, that if any would not work, neither should he eat. 2 Thessalonians 3:10

Give her the fruit of her hands; and let her own works praise her in the gates. Proverbs 31:31

❖ Planning for the Future

In planning a junior or senior high school course of study, it is obviously important to consider the future. However, the tendency among today's schools is to rely heavily on planning for, as Webster put it, "future stations," while largely ignoring or downplaying the first three provisions of education. This is particularly odd because out of the four components of education, planning for the future is the part about which there is a great deal of uncertainty. Who knows what the future will bring? How many of today's parents are employed in a field which, while still in high school, they planned to enter?

The first three parts of education should be fairly consistent for all. Correct manners, habits, temper and understanding do not change from person to person. Indeed, most would consider that a youth who has mastered the first three items is *already* fit for usefulness in many future stations.

Most high school students are not sure of their plans for after high school. In fact, many college students and many adults aren't sure what direction to go in their careers. This is normal and I hope your students won't feel too much stress about having their lives all laid out by age 14 or 15. It is probably best to encourage them to learn about many different fields, leaving open as many doors as possible.

The main idea in high school is to continue building and refining those *foundational skills* that are needed by all, while giving the student a great deal of exposure to as many different fields as possible, allowing him to work into advanced levels as he is able. Helping the student prepare for what he thinks *may* be the Lord's call on his life, while continuing to build in those areas that *all* are called to, will provide the most useful education. All need godly character; all need communication skills; all need basic skills of reading, writing, thinking, etc. However, not all need calculus, ceramics or guitar lessons.

> ❖ enlighten the understanding
>
> ❖ correct the temper
>
> ❖ form the manners and habits of youth
>
> ❖ fit them for usefulness in their future stations
>
> *- from Webster's 1828 Dictionary -*

For many families, it is helpful to have a list of basic skills that, ideally, should be covered during junior or senior high school. Some of the skills will naturally fit into one academic subject to study; others will seem more like non-school topics which anyone, whether homeschooling or not should teach their children. Skills like being able to read fluently, with understanding, will likely be on every parent's list, but you should also add any items that are important to you, even if they are not "traditional" school subjects. For example, you may want all your children to graduate from high school knowing CPR, or knowing how to type, or knowing how to make an old family recipe that you learned from your grandmother. Perhaps you think it is important that everyone know how to use basic hand tools, read music, sing four-part harmonies, or clean fish. Having a place to list the skills you would like to cover with your students will help you have confidence that you aren't going to leave any terrible gaps in their education.

I suggest keeping a list of skills you'd like to teach in your own teacher's notebook where you can easily add to it. If you are at all like me, every year you will think of things to add. If your student knows about the list, he will likely have skills to add, too. (My son regularly tries to add "earn a pilot's license" to my list.) Look at the subject list on the previous pages and take a few minutes to jot down any skills that come to mind. Part of my own list is shown on page 21.

While it is impossible to foresee everything a student will need to learn for his future, you will have more confidence if you will take time to consider what general subjects should be covered, as well as what specific skills you think are important to be taught to everyone. If you haven't done so already, take time now to start two lists.

The first list should include general school subjects you want to cover before graduation. Don't worry about *how much* of each subject to require. That will come in later chapters. For now, just list subjects, for example, Bible, English, math, etc. Include only subjects you would want *every* student to learn, not individualized subjects like "flute lessons" or "calculus," unless, of course, you think *every* child should learn one of those subjects. This list will be the start of your graduation requirements, so keep it handy to work on in Chapters 2 and 3.

The second list should include basic skills you want to teach before high school graduation. Include any specific tasks or skills you think every student should learn. As with the first list, forget about your individual student for now—list the kinds of things you thing *everyone* ought to know.

Once the basic foundational areas have been outlined (this is your list #1), elective courses and extracurricular activities which relate to current interests or future plans for a specific student may be considered. Certainly thoughts about direction for the future will be (and should be) entertained. By considering various occupations and fields of interest, the student will discover gifts and interests which may, indeed, lead him to his "future station." Often it is hard to decide which field to study, simply because there are so many from which to choose.

You may want to begin a third list of possible studies for each individual student whom you teach. This list will include possible *elective* courses. Elective courses are those classes or studies taken by a student *in addition* to his school's general requirements. Remember, as a parent, you may require one of your students to take a particular elective course. My mom made me take typing in eleventh grade even though typing was not required for graduation from my high school.

For the sake of clarity of definitions, in this book, we will refer to "required" courses as being those courses you will require every student you teach to take before graduation. "Elective" courses are those courses that some students may take, but others may not, whether by the parents' choice, or by the students'. For example, let's assume you have two high school students, Ben and Amy. Amy is gifted in music, so you will require her to continue piano lessons throughout high school. Ben, however, appears to have no musical talent at all, so even though you have given him 8 years of hopeful piano lessons during elementary and junior high school, you have decided to let him stop the lessons as he begins high school. He will graduate without any high school piano courses. Even though you are *making* Amy take piano, it is considered an *elective* course since you do not require piano of all your students.

The following guidelines should be considered in selecting elective courses as preparation for future callings or careers. Again, remember these will likely change as your student matures.

1. Personal Interest and Aptitudes
2. Achievement and Ability in various subject areas.
3. Future Vocational Plans
4. Future Educational Plans

Even though most teenagers will not know precisely what jobs they do want to pursue, most have very clear ideas about some jobs that they definitely do not want. By 14 or 15, it is already clear to some children that they will never become professional writers. These students will need to continue studying writing skills because writing is a fundamental skill which all adults need to use, but they probably do not need to spend as much time discovering all the intricacies of style that a gifted author will need to know. And you never know, more study of writing may change your student's mind. All can use improvement, but not all need perfection.

Other students who say they have no idea what they want to do as adults may already know that they do not want to work on cars. They will need to know how to check the oil, change a flat, and fill the gas tank, but probably don't need to spend a term rebuilding an engine. For each of these students there will be another who would love the idea of rebuilding a car engine for school credit.

A student heading for college or university will need to be aware of the university's entrance requirements. A student who is aiming to pass the GED or similar proficiency test at 16 or 17 and get a job or attend community college may not need to stick as close to the traditional schools' courses of study. A student desiring to enter an apprenticeship program will need to be aware of the job requirements for his chosen field.

Finally, a student heading for marriage and full time family-raising will need to focus on home skills, but should not neglect to prepare for what my mom used to call "something to fall back on." A spouse may not be in God's plan or family emergencies may arise which require full-time moms to bring in some income. Even the godly ladies in the Bible were commended for their ability to use "business sense."

Whatever your future plans or your student's future plans (or lack of plans) focus on the basics. Future plans change; the basics don't.

Schofield Family
Basic Skills List Excerpts

Bible
- ☐ Knowledge of salvation and how salvation is obtained
- ☐ How to find information in the Bible related to any topic of interest
- ☐ Use of a concordance, commentary, and other Bible study aids

Character
- ☐ Importance of keeping his word
- ☐ Consistently consider how his actions will affect others before he acts
- ☐ How to answer softly

Economics
- ☐ Biblical principles of the free enterprise system
- ☐ How to balance a check book and pay bills
- ☐ How to make and follow a budget

Fine Arts
- ☐ Able to read music on at least a basic level

Geography
- ☐ Locate the major countries and cities of the world on a map
- ☐ How to read a street map
- ☐ How to give good directions

Government
- ☐ "Think governmentally" -- discerning who or what is in charge
- ☐ Understands the different spheres of government established by God
- ☐ Able and willing to submit to proper authority
- ☐ Self-governed
- ☐ Read and understand ballot issues

Health
- ☐ CPR & basic first aid
- ☐ What a healthy diet is

Home Economics
- ☐ How to follow a recipe
- ☐ Basic sewing skills
- ☐ How to paint a room
- ☐ How to clean really well
- ☐ Ability to set up appointments, gather information, etc. by telephone
- ☐ How to organize a file cabinet, warranties, family records, etc.
- ☐ Ability to handle basic home repairs
- ☐ Ability to change a diaper, burp a baby, or entertain toddlers for an afternoon

Literacy & Communications
- ☐ Ability to read anything at any level
- ☐ How to locate any information in a library
- ☐ How to lead a meeting
- ☐ How to give a speech
- ☐ Ability to write a business letter
- ☐ How to write a paragraph on any topic

Mathematics
- ☐ Master basic arithmetic skills
- ☐ Able to measure for and plan projects
- ☐ How to figure out a waiter's tip

Science
- ☐ Not to mix bleach and ammonia
- ☐ Not to put gasoline in a washer
- ☐ Basic ability to garden

Vocational Skills
- ☐ Basic typing & computer skills
- ☐ How to give a good job interview
- ☐ How to make a resume
- ☐ How to use basic carpentry tools

Other
- ☐ How to change a tire
- ☐ How to say "no" nicely
- ☐ How to delegate
- ☐ What to look for when making major purchases like cars, furniture, houses

❖ 2 Teaching Junior High

Junior high school students[3] are a delight! I mean it. Somehow, children in this age group have a bad reputation (possibly from the quaint tradition of sticking too many of them all together in the same room all day, everyday, when they'd be much better off getting on with real life?!) But as you know, or you'll discover if you're new to homeschooling, having your children home as they go through adolescence is as fun and exciting as any other developmental milestone, and more so.

Remember when your children were just learning to walk? Thinking back, you can probably say, "I wouldn't have missed it!" Junior high is even more special than that because at this age, your children are learning to walk *spiritually*. You won't want to miss it.

According to Jewish tradition, children become adults within the community at age twelve. Most Christians do not have such a set age, but do share an understanding that at some point, children reach an "age of accountability." For most of our children, I believe this transformation from child, under grace by virtue of his parents' faith, to spiritual accountability on his own standing before God, probably takes place during adolescence.

This is the age when most students make some major decisions about what kind of people they want to be, what kind of lives they want to lead. This is the age at which many criminals turned from bad to worse, from bad childhood or petty thievery to more serious crimes. This is the age at which many mature Christians made their initial commitment to serve Christ.

Of course, salvation and decisions about what kind of person one will be may come later— in high school, college, or even once a person becomes a parent himself. But if such a change comes later in life, most of the "undoing" that must be done is because of actions and habits that first started in junior high.

Junior High is an age when students can begin to envision life as an adult (not usually very realistically, though.) Because of the God-given desire to follow one's own conscience and make one's own choices, these students'

---

[3]   In this book, "junior high school" means students approximately ages 11-14, or grades 7 & 8. Your own program may include 6th graders, or it may include 9th graders. You may even be including what would be considered 6th grade work *and* 9th grade work with the same student!

At any rate, my family calls "junior high" 7th and 8th grade. If yours calls it something else, we can still communicate about teaching adolescents.

are especially susceptible to the mistakes made when too much independence or responsibility is given too soon. The desire for independence often causes the common mistakes of making important decisions too quickly or without proper counsel. This makes junior high students particularly susceptible to false doctrines and bad company.

Well-known speaker and home educator, Jonathan Lindvall, has said that if he could only teach his children for two years, he would choose to do so during junior high. If only all parents could understand how important it is to train our students personally during junior high. The tendency among some homeschoolers to put their children "back into school" at junior high is a sad one, indeed. Just when they are on the threshold of spiritual and physical maturity, just when they are capable learning how to make wise and life-changing decisions, just when they have mastered the basics and are on to the interesting stuff to learn... what a shame to miss it!

If you are just beginning junior high at home, you will likely have to face all the questions from well-meaning friends and family that you did when you began homeschooling. (If you're new to homeschooling, you'll field questions even more than if you had started sooner.) People can grasp why you might homeschool during the early years. After all, it can't be too hard to teach kindergarten or first grade. But to actually want to teach junior high? First of all, you probably aren't a professional teacher and second, who would want to be around an adolescent all day?

Let me assure you that you don't need to be a "professional" to teach junior high and I can't think of anyone nicer to be around than your own junior high student. Parents who homeschool through junior and senior high school find that they love to be with their children. In fact, attendance at homeschool field trips, park days, and other activities dwindles as parents begin teaching junior high at home—not because it's so hard and time consuming to teach, but because the moms just aren't so desperate for stimulating conversation. They find they get plenty at home!

❖ What Exactly *Is* Junior High?

Junior high (and every other school grade level) is more an age or a stage than it is a set of skills to learn. In other words, a second grader is one who is in his second year of academic education, not necessarily one who has learned to read, add, or print. It is true that many second graders have learned those basic skills, but just as true that many have not. When our niece moved in with us and began homeschooling as a high school junior, she could not multiply or divide. She hadn't even passed all her 10th grade courses, yet was still considered to be in 11th grade.

Consider for a moment where the term "junior high" or "middle school" came from. These terms were coined by those who were involved in designing a particular educational system. For the purpose of defining those students who have mastered elementary education but are not yet entering high school (whatever that is) the term junior high may have some use.

If you were a campus-school teacher, you would find it helpful to know that all your new students were seventh graders or that half were seventh and half were sixth graders, assuming that meant they had mastered a certain level of skills. You would find it useful in planning what to teach, particularly since your students had been taught by many different teachers during past years and you would have no way of knowing exactly what had been covered by each of those teachers. Since you would not personally know your new students, you wouldn't know what they were (or were not) capable of doing, unless there was some meaningful classification of skill levels. Grade levels were originally designed as such labels.

Two things have happened since the grade-level system was begun. First, schools no longer like to hold children back if they have not mastered the material at their grade-level. Second, many schools no longer like to use clearly defined skills as a master list of requirements for each grade. Because children are still moved from class to class and from teacher to teacher, the move away from clear grade-level definitions is frustrating to many parents and teachers. How can a teacher know where to begin teaching if he does not know what has been covered?

Some schools are beginning to keep children with the same teacher for several years to solve this problem. Homeschoolers have solved this problem in a similar way. When it is Mom who just finished teaching sixth grade, she pretty well knows what to expect next fall from her seventh grader. Rather than having a list of what to do at each grade level, homeschooling parents find it most useful to have a list of skills to be taught *throughout the years of academic education*, so that after teaching one skill they can simply move on to the next.

If you have been homeschooling a long time, you can attest to this. Defining grade levels becomes harder and harder the longer you are out of "the system." Your students work at different levels in different subjects. They excel in some areas and, even if you use a very advanced curriculum, could probably skip a grade in certain subjects. In other areas, they could really use more work, but you just hate to "hold them back" because they might fall behind.

If you are brand new to homeschooling, you may be terribly confused at this point, wondering how on earth you are going to set up a seventh grade program and order books when I won't even tell you exactly what seventh grade is.

It may be helpful to realize that in most public schools, junior high offers two tracks: remedial elementary education and pre-high school. Remedial elementary is for those students who need an extra year or two of basic arithmetic before moving on to algebra, or some extra time becoming proficient at reading and understanding various resource materials before high school requires them to write reports depending on information from those materials. Remedial elementary, then, is just catching up on skills that some of the other students mastered during elementary school.

Pre-high school is typically for children who have mastered all the basics but aren't old enough for high school (they can't just send them home for two years, can they?) These students take algebra, advanced English, foreign language, computer science, and other courses that are similar to those in high school. In fact, these same classes will be offered in high school, but to students who are not ready to handle college preparatory courses.

This means that, as homeschool parents, you should feel comfortable in spending an extra two years on elementary work, or in teaching high school subjects (and giving high school credits.) If your student needs time to master the basic arithmetic facts or to learn to read better, junior high is a perfect time to work on those skills. On the other hand, if he is ready to begin advanced-level work, let him do that. If he finishes high school at sixteen, he can begin college work (at home) and at eighteen could already have reached sophomore status in college.

For our purposes, then, junior high is that two year period (or three if you prefer) before high school. Most children in junior high will range from 11 to 14 years of age and will be just entering puberty, or just finished, or getting ready to enter it. Most will know how to read, write and handle basic arithmetic problems. Some will need more work in these areas, and some will be ready for advanced studies.

So junior high encompasses many different levels and in order to work in your home, junior high will need to be better defined by *you*. In Chapter 4, we'll begin to work on an individualized definition for your homeschool. We'll do that by deciding what to accomplish in junior high, and what you and your student expect to get out of it. In short, by identifying goals or requirements.

❖ Graduation from Junior High

To "graduate" from junior high into high school is the goal of most junior high students. While the parents may have a loftier goal in mind, to the student, the practical question will not be, "Did I further my grasp of history?" More likely, it will be, "Did I further my grasp of history enough to convince Mom and Dad that I am ready to begin high school?"

Graduation from junior high school may be as large or small an issue as you choose to make it. If you choose to pattern your junior high course of study after those of the elementary grades, graduation may simply mean finishing eight years or so of elementary education and proceeding to secondary education. On the other hand, if you choose to design a junior high course of study more like those of the high school years, then your child will have earned credits, or will have passed a test; either of which sets a clear mark of achievement reached, rather than simply time put in.

Any of these methods is acceptable. Some prefer to continue in seventh and eighth grades, following the same subjects as in fifth and sixth grades, but at a little bit more advanced levels. Record keeping, report cards, etc. will look like those kept in the elementary grades. Rather than setting up separate courses to complete, each course with a title, outline, goal, or separate description, the parents may choose to continue subject areas as in the elementary grades.

Some prefer to begin to lead the student toward the type of work that will be expected in high school, which usually means having the subjects more clearly delineated into separate courses. This is because once the basic 3-Rs have been mastered, the student is ready to begin more specialized courses; i.e. American Literature, Algebra, or Biology, as opposed to studying general subjects like reading, arithmetic, and science.

Probably most will find themselves somewhere between these two choices, and that is fine, too. A parent may want to continue with basic elementary studies in some areas where the student needs more help, while planning more specific courses in other areas. Even in those subjects where the student needs more elementary level work, the parent may want to design the course after the pattern of high school courses, with clear course requirements.

I recommend setting up at least a few junior high courses more like high school because the clear distinction of what is required to "graduate" gives the student a clear and reachable goal. He does not feel he has graduated into high school just because he is 14 years old; he knows that he has earned his way into high school by mastering a set level of skills and objectives. Also, he has had a couple of "practice years" of high-school-style record keeping to learn how to use self-control, diligence, and initiative in finishing courses. By high school, parents would hope their student is ready to be doing more self-directed studies, not needing Mom or Dad at his side all the time to tell him what to do next.

Laying out courses with clear requirements will free the student to work at his own level, while teaching him the discipline to pace himself. He will learn to govern himself, to make decisions, and to follow through. The parent will also be freed from being taskmaster every day, and will be able to move more into the role of counselor and guide.

❖ Recommended Junior High Courses

The following recommendations are made considering junior high as two years, grades seven and eight.

Bible: 2 years suggested

Assuming yours is a Christian school, Bible should be required every year. Knowing that homeschooled junior high students have often had many years of Bible training already, I rarely find any "teen" studies from the local Christian bookstore very helpful. You may want to focus on Bible study skills during junior high, as preparation for high school. This would be a good time to purchase a good study Bible for your student. Teach him how to mark it up so that by the time he graduates from high school, it has become his well-worn friend.

English: 2 years suggested

In junior high, please feel comfortable to continue with the basic elementary skills of reading and writing. Many junior high students continue to benefit from regular handwriting lessons, for example. Readers may also prove valuable to continue to improve basic reading skills. However, if your student has mastered basic handwriting, spelling, and grammar, and if he can read just about anything fluently, you may want to drop the readers and spellers, and begin to focus on the study of literature and composition. All junior high students should continue to read good literature, and have it read to them, whether simply for exposure or for beginning analytical studies. Please don't stop reading aloud!! You are just now ready to read many truly wonderful books together as a family!

Math: 2 years suggested

If your student needs more time to master basic arithmetic skills, do it now! Do not feel pressured to begin higher math, like algebra or geometry if your student hasn't mastered long division or fractions. On the other hand, if your student is ready for high school algebra, go right ahead—and count it for high school credit, too.

Science: 1 year suggested

If trying to cover five solid subjects is wearing you out, it may help to realize that many junior high schools do not require 2 years of science or history. You may want to pick one for each year, or do a semester of each, or choose a type of unit study that combines both science and history. Working in a garden, participating in 4-H animal projects, earning scout badges, or doing a fun experiment each week can all help to lay an excellent foundation for the high school level sciences.

History & Geography: 1 year suggested

As with science, don't feel pressured to teach a full year of history each year of junior high, especially if you are planning to cover history thoroughly in high school. It will probably be a better use of time to focus on reading, writing and arithmetic skills in junior high, so your student is well-prepared for high school studies.

In your history plans, consider what you will likely do in high school. Don't turn history into boring reviews by covering the same material over and over, year after year. Perhaps you could do ancient world history in junior high, and modern world history in high school. Or focus on a literature approach in junior high by reading biographies and historical fiction, saving the full chronological survey course for high school. Or cover geography thoroughly in junior high, and history during high school. The ideas are endless and you'll enjoy your studies more if you think ahead.

Fine Arts: 1 year suggested

Visual or performing arts may be studied. Art, dance, drama, or music are commonly taken as separate courses, or a survey course may be designed which includes an introduction to a variety of the arts.

Physical Education: 2 years suggested

While you don't have to exercise *every* day to be physically fit, a regular program of several workouts a week is a great habit to develop. If your children take dance lessons, swimming lessons, play team sports, etc. you may have P.E. covered already. If not, maybe a good walk three days a week would be workable.

Home Economics: 1 semester to 1 year suggested

Home economics is usually considered an elective. But considering the likelihood that all students will one day have the responsibility of taking care of a home, it seems prudent to include at least a minimum requirement for home economics. Besides, if your students master basic cooking, sewing, or home maintenance skills now, in high school they'll be a real asset to your family's work!

Typing or Computers: 1 semester or more suggested

While typing is not usually required in public school junior high, most students will benefit from at least a semester to acquaint them with basic keyboard skills and computer software.

Electives: 2 semesters or more suggested

While a student is in junior high, it is most important to focus on honing the basic 3-R skills. However, if your schedule will allow, it certainly isn't too soon to begin to let your student choose some subjects to study of his own interest.

❖ 3 Teaching Senior High

By the time a student reaches ninth grade, he should have mastered the basic skills of reading, writing, and arithmetic. He should also know how to use research materials and think things through to a logical conclusion (or be getting better at it). If he has not mastered these basic skills, spend time at the beginning of high school to review, strengthen, and master them.

Assuming your teenager can read well, can express himself verbally and in writing, and has mastered general arithmetic, your job as a high school teacher at home is relatively easy. At this point, your student is ready to become an independent, self-motivated learner.

You do not need to know everything that your student is learning. Do not be intimidated by well-meaning people who ask you how you can possibly teach high school without a state credential. What your homeschooled high school student needs most is a godly counselor, an encourager, a resource person, someone to bounce new ideas off, and someone to keep him in line as he works to meet his goals. These jobs are challenging, but certainly do not require a degree or state credential.

❖ Dealing With Authorities

During the high school years you may need to work with school or government officials. Perhaps you need a transcript or a work permit from the local public high school, or maybe your student is applying for a driver's license. A positive, professional attitude cannot be underestimated.

I have had many occasions to work with public officials. In nearly every case I have been able to get the help or information that I needed. In the few negative situations, I have usually been able to avoid the negative person and talk with someone else who was more helpful. By working in a positive way with officials, you will be helping to build good relationships for all homeschoolers. If you are tempted to argue, please remember that the next homeschooler who calls may be affected.

If your state law allows homeschoolers to operate as private schools, refer to your student as a "private school student" rather than a "homeschool student." Your student, enrolled in a private school, should be treated by officials in the same way students from other private schools are treated. Use official school stationery, dress in clothing suitable for a business office, speak clearly and confidently, and you will most often not even be questioned.

Whether or not homeschoolers in your state are considered private school students, do your homework *at home*, before visiting a government office to request a work permit, driver license, etc. If you don't know the proper procedure, first ask your local homeschool leader. Second, ask your state's homeschool organization or Home School Legal Defense Association. Only after being briefed in these ways will you be prepared for handling possible questions from government agencies.

Sometimes a homeschool parent can walk right into the Labor Board office or the Department of Motor Vehicles and receive the information needed without any delay or undue questioning. However, it is also common for a homeschooler to inadvertently cause problems by not knowing how to address questions, particularly those relating to the legality of homeschooling. By being prepared ahead of time, you will be able to confidently answer questions and will more likely avoid problems.

❖ Graduation from Senior High School

There are several ways of graduating from high school, but it is hoped that "graduation" is not the only aim. As speaker Gregg Harris has said, "If graduation means the end of education and learning, then what we don't need are more graduates!"

If your student's aim is to finish high school and start a family, or begin working in the family business under his parents' training, or begin an apprenticeship program where no further formal education is desired, he may want to finish high school as quickly as possible. It may be a good idea to help him finish quickly, or it may not, depending on his maturity and on his goals. Some students may be well-prepared to live a godly life in the adult world at 16 or 17; most are not. It would be a shame to send some from the nest before they are ready, and teenagers usually think they are ready before you think so.

If a student is new to homeschooling and simply wants out of high school as soon as possible because he dislikes school, but is not necessarily ready to be out on his own, it is probably wisest to try to find out what it is that he dislikes. If he feels that what he is learning is a waste of time, he just may be right. You may want to plan courses that will have direct relevance to your student's life, so he can begin once more to see the point of education.

Following a typical high school course of study, including counting up credits or hours, will take two to four years, while studying for and passing an examination may take a year or less. You and your high school student will have to make the decision about which means of graduation will best fit your needs.

The three most common means of finishing high school are:

1. Passing a proficiency exam (either a state's own exam, or the GED),

2. Entering college (without a diploma or proficiency certificate), or

3. Following a course of study that meets pre-set requirements, with a minimum number of class credits to be earned, to receive a diploma.

The following sections will discuss these three methods.

Please bear in mind that because it is easier to explain the first two possibilities, less time is devoted to them. This does not mean that I necessarily endorse the third alternative of setting up and completing a set course of study.

My personal recommendation is usually that students take a proficiency exam like the GED (described below) and also work on completing basic course requirements as determined by the parents.

These courses will likely cover a broad range of subjects; studies in each of them will certainly not be a waste of time. If your student passes the GED, you may choose to finish the course work you had planned for high school. If finishing all the high school courses is not necessary for your student, you may decide that passing the exam is enough and "graduate" him.

❖ High School Graduation by Passing an Exam

If your student is planning to take any of the following tests, he should spend some time practicing test taking skills. The library or bookstore should have a copy of the test preparation books published by Barron's. There is a book for every test imaginable. Each book has descriptions of the test, registration information, practice tests, and chapters reviewing each section of the test.

General Education Development (GED)

The GED is designed for adults who did not graduate from high school to show equivalency to a high school education. Each state sets its own age requirement for taking the GED, but most states set the minimum for taking the GED as higher than the state's minimum age to leave school. For example, in Colorado, compulsory attendance at school is required until age 16, but a student must be at least 17 to take the GED. So the GED is useful as a means of verifying that a student's homeschool program provided an education equivalent to high school graduation, but only after the fact.

The local public library usually will have brochures and registration information for the GED, or you can call the Service of the American Council on Education at (202) 939-9490.

There are a number of books available to help students study and prepare for the GED. Your local public library probably has several, however, those that are most current are likely in the "reference only" section. Since the test is updated regularly, the older preparation books may not be as helpful anymore, so it is probably worthwhile to purchase your own preparation book. Most of the books are similar in format, however, you may want to borrow a couple of the available versions from the library to evaluate the different companies' study methods before actually purchasing one. Most large book stores, like Barnes and Noble, will have a selection of several different publishers' test preparation books.

Students who are concerned about their ability to pass the GED, or who have stopped their formal education already, may benefit from a GED preparation course. Most community colleges offer a class designed to prepare students to pass the GED.

The following chart shows the age and residency requirements by state, as of this writing. Some states have exceptions for both age and residency requirements, so check with your own state before planning to take the test.

State	Min. Age	Residency Requirement	State	Min. Age	Residency Requirement	State	Min. Age	Residency Requirement	State	Min. Age	Residency Requirement
AK	18	resident	ID	16	resident	MT	17	resident	RI	18	resident or military
AL	18	30 days	IL	18	30 days	NC	18	resident or military	SC	17	resident
AR	16	legal resident	IN	17	30 days	ND	18	none	SD	18	resident

State	Min. Age	Residency Requirement	State	Min. Age	Residency Requirement	State	Min. Age	Residency Requirement	State	Min. Age	Residency Requirement
AZ	16	none	KS	16	resident	NE	16	30 days	TN	18	resident
CA	18	resident	KY	16	resident	NH	18	resident	TX	18	resident
CO	17	resident	LA	17	resident	NJ	18	resident	UT	18	none
CT	17	resident	MA	19	resident none	NM	18	resident	VA	18	resident
DC	18	resident	MD	16	90 days	NV	17	none	VT	18	resident
DE	18	resident	ME	18	none	NY	19	30 days	WA	19	bona fide resident
FL	18	legal resident	MI	16	30 days	OH	19	resident	WI	18	voting resident or migrant worker
GA	18	none	MN	19	resident	OK	18	resident	WV	16	30 days
HI	17	resident	MO	16	resident or military	OR	18	resident	WY	17	resident
IA	17	resident	MS	17	30 days	PA	18	resident			

Standardized Testing

Although standardized tests (like the ACT, Iowa or SAT) are not designed to show graduation equivalence, some families award a diploma to a child who scores an overall average above the twelfth grade level. A student who scores at this level on standardized tests would probably also pass the GED. Having him take the GED when he is old enough will spare you from defending your diploma to a college or employer. For information about tests used for college admissions, see pages 197-198.

❖ High School Graduation by Entering College

By "entering college," I am referring to students going to college who have not passed the GED or completed high school by other means. Students who have already finished high school and now want to go to college should read Chapter 11: After High School, which deals with college admissions for high school graduates. Students who live in California should check the information in the Special California Supplement at the end of this book before trying to sign up for college courses.

Universities

Some students are entering college at incredibly young ages. These students are going straight to college without finishing high school first. Although admission to a university is no easy matter for your average twelve year old, and I don't recommend it to any that I can personally think of, if your child is incredibly gifted academically and has the maturity level to match, it may be possible to have him accepted to a university.

There is no age limit for the college entrance exams, so the first step will be to have your student take these. Often, students who score at a very high level (listed by each college in its manual) do not need to have a particular grade point average to be considered for admission. See pages 199-201 for a sample of the average scores earned by students at some well-known universities. Information about the tests themselves is in the section "College Entrance

Examinations" on pages 197-198. In addition to high scores on the entrance exams, your student will likely need several letters of recommendation; will have to be able to write an outstanding essay; and will need to be able to express himself well in person, as he will likely be interviewed before acceptance.

Another approach is for a student to begin taking university-level courses at home. This can be done informally, by choosing subjects to study, ordering materials, and working through the course at the student's own pace at home. When the student has mastered the material, he can take one of several exams available. If he passes the exam, he earns college credit. More information on receiving college credits by exam is in the "College at Home" section, beginning on page 193.

Some universities offer more formal courses by distance learning, correspondence, or even by video. While some programs require a high school diploma, others do not. Information on correspondence and other at-home college courses is also provided in the "College at Home" section.

Whether you are interested in having your high school student attend college on campus or at home, contact the university that you are interested in and purchase a catalog. *After reading through the catalog*, call the admissions office with any further questions.

Community Colleges

Far more common, and easier, than being accepted as a full-time university student, is for a non-graduate high school student to enter a junior college (also called a community college.) Students can attend junior college part-time for a class or two, while continuing most of their studies at home. Or, they may be able to take a full load of junior college classes and simply aim for a college degree rather than a high school diploma.

One strength of this idea is that junior colleges today offer a very wide selection of courses, ranging from General Arithmetic (approximately eighth grade level) to Advanced Calculus (university level), and from Basic Writing Skills to Commercial Writing. If you feel that your own homeschool has been weak in a particular area, you don't need to panic; if the junior colleges offer classes to fill the gaps left by substandard public high schools, they will certainly be able to fill in any areas you didn't give enough attention to.

There will be no social stigma if your teenager takes a remedial course as part of his program. Plus, taking a remedial class or two at junior college may offer a far better education for your teen than his age-mates are receiving in public high school.

Another advantage of doing work at the junior college rather than the local high school is that the students at the college are usually more serious about their education (they don't have to be there.) Also, there is a wide range of ages among the students, so peer pressure may be less, or at least more mature.

A disadvantage is that the public junior colleges are steeped in humanism, and can be very anti-Christian (more overtly than the high schools.) It is quite possible that your teenager will be in a class where every value he has held dear since childhood will be openly mocked and criticized. This is hard to take as an adult, and may prove too much for many teens. Use your judgment as to whether your student can handle the junior college experience.

Shun profane and vain babblings: for they will increase unto more ungodliness. II Timothy 2:16

Do not be carried about with divers and strange doctrines:
For it is a good thing that the heart be established with grace,
not with meats which have not profited them that have been occupied therein.
Hebrews 13:9

Another possible problem is lack of supervision. Absences will cause grades to fall, but usually won't be reported to you. You also won't receive the report cards; they are usually sent directly to the student.

Finally, a common problem among high-school-age students attending college is that they will likely develop a group of friends several years older than they are. At first glance, this seems good—hopefully the new friends will be more mature and, therefore, good influences. However, what is often reported is that most students of college age will have a greater amount of freedom than your younger student does. The natural tendency in the younger teen is to covet the freedom enjoyed by his older friends. He wants to stay out later, participate in more adult activities, and often begins to resent having to give account to his parents about what he is doing and where he is going.

If you have any question about your child's readiness to be treated as an adult, responsible for his own education, or if you are unsure of his spiritual maturity, then it may not be a good idea to send him to college.

You could, of course, take a course with your student for the first term. Choose something you are both interested in or a fun class like volleyball or ceramics, just to get your feet wet.

Usually, it is easier for a high school student to enroll as a part-time student than a full-time one. There are always exceptions, but be careful about insisting that your student attend full-time the first term just because you know a friend who did. Once your student has completed his first couple of classes with good grades, the college should have no problem letting him take more next term.

Parents who are trying to get their children into junior college have been told everything from, "Junior colleges have to let anyone attend who wants to," to "Absolutely no child under age eighteen who is not a high school graduate will be permitted to attend." While each state has different laws governing admission to community colleges, it is usually possible for capable high school students to take a class or two. Expect for your student to have to take a placement test. Have his high school transcripts in order and ready to send upon application for admission. Be courteous and professional-sounding on the telephone. Ask your statewide homeschool organization or Home School Legal Defense Association for help if you need it.

Your student may be given a choice of whether to count his class for college credit or high school credit. If given the choice, *choose college credit*. You can quietly choose to also count the college credits as fulfilling your high school requirements if you want. The choice of high school or college credit is a question designed with public high schools in mind, and public high school credits are not what you are after.

If your student is taking college courses, you may want to continue keeping a transcript for high school if your student only has a few high school courses needed for graduation. Simply add the junior college course to your own high school transcript with a notation that the class was taken at such-and-such college (see sample transcript on page 165.) Typically, a college semester course (3 hours a week of class attendance) will count as a year course for high school. So if your student takes a semester course of Spanish at college, you could count it as a full year of high school Spanish, or you may decide to count it as a semester-long "honors" course.

If your student has 15 or more units of transferable credits from the junior college, any prospective university will likely depend more on that record than the high school record, though the will typically want to see a high school transcript as well. If your student has completed 24-30 units or more, he should be considered a transfer student, not an incoming freshman, so you may not need to continue adding to a high school transcript. But check with the prospective university's admissions office to be sure.

A few junior colleges award a "Certificate of High School Equivalency" to a student who completes 24 units with at least a 2.5 grade point average at the college. Check with your local junior college if your student is interested in this option.

❖ High School Graduation by Completing a Course of Study

You may choose to have your student complete courses and study subjects that you have chosen as requirements for graduation. Setting up your own course of study will require you to set up your own graduation requirements and have your student study the subjects and complete the courses according to your plan. You can easily set up and keep a transcript (official record) of these courses at home.

You may choose not to require the same amount of classes that the public schools require, but you will probably want to spend at least some time in each of the different branches of study required by public schools.

Be aware that if your student plans to attend college and hopes to gain admission on the basis of his high school transcript (rather than outstanding test scores) he will usually receive more consideration if his transcript includes the normal high school courses. This is changing for at least two reasons. First, as homeschooling has become more popular, colleges are realizing the need for individual assessment. Second, with Outcome-Based Education gaining more and more ground, traditional grades and course work are being shunned in favor of outstanding students who demonstrate individuality and leadership. Some colleges will now accept a portfolio of work in lieu of grades. Those that will accept (or prefer or require) portfolios will include information about what to include in their college manual.

Whether you choose to use the public school requirements or college admissions requirements as the basis for your own private school's graduation requirements, or whether you are going to completely write your own requirements, you should take time to set up your high school course of study (list of graduation requirements) *before* you start your high school program. If you have already started high school, however, all is not lost. Begin now and set up graduation requirements as if you had not already completed any courses. Then mark off the classes already completed on your requirement list.

How will you know when your student has finished high school? It would be unfair to add three elective courses to your student's requirements when he is in his last semester of high school. A well-defined list of graduation requirements will help you plan what to study each year and will allow your student to progress at his own rate.

In writing your graduation requirements, you may want to look at the planning charts on pages 54-57, the state subject requirements on pages 8-12, and the recommended courses listed starting on page 38. Also take into consideration your student's gifts and goals. Some families have chosen to include a semester of missionary work or volunteer service in their graduation requirements. You may want to require work experience or home economics, rather than allowing your student to have the choice of whether or not to concentrate on those areas as electives. Blank charts for listing your own graduation requirements are on pages 54-55.

In following your course of study, formal curriculum (pre-planned courses by a recognized publisher or school), informal curriculum (using less traditional materials), or a combination of both may be used. If you have been homeschooling for a while, you have probably developed many unique studies in a variety of subjects. Enjoy the blessings of homeschooling by continuing to follow the vision God has given to you. Please do not feel that recording credits, writing graduation requirements, or grading classes means that you must stop homeschooling in the way that you love. The goal should simply be to take what you are *already* doing, and learn to *translate* that into the education system's language of credits, grades, and transcripts.

A course description or course outline, written before the start of each term for each class to be taken, will help you and your student keep a clear picture of what is to be studied during each course. The course description form included in this manual includes space for the student's name, grade, and school year, and for the course title, curriculum used, length of course, credits (or units) awarded upon completion, and a description of the course. You may want to make several copies of the form; it will take one form for each course.

There are many possible ways to cover the subjects you want to study. A number of sample course descriptions are included in this manual to help you design a course of study. These samples are just that. They are not meant to tell you how to teach a course, nor are they necessarily recommendations of a particular text book or study plan. My aim in including samples is simply to give you a visual idea of how you might record a similar study. If you see assignment ideas you like, by all means, use them. But don't feel like the assignments in the samples represent "the right way" to homeschool.

In addition to the course description or course outline, parents should also prepare (or help their student prepare) a "course standard" for each course. This will outline what work is required in each course to earn credits, as well as what expected to earn a particular grade. Again, samples are included to help you.

❖ Required Courses for High School Graduation

While most states have a list of subjects which must be taught in high school, the *amount* of study in each of those subjects will be up to you. An important exception is if your student is enrolled in a private school program[4], whether correspondence or independent study. If you are a part of such a program, you will need to follow the graduation requirements they have established.

Whether you will be setting all your own requirements or simply designing your courses to meet the requirements of the program in which you are enrolled, you will still need to consider your own plans and goals for deciding on subjects to study each year. Your state or program of enrollment may not require foreign language, for example, but you, as a parent, may decide to require your students to study a year or two of another language.

Most colleges set clear requirements for courses that incoming college freshmen must have taken while in high school. College admissions requirements vary, so if your student is planning to attend college, it is imperative that you check with the college to see what courses your student must take.

❖ About Credits

Sometimes homeschoolers balk at the idea of tracking credits. It can seem to undermine the whole concept of home education to have to keep records in such a public-school-looking way. It should help to remember that tracking credits *does not* mean that you have to stop your wonderful homeschool lifestyle and begin "school at home." As stated previously, credits are simply used to translate all the things you have done in your homeschool into the commonly understood education language.

In addition, knowing the language of credits is very useful as a planning tool. If you have an idea of how much study of a particular subject area will usually translate into a semester's worth of credit, then you will be able to plan your own studies effectively. While most parents who are learning the process are concerned that considering

---

[4]   Please remember that if your student in enrolled in a *public* school program, he is a public school student, subject to the requirements set by the public school system in your state. This book deals with homeschooling privately, that is, *apart from* the government or "public" school system.

credits will force them into doing *more* work, the opposite is usually true. Knowing how to figure out credits typically helps the homeschool parent to tone down a bit on requirements.

For example, most of us, as parents, want to teach our children as much as we possibly can while they are young. We want to equip them to avoid many of the mistakes we made through lack of knowledge. As our children become teens, it is easy to feel the pressure of the end of our homeschooling years in sight. When my own children were young, it was fairly easy for me to choose which topics to study *this* year, knowing that next year would provide an opportunity to focus on other subjects. Once they reached 12 or 13, however, I began to sense that my "next years" were limited. If there was something I wanted to teach, I had better think about beginning it soon!

This put me under pressure to begin to try to "cover it all." I was afraid that I might leave gaps that would damage my children's ability to function as adults. I knew that some gaps were inevitable; I certainly have many in my own knowledge. But I wanted to give my children as fine an education as possible, and I began to wrestle with my tendency to cram in as much as I could.

Learning to understand credits means recognizing that it is impossible to teach our children everything they will ever need to know. Rather than making me feel that I have to do *more*, working with credits has helped me to prioritize all those things I want to teach, recognizing that I will have to make decisions about what is important to learn in junior or senior high school, and learning to let some of the peripheral topics go.

Before we move on, let me first offer this important disclaimer: I do not advocate clock-watching while homeschooling. It is far more important to me that my children have learned something than that they have spent an hour sitting at a desk. I become easily annoyed when held too often to a tight schedule. I wear a watch so seldom that I usually forget to pack one when I need it, so I have often had to rush out and buy a watch on my way to a homeschool convention so that I'll know when to be at my own workshop. If you are at all like me in this way, it is especially important to remember that *I don't watch clocks when homeschooling*—I won't ask you to, either.

I simply use the time computations for credits as a *planning tool* when I'm setting up courses. This will be covered thoroughly in Chapters 4, 5, and 6, so be patient if it begins to look like you have to begin timing your students' work—you don't! For now, in looking at common college entrance requirements and my list of recommendations for graduation requirements, you just need to know that for the purposes of this book, including the following list, one semester of work is equal to 5 credits, and one year of work is equal to 10 credits.

Many states use the system in which one semester is equal to ½ of a credit, and one year is equal to 1 credit. This is also the system used by the vast majority of colleges. If you prefer to use the 1 credit per year system, it is very easy to translate your courses when entering credits on a transcript. You will simply move the decimal place one place to the left once courses are completed. 5 credits will become .5 credits; 10 credits will become 1 credit.

Why all the trouble? Why not just start out planning with the 1 credit system? The reason is that when using credits as a *planning* tool, not just a *translation* tool, it is easier to use the 10 credit system. Ten credits can more easily be divided into small units as parts of a course than 1 credit can. At any rate, if you're still not convinced, you can convert all the courses in this book by simply adding in a decimal.

Finally, you should know that the term "units" is often used in place of "credits." Because a "unit study" has a different meaning for most homeschoolers, I have chosen to use the term "credits" in referring to the tallying of work a student has completed in a subject. I use the term "unit" when talking about a focused topic of study, like a unit study on the Civil War, regardless of whether it will earn 5 credits or 10 credits when completed.

> 5 credits = 1 semester
> 10 credits = 1 year

❖ Total Credits Needed for High School Graduation

Most public schools require between 200 and 240 credits for graduation. This allows for study in the basic core subjects, plus allows the student to select some elective courses to pursue his own goals and interests.

If a student completes all the recommended courses listed beginning on page 38, the total credits earned will be about 210. If you require an additional 30 or 40 credits from elective courses, the total accumulated by graduation will be 240-250. If you choose to follow this plan, your student must take an average of six courses each semester for four years in order to earn a total of 240 credits.

Regardless of which basic courses you require, the total number of credits required for graduation should include some credits from electives. This will give your student the opportunity to explore a few areas of special interest through his school studies. Some ideas for elective courses are listed on pages 175-177.

Often, homeschooled high school students will have more than the required number of credits by the time they graduate. Most students continue studies during the summer, either with a job (work experience) or with an activity that is counted as Physical Education or with extra studies in another subject area. Many students also take special classes with church youth groups (choir, baseball, missions) or at a local community college or at a local private campus school.

The most important thing is to have well-defined requirements spelled out at the start of high school so that your student will be able to plan courses ahead. It would be difficult to save all of the history courses for twelfth grade.

In the next chapter, "Setting Requirements & Planning Your Year," there are charts to help you plan a course of study. There are samples to show several ways to plan your requirements, whether heading for university or not, whether desiring a traditional course of study or not.

If you are planning to attend college, check the college manual for entrance requirements and adapt your high school course requirements accordingly.

❖ Recommended High School Courses

Ideas for the amount of courses in each subject area are listed below. These suggestions include all of the typical public school course requirements, plus a few extra courses you may want to include. Remember, this is a suggestion only; you should feel free to set your own requirements.

Also remember to set graduation requirements just once for your family. If one student will take four years of math, but another will likely take only two, then your graduation *requirement* should be two, not four. The more mathematically gifted student will use his elective choices to fill in the extra two years of math.

Bible: 20-40 credits suggested (5-10 credits per year for 4 years)

Assuming yours is a Christian school, Bible should be required every year (9th-12th). Can you in good conscience award a diploma from your Christian school to a student who has not had training in Bible? The decision of how many Bible credits to require will likely depend on how much the Bible is used in the other school subjects. If all the other subjects are Bible-centered, you may choose to require less time in a stand-alone Bible course, because your student will be learning Christian principles throughout his day. However, if many of your other subjects rely on non-sectarian materials, or lack a depth of Christian content, you may decide to require a full 10 credits per year.

The required number of Bible credits could be adjusted for students transferring out of a school which did not require Bible. For example: If a student is homeschooled for grades 11 & 12, after attending a non-Christian school for grades 9 & 10, he may be required to have only two years of Bible.

English: 40 credits suggested (4 years)

High school English should stress writing skills and literature. Commonly, ninth and tenth grade English courses are more general in nature, reviewing basic grammar, introducing a variety of literature forms, and developing writing skills. The third and fourth years (if you require a fourth) may be advanced literature courses or specialized subjects like Journalism, Creative Writing, etc. Most colleges and universities expect 40 credits (4 years) of English, including American Literature and English Literature.

Math: 20 credits suggested (2 years)

Remedial and consumer math courses meet most public schools' math requirement for high school graduation, but colleges usually expect students to have two years of Algebra and one of Geometry, and higher math is strongly recommended. If your student plans to attend a college or university and major in mathematics, business, or any of the sciences, plan to include mathematics every year of high school.

Science: 20 credits suggested (2 years)

These courses should usually include biological and physical sciences. Most high schools recommend that students include 10 credits of a life science and 10 credits of a physical science. They also recommend that at least one of the science courses be a laboratory class. (A laboratory class means experiments and hands-on activities are stressed.) Colleges usually require at least one year of Biology and one year of Chemistry, often expecting a third year of Physics. Of course, if your student plans to attend college as a science major, he will want to cover more science in high school.

World History & Geography: 10 credits suggested (1 year)

One year of world history is often required by public schools. It may be taken any year, ninth through twelfth. Be sure to stress current events throughout the course - the chronological order used in texts often means running out of time at the end of the year, so current world leaders are covered too briefly to prepare students for understanding events taking place today.

United States History: 10 credits suggested (1 year)

One year of U.S. history is usually required in public schools. It may be taken any year, ninth through twelfth. Usually, U.S. History is taken before American Government, as a foundation for understanding how and why our government is set up as it is. But this order of courses is not mandatory.

State History: 2-5 credits suggested (up to one semester)

Many states require state history to be taught in high school. At least a short unit (maybe 6-10 weeks) should probably be required. Be sure to include your state's constitution and government.

American Government & Civics: 5 credits suggested (1/2 year)

One semester of government, taken any year, ninth through twelfth. If you do not cover state and local government in a state history course, be sure to include it here. While U.S. History is commonly taken before American Government, if your students have a good foundation in U.S. History, it may not be necessary to follow this pattern. Many homeschool families choose to cover American Government during whichever year of high school includes a presidential election.

Economics: 5 credits suggested (1/2 year)

One semester is usually by public schools, any year, ninth - twelfth.

Fine Arts: 10 credits suggested (1 year)

Visual or performing arts may be studied. Art, dance, drama, or music are commonly taken as separate courses, or a survey course may be designed which includes an introduction to a variety of the arts. Colleges vary in their fine arts and foreign language requirements. Most will expect at least 5 credits of fine arts even if a year of a foreign language has been taken. Many colleges require two years of the same foreign language in addition to one year of fine arts. Consult the catalog of the college you plan to attend; or if you have no idea what college you will consider, it is probably safest to take two years of the same foreign language plus one year of a fine art.

Foreign Language: 10 credits (1 yr) - 20 credits (2 yrs) suggested

Any foreign language, including Sign Language. If advanced studies will be desired in college, check ahead to see that the college in question offers the language you plan to study. Public schools often require one year of foreign language for high school graduation. Colleges vary in their foreign language requirements. Many universities require two years of the same foreign language in addition to a year of fine arts. Consult the catalog of the college you plan to attend; or it is probably safest to take two years of the same foreign language plus one year of a fine art.

Physical Education: 20 credits suggested (5 credits per year for 4 years)

Many homeschool families require P.E. every year, as a way to instill the healthy habit of exercise while their children are still living at home. Our family requires P.E. each year, but only three days per week. So we require 5 credits for each year, but it takes the whole year to earn them.

Home Economics: 5 - 10 credits suggested (1 -2 semesters)

Home Economics is not usually required for public school graduation. But considering that most students will one day have the responsibility of taking care of a home, it seems prudent to include at least a minimum requirement for home economics.

Vocational Arts: 5 - 10 credits suggested (1 -2 semesters)

Since high school students will enter the business world, either as job holders or as consumers, families may want to require credit in vocational skills.

Typing or Computers: 5 credits or more suggested (at least 1 semester)

While typing is not usually required for public school graduation, most students will benefit from at least a semester to acquaint them with basic keyboard skills and computer software.

Driver Education: 2½ - 5 credits (½ semester or ½ year)

This is a course most students look forward to taking in high school. Each state has different requirements on what is needed to earn a driver's license, however, whether or not your student gets a license before graduation, it is probably a good idea to teach them safe driving skills and traffic laws while they are under your authority.

Driver Education is often paired with a course in health education. Each subject may be given one quarter of the year, to fill a one-semester time slot; or Driver Education and Health may each be given a whole semester so that combined, they create a full year course.

Health: 2½ - 5 credits suggested (½ semester or ½ year)

Homeschool families may want to require basic CPR and emergency first aid training as part of a health course.

Electives: 40 credits suggested (5 per semester for 4 years)

In order to become well-rounded adults and to help to uncover what may be undiscovered gifts and abilities, students should be exposed to a wide range of subjects. For ideas on elective courses, see pages 175-177.

Other:

If it is important to you that your students have exactly the same courses as their public school counterparts, ask your local high school for a copy of its graduation requirements.

❖ 4 Setting Requirements & Planning Your Year

Once the parents have set general educational goals, they must determine what should be required for entrance into high school, and what should be required to graduate from high school. Rather than setting requirements for each grade individually, graduation requirements are set as a *whole*. Once the graduation requirements are set, it is easier to decide what to study each year or semester.

Two major problems can trip you up in setting your graduation requirements. I stumbled over both of them the first time through.

The first problem was that I wanted my student to study *too much* (and you were worried you might miss something!) I have not yet met a homeschooler in very much danger of missing a major academic area of study. Most of us err the opposite way, wanting to cram so much knowledge into our children that their brains can't absorb it all and they have no time for *life*.

My own case happened this way... In trying to decide on high school requirements, which are organized by credits, I was aware that most public high schools require from 200 to 240 credits to graduate, which would mean taking five or six courses per semester. When I began to list all the courses I wanted us to cover, I was well over 300 and still not slowing down.

❖ Has Your Student Already Completed One or More Semesters of Junior or Senior High?

If you are not setting up your course of study from the beginning of junior or senior high, do not waste your time thinking about what you *wish* had been done during previous years. Begin from where your student is right now, and set your graduation requirements according to the time you have available starting now. For example, if your student has completed grades 9 and 10 in public school, set up a two-year course of study for grades 11 and 12, taking into consideration the courses he has already covered.

If you are not sure where you student is academically, you may want to arrange for an assessment test right at the beginning. Ask your local homeschool group leader for a referral to someone in your area. I recommend avoiding the "free" public school testing opportunities, since there is a strong tendency for the officials to misconstrue their "free service," and instead try to push their recommendations on you.

Because I love foreign languages, I want my children to have a chance to study several. Growing up in the Southwest, I can see how valuable it would be to speak Spanish, and anything close to fluency would require at least three years. As a Bible student, I'd love to see my sons know some Greek, maybe two years? Of course, the Old Testament was originally written in Hebrew, which would require at least a year just for exposure, and Latin, being the Classical language, should certainly require two years. So foreign language could easily work up to seven or eight year-long courses, or 70 to 80 credits! And I was just getting warmed up!

The second problem was related to my son's special gifts. He loves music and has a talent for playing piano. He studies very seriously and I felt that his lessons and practice were deserving of high school credits. Since he would likely continue his studies throughout high school, that would be four year-long courses, or 40 credits in music. He also loves computers and is good at math. So rather than the typical public school requirement of two years math, He would take two years of Algebra, a year of Geometry and Trigonometry, and a year of Calculus. Plus he'd need a year's worth of credits for typing and keyboarding skills, and computer science, and maybe some computer repair.

My second son has different gifts, so I would change my requirements for him. Writing graduation requirements all over again for my next child began to look like a huge task (which it would be!) so I began to re-think my requirements.

How do all those other schools do it anyhow? Since the Bible doesn't mention high school graduation, how could I find out what that meant? More study revealed that a list of graduation requirements is actually a list of *minimum* graduation requirements. The list shows the least amount of study required in each subject in order to graduate.

This made me consider that rather than requiring four years of math because my son is good in math, I should ask what would be the minimal expectation. For example, what if he got great grades for three years, but then found he *hated* Calculus. Could he quit the Calculus book and still graduate? Not if I had made Calculus a graduation requirement. Of course, I could simply change the requirement, but then my son would feel like I was "dumbing it down." Besides, what good is a requirement if it changes so often you can't tell what is required?

It seems so simple now, but I had to realize that our graduation requirements should simply include those subjects we feel our children *must* cover in order to have a good *start* in their adult lives. We all know that education will continue throughout their lives, but it's hard to restrain ourselves from trying to "teach them everything" while they are under our care.

Before you can determine all the subjects to require and the amounts of study to require in each subject, you have to know how much time you have in which to complete all the courses. "Easy," you say, "two years for junior high and four years for high school." Exactly. But how many days out of the two years will you be studying each subject? And how much time each day?

❖ How Many Days in a School Year?

Most states require students to attend school for a minimum number of days each year, not counting excused absences. In some states, the schools are in session for more than the required number of days, usually because funding is provided for more days. In California, for example, public schools must operate 175 days per year. However, most schools are in session for 180 days because they can receive funding for that many.

Even if a school is open for 180 days, sometimes children are absent. Students who miss classes are generally expected to make up the missed assignments and tests, but not the class time. Teachers do not stay at school for extra days during summer for all the children who missed days. You should not have to add days to your schedule at the end of the year to make up for absent days, either. Generally, if your student misses a couple of weeks each semester, but completes the required course work, you should not worry about making up the missed time. So even though your schedule planned for 180 days, if you actually taught for only 160 to 170, I wouldn't worry about it.

Many states set a minimum number of days for public schools to operate, but not for private schools or homeschools. The number shown is based upon either specific laws for private or homeschools or upon the number of days offered by public schools in the state. The following chart shows the minimum number of days usually recommended for homeschools to schedule. This chart is intended as an aid in planning your schedule, not as legal advice. Remember to check with your statewide homeschool organization or HSLDA to verify your own state's requirements.

State	Days Recommended	State	Days Recommended	State	Days Recommended	State	Days Recommended
AK	180	ID	same as local district	MT	180	RI	same as local district
AL	180	IL	176	NC	180	SC	180
AR	180	IN	185	ND	175	SD	175
AZ	175	KS	180	NE	1080 hours	TN	180
CA	180	KY	185	NH	180	TX	170
CO	172	LA	180	NJ	180	UT	same as local district
CT	180	MA	180	NM	same as local district	VA	180
DC	180	MD	180	NV	180	VT	175
DE	180	ME	175	NY	180	WA	990 hrs - jr high 1080 hours - sr high
FL	180	MI	180	OH	182	WI	875 hours
GA	180	MN	170	OK	180	WV	same as local district
HI	same as local district	MO	1000 hours	OR	same as local district	WY	175

Since about half of the states require 180 days per year, most of the examples in this book figure you will be teaching about 180 days (not counting excused absences.) If you plan to teach less than 180 days, it is easy enough to cut back. However, if you live in Indiana, Kentucky, or Ohio, you'll have to plan ahead for the additional days required by your state.

If you live in one of the states which require you to track hours, you may be used to marking down each day's starting and ending times already. If so, and if it works well for you, by all means, continue that method of record-keeping. If you need to simplify, however, here's what I'd consider doing: plan your courses to include about the right number of hours and figure that your student does extra things like help with meals and chores (home economics), read good books (literature), and review subjects for tests. You'll more than likely surpass the required number of hours and although you may not have recorded every minute of every subject, your course records will provide an example of how much time has been spent during the year.

❖ How Many Hours of Study?

First, most states do not require homeschoolers to keep track of hours and minutes at all. Second, I have much better things to do than keep track of every minute spent studying every subject. Third, we do lots of studies that fit into more than one category, so it would be hard to figure out where to write them. And fourth, I would have a tendency to get very legalistic over hours and minutes if we tried to record them all as a requirement for passing a course. I want to avoid the idea that putting in a certain amount of time makes one "educated." So I don't watch the clock all day, tracking every minute, to figure out if we're "done" yet. However, I *do* consider the time required in setting up the courses, just to give me an idea of how much we can expect to accomplish each year.

I had always figured that with 180 days in a school year, a year course was approximately 180 hours of work, or 90 hours for a semester course. Barbara Shelton, in High School: A Home-Designed Form+U+La, freed me up in this area. First, she reminded me that high school courses are not typically an hour a day. They are usually 50 minutes. 50 minutes of class time for 180 days is only 150 hours for a year-long course, or 75 hours for a semester.

Barbara went further and said that most classroom teachers would be delighted if, out of the 50 minutes of class time, they actually got in 40 minutes of instructional time. And, of course, even 40 minutes in a typical schoolroom would be much less productive than the uninterrupted study of an individual without 25 peers around him. So Barbara feels very comfortable with figuring that the rule of thumb for class hours could be just 120 hours per year-long course.

For your own school, you may decide what you feel comfortable with. Carnegie units, sometimes referred to for college admissions, are based upon 160 hours of study. However, if you figure in outside reading and a little extra studying before tests, a planned 150-hour course will usually cover about 160 hours. Of course, you have to remember that those 160 Carnegie hours are spent mostly in a group-setting classroom. Surely your hours of independent study count as more.

Whatever amount of hours you decide will represent the "average" high school course, it need only be your rule of thumb—used for planning, but not to put you into the bondage of recording every hour of every subject. For my own family, 150 hours is used as a guide. We figure that it takes into account that most high school students have some home work to do in addition to the class time. You may figure 180 hours, or 120 hours if that makes more sense to you.

The sample courses in this book are shown according to my own family's general rule:

- A one-year course will take approximately 150 hours to complete;
- A one-semester course will take approximately 75 hours.

❖ Awarding Credits

Credits (also called units) are awarded for work completed to show how much study in an area has been done. For a college admissions officer, seeing one student's transcript with 10 credits for Spanish, compared to a student with 30 credits for Spanish, will tell him approximately how many years of study each student has done. Remember when awarding credits that you are trying to show a reasonable comparison of how much study in a subject your student has completed, compared with the "average" high school.

The 5-credits-per-semester system is not used in every state, however it works particularly well for home educators because the credits can be divided into units of study or subsections of a subject so easily. If your state uses a different system (most likely in which ½ credit is given per semester course) it is easy to translate your courses once they are completed and you are ready to record them on a transcript. Chapter 9 covers recording courses on transcripts.

The 5 credit per semester, 10 credits per year system is used in this book. It is easy to use and understand:

- 5 credits = 1 semester course
- 10 credits = 1 year course

To be able to set graduation requirements using this credit system, and to fully take advantage of the flexibility of home education at the same time, you will want to be able to set subject requirements two ways:

1. Set the requirement based on the number of credits you want to award (and figure out the amount of time it will take to earn them), or

2. Set the requirement based on the approximate amount of time you want the student to spend on a subject (and figure out how many credits that amount of time will earn.)

Converting Credits into Time

If a semester course receives 5 credits, and as stated in the previous section, a semester course takes approximately 75 hours to complete, then

5 credits will take approximately 75 hours to earn.

This makes 1 credit equal to about 15 hours. (75 hours ÷ 5 credits = 15 hours for each credit.)

Examples:

If you want to establish your English requirement following the typical college entrance requirements shown on page 56, you will require 40 credits of English. This would work out to an average of 10 credits per year, or 150 hours of study in English each year.

If you require 10 credits of home economics for graduation, you will plan to record about 150 hours of home economics work during high school. You may choose to do this in the institutional-school mode of planning all 150 hours during one year, or you may do a little here and a little there each year, just so that when you are ready to graduate, you will have completed the 150 hours.

Converting Time into Credits

The obvious opposite is also true: if a student works approximately 75 hours in a subject area, he could be awarded 5 credits. Or if a student works about 15 hours, he could receive 1 credit.

Examples:

If your student participates in a missions project with your church, which includes 30 hours of work, you could award him 2 credits. (30 hours work ÷ 15 hours per credit = 2 credits.)

Our family studies every subject from the Bible, but we also wanted to require a separate Bible course. We want to instill the habit of an independent daily devotional each day and decided a ½ hour each morning would be our *goal*. I have to confess that we have missed our individual devotional time pretty often, so we set our *requirement* based upon ½ hour, 4 days per week.

This works out to two hours per week, or a total of 72 hours for the whole school year (which is 36 weeks.) 72 hours is close enough to 75 hours for me, so we require 5 credits of Bible per year, and set up our course outline with about 72 hours in mind.

Physical education is required for two years in many public high schools, but during the other two years the students aren't required to take P.E. at all. This makes no sense to me since the whole purpose of P.E. is to develop a habit of physical fitness. I don't see how you can be physically fit when you only work out every other year.

An ideal amount of workout time for fitness is about 45 minutes per session, three times per week. If we required 40 minutes of exercise, three times per week, that would total 120 minutes (or two hours) per week. Since two hours per week over the 36-week school year equals 72 hours, I will award 5 credits for our P.E. program. Again, 75 hours is only my ball-park figure for a semester's worth of credits; 72 hours is close enough. My students must earn 5 credits in P.E. each year, for a total of 20 credits toward high school graduation (or 10 credits toward junior high graduation.)

❖ Keeping Track of Points vs. Keeping Track of Hours

Remember that I said I don't like to keep track of hours and minutes? I don't. You may decide you like to keep track of hours and minutes, and, if so, go right ahead. Remember, you're in charge of your homeschool, so you have the authority to decide how records will be kept. For me it would be absolute bondage and a waste of time and energy, so I almost never keep track of hours.

I just use the rule of thumb on hours in a course for *planning* my courses. I keep a rough idea in mind of how much study I am going to require. If I am going to require around 150 hours of history, and I want to include a special research project, I will keep in mind how long such a project would take. If, for example, I want my son to do some research in the library, write an outline, prepare a rough draft, and write a good final draft, I may decide that he should spend time *approximately* as follows:

2 hrs.	=	research at library and note taking
1 hr	=	outline
1 hr	=	rough draft (in my house, this is for a report about 2 pages in length)
2 hrs	=	final copy
6 hrs	=	total report

When I plan our history class, I will figure that the history report is worth 6 out of 150 points. Once I do the initial planning of the course, I don't worry about whether the library research actually took 1½ hours or 2½. If the whole report takes only 4 hours or if it takes 8 hours, I am not concerned. Some assignments and projects will take longer than I thought, and some will take less time. It all works out pretty well in the end.

In the case of the history report, I would simply make sure that when I was ready to assign the report, I explained what I had in mind: a report of about two pages, with an outline, a rough draft, and then a final copy, based on research done at the library.

Each student and each course will vary. My intent is to set a guideline to help you, not to limit or control your homeschool. Some students may work through a course in two months, while spending 8 months on another. Try to allow for maximum flexibility while being assured that your homeschool graduates are deserving of a diploma.

For some courses, I don't worry about how many hours it will take at all. For example, if I buy a textbook for Algebra I, which is intended by the publisher to be a one-year course, I don't bother planning for hours or points in my course outline. I just figure that when we are done with the book, I will award the student 10 credits.

❖ Your Own Graduation Requirements

At this point, you should be ready to decide how much study makes a "full-year course" (are you going with 150 hours, 120 hours, or what?) You also should have a general idea of your educational goals and what studies you want to cover, although you may not have decided which years to cover them. The next step is to decide which subjects to require, and how many credits or approximately how much study time to require for each course.

To determine the courses you will require, you should consider both ways of planning credits. Some decisions about courses will be easiest to make by figuring out *how much time* you want to spend on the subject, and others will be easiest if you figure out *how many credits* you want to require.

Look at the samples and charts on pages 54-57 and 61-63. Either make several copies of one of the blank charts, or start out with a scratch piece of paper so you can revise your first drafts. Begin by listing the subjects you want to require for graduation in the column on the left, then pencil in your ideas for requirements on the right. Don't be frustrated if you have too many requirements the first time through. Pray about it, considering the *essential foundation subjects* everyone should learn.

I have found through all our years of home education that the whole course of study comes together easiest if we begin with the planning of Bible.

> *But seek ye first the kingdom of God, and his righteousness;*
> *and all these things shall be added unto you. Matthew 6:33*

❖ Writing Your Graduation Requirements

Beginning on page 52, there are six different charts of graduation requirements. Three are blank, ready for you pick one to photocopy and use, and three are filled-in samples. Look at the samples and use the ideas you like, but don't feel pressured to follow them; you are the one God has appointed over your own homeschool.

At this point, focus first on the left column of the chart you want to use. Start by writing in the subjects you want to cover in junior high or high school. Look back to pages 8-12 if you want to see what subjects your state requires, but write in the subjects primarily based upon the vision God has given you. It's easiest to keep the subjects very general on this part of the chart. For now, just write in "math" rather than "algebra." You will fill in more specific courses in each subject area later.

Once you have listed the subjects, write in the total amount of credits required for graduation in the left column. Use a pencil because, if you're at all like me, you will need to adjust your figures several times before you're through.

When you are through with your first draft, total all the credits you have listed. If your total is between 100 and 120 for junior high or between 200 and 240 for senior high, you are right in the average range. If you are much higher or lower than the average figures, you may want to adjust your requirements. If your figure is high, you may need to realize that you simply can't teach everything! Pray about it and see if you can cut back a bit without compromising your goals. On the other hand, if your figure is low, you may need to check that you haven't left out a major subject area.

When you think you are satisfied with your chart, double check by figuring out the amount of work you will need to complete each year in order to meet your graduation requirements. First, divide your total credits by the number of years you are planning to see how many credits you will need to finish each year on average. Then multiply the credits per year by 15 hours (assuming you are planning around 150 hours for each 10 credits) to get an approximate idea of how many hours per year you are considering. Finally, divide your total hours per year by the number of days you plan to teach.

For example, if your total number of credits is 220, the math will work out this way:

1. 220 credits ÷ 4 years = 55 credits per year

2. 55 credits per year × 15 hours each = 825 hours per year

3. 825 hours ÷ 180 days = about 4½ hours per day.

If this seems to be a reasonable amount of work, you're done with this step! Write the number of hours on the back of your graduation requirements sheet to use as a reference point later when you are working on lesson plans. If you are in one of the states which require you to track hours, you will want your graduation requirement to reflect an average amount of study time that is within an hour or so of the required amount. For example, if you are supposed to be tracking 6 hours per day of school, try to set your graduation requirements at a minimum of 5 or 5½ hours. You will be able to add extra reading, household chores, church or community activities, work experience or hobbies to your actual study time, thus bringing your total number of school hours easily within the requirement.

❖ Notes on the Sample Graduation Requirements

On each of the sample charts, I have listed the number of credits required. The credits are based on the formula that approximately 75 hours/points = 1 semester = 5 credits. The "College-bound Student" sample is based upon the necessity of meeting both the typical university admission requirements and the usual public high school graduation requirements. There is room for flexibility. Check out the graduation requirements of public high schools in your area (most will have a list of course requirements available at the counselors' office), look at the sample college admission requirements in Chapter 11 of this book, and check out a couple of local colleges' catalogs at your local public library if you need more help.

Notes on the Schofield Family Graduation Requirements:

I'm always hesitant to show exactly what our family is doing because so often people will misconstrue it as my recommendation for everyone else. I fully expect and hope that you will take the time to set your own family's requirements rather than just using ours. However, I am aware that it sometimes helps to see just how another person has done it, so I'm including our own family's requirements for that purpose. If you like some of our ideas, use them with our blessing. If you have other ideas of your own, use them with our blessing, too.

Please note that these are our minimum requirements. Our students exceed these in many areas, depending on each student's gifts and interests. You should also be aware that in junior high, our graduation requirements are used more as goals to strive for. We did not meet them in every area, going over and under in some subjects. We used our junior high requirements as a planning tool, and as a practice for the kind of record-keeping we would be doing in high school.

Bible: Our requirement is explained and displayed on pages 109-114.

English: We require 10 credits each year. We feel literacy warrants this because the basics of reading and writing affect all subjects. Plus, it takes years to master all the different subjects included in English: reading (including literature and comprehension), writing (including composition of reports, essays, letters, etc), grammar, spelling, speech, and listening.

Math: We require 10 credits each year of junior high because we are either finishing work on basic arithmetic skills which must be mastered, or because we are beginning more advanced mathematics studies like Algebra. For high school, we require at least 2 years, or 20 credits. However, since our first homeschooled high school student had not mastered basic arithmetic by 11th grade, I had no qualms about making her use elective courses to continue in arithmetic.

Science: We require one semester's worth of credits (5) each year (but we may spread it out to take a whole year to complete the semester, or we may pour it on and do a semester's worth in a couple of months.) Our basic program in science for high school is a bit different—we are planning to study one semester each of Creation Science, Biology, Chemistry, and Physics. For junior high, we are studying one semester of life science (basic biology) and one semester of physical or earth science.

Physical Education: Our requirement is explained on page 48, and displayed on pages 119-120.

History: For junior high, we are requiring 5 credits each year. As with science, the 5 credits may be spread out and take the whole year to finish, with history one year and science another year, or we may do all of our history in one semester and science in another. Our junior high history courses have a heavy focus on geography. For high school, we are requiring the typical 10 credits of U.S. history and 10 of world history, but with a heavy focus on political events, people, and literature. In addition, in high school, we require 2 credits of state history, which is about a 30-hour unit (about 6 weeks.)

Vocational Education: Our family divided this course into units. Our course description is on page 88, example 3. This is a requirement, not an elective in our school.

Home Economics & Family Living: We also divide this course into units, as described on page 87, example 1. This is a requirement, not an elective in our school.

Typing: Also required in our school—not an elective.

Fine Arts, Foreign Language: We are requiring one year of each in high school, and a brief exposure to several different arts in junior high.

Health & Driver Education: Since a typical drivers education classroom course in our state takes about 30 hours in a private driving school, we are giving 30 points (2 credits) for our students' completion of that. They don't get any points at all for the behind-the-wheel part of driver education, since that brings its own reward—a license. The 45 points (3 credits) allocated for health is what is left over after driver education to round out a semester's worth of credit.

Electives: In both junior and senior high, this is what we had left to make a nice round number of credits required for graduation.

JUNIOR HIGH
Graduation Requirements

SUBJECT	7th	8th	REQUIREMENTS
Total Credits:			Total Credits
Cumulative Total:			Required: _____

Schofield Family Junior High Graduation Requirements

SUBJECT	7th	8th	REQUIREMENTS
Bible			10 credits (5 each year)
English			20 credits (10 each year)
Mathematics			20 credits (10 each year)
Science			10 credits
Physical Education			10 credits (5 each year)
Social Sciences			10 credits (5=World, 5=U.S.)
Vocational Education			5 credits
Home Economics & Family Living			5 credits
Typing/Computer Keyboard Skills			2 credits
Fine Arts			5 credits
Electives			3 credits
Total Credits:			Total Credits Required: __100__
Cumulative Total:			

- 1 credit = 15 points/hours
- 5 credits = 1 semester course (about 75 hours/points)
- 50 credits = required to pass to next grade level
- 100 credits = junior high graduation

High School Graduation Requirements

SUBJECT	9th	10th	11th	12th	REQUIREMENTS
Total Credits:					Total Credits Required: _____
Cumulative Total:					

High School Graduation Requirements
(with semesters separated)

SUBJECT	9th	10th	11th	12th	REQUIREMENTS
Total Credits:					Total Credits Required: _____
Cumulative Total:					

Typical College-Bound Student's Graduation Requirements

This chart covers common university requirements for incoming freshmen.
Check the manual of the college you plan to attend for additional requirements.

SUBJECT	9th	10th	11th	12th	REQUIREMENTS
Bible					20-40 credits 4-8 semesters
English					40 credits 8 semesters
Mathematics					30-40 credits 6-8 semesters *Students planning to major in math or science should take 40 credits.*
Science					20-40 credits 4-8 semesters *Students planning to major in math or science should take 40 credits.*
Social Sciences					35 credits 7 semesters
Fine Arts					10 credits 2 semesters
Foreign Language					20 credits 4 semesters *all of one language*
Physical Education					20 credits 4 semesters
Health and Driver Ed.					5 credits 1 semester *usually combined into 1 semester*
Electives					40 credits 8 semesters *Typing & Computer recommended. Extra courses in above subjects may count here. Include some electives which show your unique interests.*
Total Credits:					Total Credits Required: _____
Cumulative Total:					

Schofield Family High School
Graduation Requirements

Sample

SUBJECT	9th	10th	11th	12th	REQUIREMENTS
Bible					20 credits (5 per year)
English					40 credits (10 per year)
Mathematics					20 credits
Science					20 credits (5 Creation Sci; 5 Biology; 5 Chemistry; 5 Physics)
History & Geography					22 credits (10: world, 10: U.S., 2: state)
Government & Economics					10 credits (5: govt., 5: economics)
Physical Education					20 credits (5 per year)
Vocational Education					5 credits
Home Economics & Family Living					10 credits
Typing & Computers					10 credits
Health & Driver Education					5 credits (3: health, 2: driver ed.)
Foreign Language					10 credits
Fine Arts					10 credits
Electives					23 credits
Total Credits:					Total Credits Required: 225
Cumulative Total:					

❖ What Courses to Require Each Year

Once you have set your overall educational goals and your graduation requirements, you are ready to decide which subjects to work on this year and which to leave for a different year. I hope you will feel free to depart from the typical school schedule of courses in your area if another plan will better meet the needs of your own family. I once met with a family who was concerned about their desire to study the history and geography of South America for a year. They were embarking on a year of living aboard their sailboat and traveling around South America. "But," the mother said, "all my son's friends at school are studying U.S. History this year." The family ended up relieved that they could leave U.S. History for next year and pursue their own plans while on their trip.

It is usually necessary for a large institutional school to set a program in which all students will study a particular subject during a set semester or grade, so that the school can know ahead of time how many teachers and classrooms will be required. For example, if one semester of economics is required of all high school students, but they are free to decide when they want to take it, they could all decide to take the class at the same time, creating an overcrowding in the fall, and a complete lack in the spring. This would obviously be a waste of the school's resources, so a more structured schedule is set.

Likewise, if students were required to complete 150 hours of science during a year, but were allowed to choose the hours, the same instability of classrooms and equipment would result. Imagine a student who becomes completely engrossed in today's science experiment. He is so interested that the teacher decides he will learn more by continuing his study than by interrupting it to go to history class. Multiply this by several hundred students and many teachers and classrooms, and utter chaos would result.

But what would happen if this same scenario took place in the homeschool? The student could simply say, "Hey Mom! I'm right in the middle of this experiment. I don't want to quit yet, so I'm going to finish it this afternoon and work on history and grammar tomorrow, okay?" The homeschool has a great deal of flexibility that institutional schools, whether public or private, cannot possibly have.

For most basic subject requirements, the institutional schools assign a grade level during which all students will take a particular course, leaving them free only in the selection of their electives. It is a real blessing of home education that parents and students may choose not only *what* to study, but *when*. Having the opportunity to take a trip which relates to one subject, or having access to materials or equipment that would enhance a subject can be considered in planning each year's studies. Arbitrarily deciding U.S. History must be covered in eighth grade and again in eleventh because that is what your local public school requires, will not make sense for most homeschools.

Rather than choosing this year's subjects according to what others are doing, I suggest you choose subjects according to what *you* are doing. Leave room to flex a bit. The homeschool lifestyle will work best for your family if, rather than adapting your entire family life to fit "schooling," you adapt some of your schooling to fit your family's "lifestyle of learning."

As Barbara Shelton and Marilyn Howshall explain in Senior High: A Home Designed Form+U+La,[5] "Traditional school is something you *do* six hours a day; lifestyle of learning is a way you *live* twenty-four hours a day."

They remind us that in institutional schools, the junior or senior high student typically attends six hours a day, five days a week for nine months, studying each subject for one hour each day. In contrast, most homeschool families have found that at home, learning takes place in less-even chunks. For example, for many families, the winter season,

---

[5] Shelton, Barbara Edtl. Senior High: A Home-Designed Form+U+La (Kelso, Washington: Triune Bible Institute & Seminary Press, 1993) p. VII-2.

with its cold weather and short days, lends itself to *inside* studies: workbook drills, literature readings, history research, etc. The spring, on the other hand, draws the family out of doors, for nature studies, physical education, or vocational education (also known as wood-cutting or changing the oil in Mom's car.)

Another area of flexibility is that in homeschools, each course does not have to begin and end on the same date. Once a family has homeschooled a year or more, they have realized that some books are finished earlier than planned, while some may take longer. After several years, there is quite a bit of staggering of the beginning dates for various textbooks and subjects. If the math book is finished in April, the new one is started and may be finished the following February. The history book may not be finished until July, with the new one stretching a year and a half into the following November. This makes it difficult to figure out where to put each course on a planning chart, and even harder to put it in a specific grade level on a final transcript. For example, would a 10-credit, year long history course which was actually worked on beginning in November 1992, and continuing a year and a half until April 1994, be counted in the 92-93 school year or the 93-94?

For families who plan some of their own courses, perhaps using a textbook, but not necessarily using it in the same way as a classroom teacher would, this staggering of dates can get pretty confusing by high school. Also, trying to fit in a tidy six-week course in cooking, or auto mechanics, or art may stretch the busy family's schedule to the breaking point—especially if it is a large family. It's hard enough just to fit in time for all the basics!

Once we began homeschooling our sons at junior and senior high level, we found that some subjects, like home economics, fine arts, and others were difficult to pigeonhole into a semester or year course. During the elementary years, we had spent some time in many of these subjects, but not all in one chunk. In Form+U+La, Barbara Shelton enlightened us by convincing us that we could continue to work part time in many different subjects during every high school term, and it would all come out the same in the end. So our family's graduation requirements take that into consideration. We may require one year's worth of home economics credits to graduate, but the course will be worked at during all four years of high school, until it is completed. We don't worry much about trying to squeeze in enough cooking assignments to get a whole year's credits in one calendar year.

However, the opposite is true of some subjects, like English. In courses like English, in which fundamental skills of literacy must be slowly built by regular practice over a long period of time, you will probably want the student to have some assigned work every day. This means that the course must be paced, so that it does not get put off to the point that your student has three or four years of English to complete in twelfth grade. So for some courses, a more rigid schedule is necessary.

Of course, families who want to plan their courses in the traditional way may still do that, whether the student is aiming to meet university admission requirements or not. Consider your own lifestyle. What will fit best into your home? Choose the ideas that seem workable to you and don't worry about whether it looks different from what everyone else is doing. Chances are that when your student graduates from high school, he will have mastered the same basic 3-Rs and he will have been exposed to many of the same peripheral subjects as most other students.

Many of the outlines for my family's courses are included in Chapter 6: Designing Courses. I've also included samples from others who have covered courses in different ways. The samples are shown as examples only and are meant as a place for you to start your own ideas flowing. Your own requirements and course content will be different from ours.

❖ Choosing This Year's Courses

In determining which courses to teach this year, it helps to consider a balance between those classes that require a lot of your time as teacher and those which the student can do more independently. Also consider which courses require more serious study and which are aimed more at exposure and appreciation of a subject.

First, is there any subject which is a real priority to you this year? For example, have you been battling spelling so long that you now feel that even if nothing else were accomplished this year, if your student learns to spell, you will feel successful at the end of the year? Does your student hate to read and you wish you could just focus on sparking his interest? Are you wondering about your student's salvation or walk with the Lord? Do you see a need to focus on a particular character trait, like honesty or diligence? By deciding to put the real priorities first, you will save a lot of grief later in the year. You don't want to find yourself wondering, in March, about whether you have missed the most important educational development opportunity. Whatever the most important aspect of this school year is to you, mark it on your chart so you will remember to focus on it when you are laying out course content and lesson plans.

The next thing is to write in the subjects that must be evenly paced. For example, if your graduation requirements call for 40 credits of English, you know you will need to cover 10 of them this year. You will probably be able to fill in several basic subjects that you want to cover each year. Once that is done, go back and put a checkmark next to those subjects which will require a lot of your time as the teacher. For example, if your student needs you to read through his math lesson with him and help him with most of the problems, then you'll want to put a checkmark next to math. How many checkmarks did you make? Unless you have a special needs student or you are only teaching one child, you will probably not want to teach more than two or three subjects which require a check mark.

Now, is there any subject you have been putting off for the past few years? If so, why not take the plunge and write it in for this year? You will probably find it isn't as tough to teach as you thought. What about any special gifts, hobbies, interests, or subjects you have particularly enjoyed in the past couple of years? You will want to balance your year by including a class or two that is lighter or of special interest.

Are you struggling to decide between history and science? Just *decide*. Pray about it, consider the other courses you will be doing, make your best decision, and forget about wondering if it would have been better to do something else. If you decide to teach history this year and science next, it probably won't make much difference in the long run.

Finally, consider electives or non-academic courses like Home Economics or Auto Mechanics. Are you planning to cover these kinds of courses all in one semester, or are you planning to do a little each year? If you are planning to spread any courses over several years, then you don't really have to add them to your chart at this point. For example, if you have already written in 40 or 50 credits of specific subjects out of a yearly total needed of 55-60, but you plan to do a little cooking and car repair and work experience throughout the year, you know you will finish the year with a reasonable amount of work completed.

When you are considering the sample filled-in charts on the following pages, remember that each chart shows how the graduation requirements might have been met *after the fact*. It is not necessary for you to decide on a course title or outline for every high school course all at once. Go ahead and jot down definite future courses in their appropriate columns if you like, but concentrate primarily on this year's courses.

Schofield Family Junior High Graduation Requirements

(As it might look with all the credits recorded at the end of each year)

SUBJECT	7th	8th	REQUIREMENTS
Bible	5	5	10 credits
English	10	10	20 credits
Mathematics	10	10	20 credits
Science	5	5	10 credits
Physical	5	5	10 credits
Social Sciences	5 *World Geography*	5 *United States*	10 credits (5=World, 5=U.S.)
Vocational	2	3	5 credits
Home Economics	3	2	5 credits
Typing/Computer	2		2 credits
Fine Arts	1	4	5 credits
Electives	3 *guitar*		3 credits
Total Credits:	51	49	Total Credits Required: _100_
Cumulative Total:	51	100	

- 1 credit = 15 points/hours
- 5 credits = 1 semester course (about 75 hours/points)
- 50 credits = required to pass to next grade level
- 100 credits = junior high graduation

 Typical College-Bound Student's
Graduation Requirements

A sample transcript for this student is shown on page 165.

Example of the chart on page 56 as it might look when plans are filled in.
Check the manual of the college you plan to attend for additional requirements.

SUBJECT	9th	10th	11th	12th	REQUIREMENTS
Bible	O.T. Survey (5 credits)	Life of Christ (5 credits)	N.T. Church (5 credits)	Biblical World View	**20-40 credits 4-8 semesters**
English	Grammar & Composition	Composition & Intro to Lit.	American Literature	English Literature	**40 credits 8 semesters**
Mathematics	Algebra 1-2	Algebra 3-4	Geometry/ Trigonometry	Calculus	**30-40 credits 6-8 semesters** *Students planning to major in math or science should take 40 credits.*
Science		Biology	Chemistry		**20-40 credits 4-8 semesters** *Students planning to major in math or science should take 40 credits.*
Social Sciences	World History & Geography	U.S. History	State Hist. (5 credits)	Govt/Civics (5 credits) / Economics (5 credits)	**35 credits 7 semesters**
Fine Arts	Survey of Fine Arts				**10 credits 2 semesters**
Foreign Language		German 1-2	German 3-4		**20 credits 4 semesters** *all of one language*
Physical Education	Soccer Team	Soccer Team	Soccer Team & Coaching	Soccer Team & Coaching	**20 credits 4 semesters**
Health and Driver Ed.		Taken in Summer			**5 credits 1 semester** *usually combined into 1 semester*
Electives	Typing/ Computers			Missions (5 credits) / Carpentry (10 credits)	**40 credits 8 semesters** *Typing & Computer recommended. Extra courses in above subjects may count here. Include some electives which show your unique interests.*
Total Credits:	60	70	60	60	Total Credits Required:
Cumulative Total:	60	135	195	255	240

A sample transcript for this student is shown on page 167.

Schofield Family Graduation Requirements

As it might look with credits recorded at the end of each year.

SUBJECT	9th	10th	11th	12th	REQUIREMENTS
Bible	Fund. of Faith 5	Christian Apologetics 5	Christian Living 5	Christian World View 5	20 credits (5 per year)
English	Fund. of Lit & Comp 10	Elements of Lit & Comp 10	American Literature 10	English Literature 10	40 credits (10 per year)
Mathematics	Algebra 1-2 10	Algebra 3-4 10	Geometry & Trig. 10	Calculus 10	20 credits
Science	Creation Science 5	Intro to Chemistry 5	Field Biology 5	Physics 5	20 credits
History & Geography	World History 8	World Hist 2 U.S. Hist 5	U.S. Hist 5	State History 2	22 credits (10: world, 10: U.S., 2: state)
Government & Economics		Government 1	Government 2	Government 2 Economics 5	10 credits (5: govt., 5: economics)
Physical Education	Soccer 5	Swimming & Soccer 5	Beg. Karate 5	Int. Karate 5	20 credits (5 per year)
Vocational Education	2		1	2	5 credits
Home Economics & Family Living	Cooking 2 Fam Living 1	Auto Care 2	Fam Living 1 Sewing 2	Home Maintenance 2	10 credits
Typing & Computers	Typing 5	Computer Science 2	Computer Science 5	Computer Science 3	10 credits
Health & Driver Education		Driver Ed 2	Health 3		5 credits (3: health, 2: driver ed.)
Foreign Language	Latin 1 5	Latin 2 5			10 credits
Fine Arts	Survey of Fine Arts 1	Survey FA 4 Int. Piano 7	Survey FA 2 Int. Piano 3	Survey FA 3 Adv. Piano 10	10 credits
Electives	Logic 5	See Fine Arts, Math & Computers			23 credits
Total Credits:	64	65	59	64	Total Credits Required: 225
Cumulative Total:	64	129	188	252	

❖ 5 Course Descriptions

A course description should be written for each class your student takes. It can be as simple as a short paragraph or two telling what the course is, along with a list of books and materials used. You may find that your course descriptions vary, depending on the subject area.

Even if you are using a pre-programmed curriculum that includes materials for every subject, you will probably find it helpful later if you have taken time to write at least a few notes describing each course. It would be hard to remember all the details from years of study when you are answering a college admissions officer's questions. Descriptions of pertinent courses may be useful in a portfolio, job interview or college admissions interview. A student who wants to enroll in the local community college for a computer course may find it helpful to have course descriptions of related classes he has already taken at home. It can help make the home education program look professional, serious, and well planned. Even if you never show your descriptions to anyone, taking the 10 minutes or so needed to write a description for each course will help you be organized and focused on your goals.

Knowing you are keeping written records will help you plan carefully, considering courses and requirements ahead of time. It is too easy to fall in the habit of doing what everyone else is doing, rather than making thoughtful, meaningful choices based on one's own conscience and study. Christians should be cautious when modeling their educational programs after a secular system that has fallen far short of the biblical discipleship and training called for in the Bible. Taking time to study, prepare and plan ahead will make your junior and senior high school years profitable. Writing clear course descriptions and keeping good records will give you confidence in your high school program, by assuring that you have taken time to make wise decisions, and by having a clear goal that both you and your student can refer to.

The prudent man looketh well to his going. Proverbs 14:15

*The Lord answered me, and said, Write the vision
and make it plain upon tables, that he may run that readeth it. Habakkuk 2:2*

*Now go, write it before them in a table, and note it in a book,
that it may be for the time to come for ever and ever. Isaiah 30:8*

You may choose to allow your student to select many of his own courses and to write proposed descriptions for you to approve. He could use your graduation requirements as a guideline and design courses to fit. Of course, you, the parent, retain veto power.

Whether you set structured courses for each year or begin many courses all at once, intending to take several years to complete them, you will want to consider course descriptions or course designs before the actual class begins. Beginning with a clear goal and purpose for each subject will help you plan your day-to-day assignments, keeping in mind the point of the class. It is easy to be sidetracked into "finishing books," rather than focusing on the knowledge you want learned.

The course description should include:

1. Name of Student
2. Title for each course being taken
3. Date the course was started and completed (fill this in at the end of the course)
4. Brief description of each course, or an outline (course design)
5. Primary materials used for each course
6. Number of credits for each course

In order to write a description or design for each course, you must make decisions about what to include in the course, or what the content of the course will be. If my course includes a variety of materials or components, I find it easier to write out an outline that I can follow as I make assignments. If the course depends primarily upon one main text, project or activity, and if I don't need an outline to follow when I teach, then I will just write a brief description.

Beginning on page 69, there are many sample course descriptions. Other sources of help in wording your descriptions may be found in the textbooks you are using (look in the introduction or on the back cover), in curriculum catalogs, in scope and sequence charts provided by textbook publishers, in college catalogs (available at your local public library) and in local high school manuals. I follow the suggestion of my friend, Andrea Tawney, and use the standard bibliography format in listing materials used. This lends a professional look and ensures I have all the information I need if I ever want to find a particular resource again.

A blank course description form is included on page 90 for your use. You may make a photocopy for each course you plan to take.

❖ Course Titles

Courses are usually listed by title on high school transcripts, in catalogs, and on course descriptions. Titles should be short and should make it easy to identify the field and, if applicable, the level of study.

Subjects covered several years, at progressively more advanced levels, may be titled several different ways. The usual way is to title the course by grade level if it is a course covered in every grade or in several common grades. You may want to include a letter in the title to designate the semesters. For example:

Bible 9a & **Bible 9b** for the two semesters of 9th grade, **Bible 10a** & **Bible 10b** for the two semesters of 10th grade, etc.

English 9a, **English 9b**, etc.

If a course is not specific to a grade level, but has several levels which are completed in order, it is usually numbered, but beginning with number 1. There are two common ways to number these courses. For example:

Algebra 1 and **Algebra 2** for first and second semesters of the first year course, and **Algebra 3** and **Algebra 4** for the two semesters taken in the second year, or

Algebra 1a & **Algebra 1b** for the two semesters of the first year, and **Algebra 2a** & **Algebra 2b** for the second year. (Both examples for Algebra designate four semesters of Algebra, and either method may be used.)

Drama 1 & **Drama 2** for two semesters of drama, or **Drama 1a** & **Drama 1b** for the same two semesters.

Use the method you like, just be consistent so your records are easy to decipher. Of course, if there is a specific content to the course, or emphasized area of study, you may use that for the title. For example:

Introduction to Old Testament, **Introduction to New Testament**, or **Christian Apologetics** for Bible courses, or

American Literature, **Fundamentals of Literature**, or **Creative Writing** for English courses.

There are many common terms used to describe give a sense of the level or type of course. Fundamental, Basic, Introduction, or Beginning all give the sense of a beginning course. Survey or Overview implies a general look at a range of related topics within a subject area. Review or Remedial can be used to describe courses which are somewhat below the typical grade level of the student. Advanced should be used to describe a course which truly is advanced, for example a third or fourth year of a foreign language or art.

❖ Sample Course Descriptions

Before you read the sample course descriptions and designs, please consider this disclaimer. First, this book is not a curriculum guide. Except for specifically marked sections, like the literature suggestions and other resources listed in Chapter 10, nothing here is intended as a blanket recommendation. I have my own favorite books and publishers, as I'm sure you do. My intent has been to show examples which include materials from a wide variety of publishers, and which demonstrate the use those materials in a variety of ways.

With more than ten different examples for science courses alone, it should be obvious that I have not used every item nor taught every course shown. I have tried to consider as many of the curriculum possibilities that *you* might be using as I could fit into the book. So remember, just because you see a title listed doesn't mean I am recommending it.

The first few course descriptions are shown as they would be done on the course description form. A blank course description form is on page 90. To conserve space, additional courses are listed in paragraph form rather than on a course description sheet. Beginning on page 73, there are samples included for nearly every school subject, listed alphabetically by subject. The samples are given as a source of ideas only. You may use these samples if they fit your family's needs, or create your own.

Remember that in some courses, it may better serve your needs to have a full course outline in addition to or instead of the kinds of brief course descriptions shown in this section. You may be planning a Bible course, for example, which uses several different materials. If you need to figure out how much you will use each of several books and where various assignments will fit in, as well as how much time will be spent in each component of the course, you will likely need a course outline that you can follow throughout the year. Often such an outline can also be used to fill the need of a course description, without having to write out both. Course outlines are covered in Chapter 6: Designing Courses.

The choice of whether to write both a course description and a course outline, or to choose one or the other, is yours. For courses which are already well-laid out by the publisher of a teacher's manual, I usually just need a course description. For courses in which I use more of my own ideas, or in which I combine materials from several sources, I use a course outline. Occasionally, I will make both a course description and an outline.

About the Sample Course Descriptions in this Book

(JR) = courses used in junior high, (SR) = courses used in senior high. But some of the course descriptions would work for either level. In the pre-designed courses, most of the descriptions are taken directly from the course description provided by the publishers of the material used. For self-designed courses, information may be taken from catalog descriptions, tables of contents, or course outlines. Where applicable on the sample descriptions, the source of the description is listed. Many of these courses are also used as samples in Chapter 6: Designing Courses and in Chapter 7: Evaluating Progress and Setting Standards. Where applicable, such courses are cross-referenced.

Pre-Designed Courses

"Pre-designed" courses require very little in the way of description since you are using a preplanned course by a recognized publisher or school. Usually, you can just look in the catalog and use the description given by the publisher. Be sure you list the texts used and the publisher. Or list the name and address of the school where the course was taken. (Count community college courses toward high school credits even if the student is receiving college credit.)

Your Own Designed Courses

Courses designed by a student or parent, rather than by a textbook publisher or school, may require more description. If you ever need to show what was covered in school, whether in a portfolio, interview, or admissions process, the books and materials you used and what you included in the course will not be as easily identified as it is in courses where a common textbook was used. Curriculum listed can include a variety of materials (library books, encyclopedias, specialists in the field of study, jobs, field trips, magazines, videos, hands-on activities, etc.)

If you use a well-known publisher's materials, but use them in a different way than planned for the traditional classrooms, you should also give more description of the course. You don't want someone familiar with a particular text to assume you spent a full year studying it if you actually used it only as a reference book.

Try to keep your course description to only one side of one page, so that it is easy to use, but do include all the major components of your course. Self-designed does not mean unprofessional. Your own course descriptions can look every bit as good as those of the big publishers or traditional schools. Use your computer and create your own form, or use the blank one in this book and type or print neatly on it.

Sample Course Description

Student's Name: Steven Schofield		
Grade: 7	Credits: 10	___ Semester Course ✔ Full Year Course
Start Date: Sept. 8, 1992	End Date:	Semester 1: March 10, 1993 Semester 2: July 10, 1993

Course Title: **Math 7**

Course Description:

A general math course including the following concepts:

a review and extension of basic arithmetic taught in previous grades,
changing equivalents in fractions, decimals and percents,
reading problems with two-step problems and irrelevant information,
an introduction to banking, with deposits, withdrawals, and simple interest on accounts,
figuring volume,
24-hour clocks,
graphs and tables.

Curriculum:

Understanding Numbers: Grade 6. Crockett, KY: Rod & Staff Publishers.

Test Booklet for Understanding Numbers: Grade 6.

Note: The description for this course was taken directly from the Rod & Staff catalog description and uses a 6th grade book for a 7th grade student.

Sample Course Description

Student's Name: Scott Schofield		
Grade: 9	Credits: 10	_____ Semester Course ✔ Full Year Course
Start Date: August 1992		End Date: June 1993
Course Title: **Bible 9**		

Course Description:

    This Bible course will include a study of basic doctrines of Christianity. The student will also be introduced to great Christian authors through the study of five Christian classics.

    Developing a habit of quiet prayer time with the Lord each day, implementing a habit of Scripture memorization, and independent reading of the Bible are key elements of this course and the entire four-year high school plan.

    The student will also complete a service project of his own choosing.

Curriculum:

Bible Study Books:

        Arthur, Kay. <u>How to Study Your Bible</u>. Eugene, OR: Harvest House, 1994

        The Navigators. <u>Design for Discipleship</u>. Books 1, 2 & 3. Colorado Springs: Navpress, 1980.

Memorization is from the King James version of the Bible

Independent reading is in the New King James version

Five Christian Classics, to be approved by instructor

Note: The complete outline, planning sheets and contents of this course are included on pages 109-114. The course standard is on pages 146-147.

Sample Course Description

Student's Name: Scott Schofield		

Grade: 9	Credits: 10	___ Semester Course ✔ Full Year Course

Start Date: September 9, 1995	End Date: June 30, 1996

Course Title: **English 9: Fundamentals of Literature and Composition**

Course Description: This course will emphasize literature and an introduction to high school level composition skills.

1) The introduction to literary analysis will focus on six areas: conflict, character, theme, structure, point of view, and moral tone. The reading selections in the text represent a wide range of authors and a broad sampling of literary forms, including short stories, essays, poetry, and drama. The final unit will be a study of Rostand's drama *Cyrano de Bergerac*. Outside readings will be required, selected by the student from a list of classic novels.

2) The composition skills covered will focus on how to write good paragraphs, how to do 5 paragraph essays, how to organize major papers, and other basic composition skills.

3) In addition, the student will study aspects of correspondence and its uses.

4) Five novels of his own (pre-approved) choice will be completed & reported on.

5) The final portion of the course will be devoted to the student's 9th grade project -- an in-depth study and analysis of a selection from Scripture, including researching the meanings of words, reasoning through the meaning and instruction, relating the scripture to his own life, and recording his findings through a thesis paper.

Curriculum:

Hess, Donna L. and June Cates. <u>Fundamentals of Literature</u>. Greenville, SC: Bob Jones
      University Press, 1988
Jensen, Frode. <u>Format Writing</u>. Grants Pass, OR: Wordsmiths, 1994.
Sebranek, Patrick and Verne Meyer. <u>Basic English Revisited</u>. Burlington, WI: The Write
      Source, 1985.
Dictionary, Bible, concordance, lexicon, commentaries.
Five novels of students choice (from approved list)

Note: The first two numbered items in this course description were taken from the catalog description or the table of the contents for the texts used.

The outline of this course is included on page 117. The course standard is on page 153.

Sample Course Description

Student's Name: Steven Schofield		

Grade: 9	Credits: 5	✔ Semester Course ____ Full Year Course

Start Date: September 15, 1996	End Date: March 22, 1997

Course Title: Logic and Critical Thinking 1

Course Description:

   The course covers informal and formal logic. The objectives include development of discernment in reading and listening and clarity of thought in speaking and writing.

   Through readings and class discussions, students consider and analyze a variety of realistic situations. Exercises are drawn from newspapers, newscasts, advertisements, conversations, political speeches, and government regulations. Student will complete exercises from the text, as well as additional assignments based on the current presidential election, other current political campaigns, current television broadcasts, and his own local newspaper.

   Topics include basic concepts in critical thinking, use and misuse of words and statements, propaganda and advertising techniques, logical reasoning fallacies, quantified statements, probability of truth and falsity, characteristics or arguments, and applied logic. The course will end with a unit on formal debating.

Curriculum:

Harnadek, Anita. Critical Thinking Book One. Pacific Grove, CA: Midwest
    Publications, 1976.

Local Newspaper; political campaign booklets and brochures; magazine articles and editorials; television
    newscasts and news-oriented programs.

Note: The course description was taken from the description of the course printed on the back cover of the text.

        The course standard for this class is on page 156.

❖ Sample Course Descriptions by Subject

Bible

1. **Bible 9** (SR)   1 year course - 10 credits

    See the sample course description form on page 70.

2. **Christian Living** (SR)   1 year course - 10 credits

    This course emphasizes preparing students for making decisions as Christians.
    The first part of the course will cover the person of Christ, salvation, the inerrancy of the Bible, rebellion, finding God's will, self-control, and leadership. Second semester includes bitterness, Christian liberties, separation, evangelism, prejudice, and suffering.

    Patterns for Christian Living: Bob Jones University Press

    (Description from Bob Jones University Press catalog.)

3. **Bible 7** (JR)   1 year course - 10 credits

    This course covers the character traits that should be evident in Christians. The theme is the study of the Fruits of the Spirit in Galatians 5:22-23. The course includes workbook studies, Bible readings, interviews and visits with mature Christians who exhibit the traits studied, and essays on each character trait studied.

    MacKenthun, Carole and Paulinus Dwyer. Fruit of the Spirit Series, Nine Volumes. Carthage, IL: Good
       Apple, 1986

4. **Intro to the Bible** (JR or SR)   1 semester course - 5 credits

    Study of the Gospel of John is emphasized in this beginning course in Bible study. Discussion of the basic plan for salvation is the central theme. How to apply the principles for living from the Bible to our lives today and the life and teachings of Jesus Christ are studied in depth. Portions of the books of Genesis, Psalms, Acts, I Corinthians, and Proverbs are also included.

    The Bible (King James, The Living Bible and Amplified versions) Also, Bible study aids including a concordance, a dictionary of Greek words, and Bible study aids by the Navigators.

5. **Spiritual Health** (JR or SR)   1 semester course - 5 credits

    See description under Health, Example 4.

6. **Christian Principles of Marriage and Courtship** (SR)   1 semester course - 5 credits

    A discussion of the Bible's teachings on male/female relationships, including dating, courtship and marriage.

    Elliott, Elisabeth. Passion and Purity. Grand Rapids, MI: Revell, 1984.

    Elliott, Elisabeth. Quest for Love. Grand Rapids, MI: Revell, 1996.

    Ludy, Eric and Leslie. His Perfect Faithfulness: The Story of Our Courtship. Littleton, CO: Family
       Foundations Publishing, 1996.

    Myers, Jeff and Danielle. Of Knights and Fair Maidens: A Radical New Way to Develop Old-fashioned
       Relationships. Colorado Springs, CO: Myers, 1996.

Economics

1. **Economics** (SR)   1 semester course - 5 credits

    This course covers the basics of economics, including the concepts of competition and market structure, freedom of choice, private ownership, and profit and loss. Basic terms related to economics are covered, and a unit on personal finance and Biblical financial principles is included.

    Burkett, Larry. Using Your Money Wisely. Chicago: Moody Press, 1985.

    Maybury, Richard. Whatever Happened to Penny Candy? Placerville, CA: Bluestocking Press, 1993.

    Nash, Ronald. "The Economic Way of Thinking" Parts 1-8. The Freeman. October 1993 - May 1994.

2. **Economic Principles & Problems** (SR — Adv. Placement)   1 semester course - 5 credits

    Principles of economic analysis, economic institutions, and issues of economic policy are covered in this course. Special topics include the allocation of resources and distribution of income through the price system, as well as aggregative economics, including money and banking, national income, and international trade.

    Ruffin and Gregory. Principles of Economics. 3d ed., Scott, Foresman & Co., 1988.

    (Description taken from University of California Extension Correspondence Courses Catalog.)

3. **Economics** (SR)   1 semester course - 5 credits

    The theme of this course is "America's Market Economy." Essential concepts such as competition in the marketplace and private ownership of capital are discussed from a conservative perspective.

    Kirk, Russell. Economics: Work and Prosperity. Pensacola, FL: A Beka Books.

    (Description from the A Beka Books Catalog.)

English

1. **English 9: Fundamentals of Literature & Composition** (SR)   1 year course - 10 credits

    See sample course description form on page 71.

2. **Reading / Composition** (JR or SR)   1 semester course - 5 credits

    A remedial course covering reading and writing skills. Five books will be read during the semester and various essays and short stories by known authors will be assigned. Written work will consist of weekly essays, a daily journal, vocabulary and spelling work, correspondence, and grammar.

    Jensen, Frode. Format Writing. Grants Pass, OR: Wordsmiths, 1994.

    Developing Better Reading. Crockett, KY: Rod and Staff Publishers, 1973.

    Warriner, John E. English Grammar and Composition: Complete Course. New York: Harcourt, Brace and Co., 1957.

    Additional Reading List attached.

3. **English 7** (JR)   1 year course - 10 credits

This course covers reading, composition, spelling, grammar, handwriting, vocabulary, research skills, and literature. Reading skills will be improved with regular oral readings, comprehension exercises, vocabulary and spelling words, and literature (both independent readings and read-aloud selections.) The student will also read and report on at least three books independently. Basic grammatical terms will be reviewed and mastered. Handwriting will be practiced daily. Dictionary and library skills will be practiced regularly.

Erwin, Paul. Winston Grammar. Calimesa, CA: Home Grown Kids, 1982.

McGuffey, William H. Second and Third Readers. Ed. Raymond and Dorothy Moore and Jane Thayer. Washougal, WA: Hewitt Research, 1983.

Stout, Kathryn. Natural Speller. Wilmington, DE: Design-a-Study, 1989.

Welch, Diane and Susan Simpson. Learning Language Arts Through Literature. Hawthorne, FL: The Family Learning Center, 1990.

Sample course design for this course is on page 116. Sample course standard is on page 152.

4. **Introduction to English Literature** (SR)   1 year course - 10 credits

This course traces the development of English literature from the Anglo-Saxon period through the age of the Puritans and features such major literary figures as Bede, Chaucer, Malory, Foxe, Spenser, Marlowe, Donne, Shakespeare, and Milton. *Macbeth* and *Pilgrim's Progress* are included in their entirety, complete with backgrounds, footnotes, and study notes.

A Beka Books. Introduction to English Literature. Pensacola, FL: A Beka Books.

(Course description taken from A Beka Books Catalog.)

5. **American Literature** (SR)   1 year course - 10 credits

A study of significant American authors, illustrating the drift of American thought and the changing ideals of American patriotism. Emergence of the American character and influence in literature will be covered through in-depth studies of some of the most important American authors.

Boynton, Percy H. A History of American Literature. Boston: Ginn and Company, 1919.

Slater, Rosalie J. "The Christian History Literature Program" from A Guide to American Christian Education for the Home and School by James B. Rose. Camarillo, CA: American Christian History Institute, 1987. pp.323-392.

----------. A Family Program for Reading Aloud. San Francisco: FACE, 1991.

----------. Syllabus for Teaching and Learning an American Christian Novel: The Deerslayer. San Francisco: Foundation for American Christian Education.

6. **Modern U.S. and World Literature** (JR or SR)   1 semester course - 5 credits

[This course is part of a literature approach to history. The course description is included in the history section, example 2.]

7. **Creative Writing** (JR or SR)   1 semester course - 5 credits

This course will address several aspects of creativity and writing: learning basic technical concepts of good writing, viewing films, reading great literature, student writing projects, keeping a journal, and biblical principles which govern writing. A unit on selling one's writing and various markets and tips on being published will also be included.

Felleman, Hazel, Ed. <u>The Best Loved Poems of the American People</u>. New York: Doubleday, 1936.

<u>Learning Essay Writing</u>. Crockett, KY: Rod and Staff, 1989.

<u>Poetry Pointers</u>. Crockett, KY: Rod and Staff, 1989.

Roddy, Lee. <u>Writing a Story: A Step by Step Method for Understanding and Teaching Basic Story Writing Techniques</u>. Penn Valley, CA: Roddy Publications, 2004.

Roget, P.M. <u>Thesaurus of English Words and Phrases</u>. 1979.

Sebranek, Patrick and Verne Meyer. <u>Basic English Revisited: A Student Handbook</u>. Burlington, WI: The Write Source, 1985.

<u>Short Story Writing</u>. Crockett, KY: Rod and Staff, 1989.

Strunk, William, Jr. and E. B. White. <u>The Elements of Style</u> New York: MacMillan, 1972.

Williams, Becky Hall, Ed. <u>Writer's Market: Where to Sell What You Write</u>. Cincinnati, OH: Writer's Digest Books.

8. **Journalism** (SR)   1 year course - 10 credits

This course includes an in-depth study of the principles which govern American journalism: freedom of the press, protection of the public interest, the Fairness Doctrine, confidentiality of sources and restrictions on the press. Projects are included in the five fields of journalism: Newspapers, news services, magazines, radio, and television.

Sample course design is on pages 100-104. Sample course standard is on page 155.

9. **Journalism** (SR)   1 semester course - 5 credits

The student will be the editor our homeschool group's monthly newsletter for the school year. Included will be gathering news related to events like field trips, classes, and meetings, and writing news articles related to each. The student will also solicit articles from our group members, edit the articles and prepare them for publication, including learning about copyright law. Layout and graphic design will be learned using computer software publishing programs. Printing and distributing within a budget will also be included.

Fine Arts

1. **Choir 1** (JR or SR)   1 semester course - 5 credits

Jane is a member of the Community Church choir. She attends practice once a week, sings at our church services, and travels with the choir to perform for other churches. She practices the music at home and sings occasional solos at church. Jane will also study the background of some of the composers of her favorite hymns and will attend several performances by other choirs.

2. **Survey of Fine Arts** (JR or SR)   1 year course - 10 credits

This course will introduce the student to a variety of the arts. The student will attend ten concerts, ten plays, and ten museums during the course, and will prepare an evaluation of each. Units will be included on music styles, film and radio production, architecture, art history, photography, drawing, and crafts.

Sample course design is on page 124.

3. **Advanced Piano** (JR or SR)   1 year course - 10 credits

The student will attend private professional piano lessons once weekly throughout the year, and will practice lessons daily. In addition, the student will study a variety of composers, including their music and their lives. Four performances will be required.

Sample course design is on page 121.

4. **Practical Photography** (JR or SR)   1 semester course - 5 credits

Working with equipment the average person might own, without spending the time or money a professional would have to spend, students will be introduced to the fundamentals of 35 mm. photography. Most of the course will be a variety of photo assignments, designed to encourage the student to learn by doing. Assignments will include portraits, architecture, action, photojournalism, landscapes, close-ups and stills, and lighting experiments.

Sample course design is on page 122.

5. **Drawing and Painting** (JR or SR)   1 semester course - 5 credits

The student will take three six-week courses through the Community Services Education program offered by our local community college.

"Basic Drawing Workshop" will cover classic techniques and the basic concepts essential for good rendering ability. Topics covered include: tonal scale and value studies, perspective, pictorial composition, and various qualities of line to describe shape, volume and form in space.

"Painting in Watercolor" will cover the fundamental elements of color harmonies, light, shade, line and shape. Students will experiment with different pigments and color washes.

"Painting in Oils" will incorporate basic drawing skills with the principles that make for sound painting. Skills covered will include: the mixing of colors, brush handling, painting techniques and applications, organization for a painting, and use of direct and indirect methods.

(Course description from Glendale Community College Community Service Catalog.)

6. **Advanced Ballet and Performance** (JR or SR)

1 year course - 10 credits for Fine Arts, plus 10 credits for Physical Education.

Classical ballet study including four lessons per week at La Crescenta School for Dance. The course builds upon previous study, focusing on advanced ballet techniques, daily practice, and performance. The student will work to develop grace and poise through the execution of dance movement en pointe, demi-pointe, and pas de deux. She will continue to build a repertoire of classical ballet selections through classroom study and performance. Also included will be attendance at professional ballet productions, and viewing of ballet on film. Through her own performances and through viewing other performances, the student will study theatrical techniques including music selection, lighting, costuming, stage make-up, and sets.

Foreign Language

1. **Latin 1-2** (SR)   1 year course - 10 credits

This beginning course in Latin will to teach the student to read and understand Latin literature without recourse to English. The student will master a Latin vocabulary of approximately 700 words well enough to recognize the meaning in context. Of these, the student will have an active control of approximately 300, which he can use in constructing Latin sentences.

Sweet, Waldo E. and Judith B. Moore. <u>Artes Latinae: Level One</u>. Wauconda, IL: Bolchazy-Carducci Publishers, 1991.

(Course description taken from Artes Latinae Teacher's Manual.)

2. **Greek 1** (SR)   1 year course - 10 credits

This course is a beginning study of the exact meaning of words, the various forms of words, and the correct use of words—the grammatical principles by which words are used correctly in sentences. Exercises in translation include translating from Greek to English and from English to Greek. The Greek New Testament will be the source of many of these exercises.

Mastery of Greek 1 will put the student in control of the essentials, and will provide the student of the Word and of the language of the Word the basic tools for a lifetime of fruitful study.

Alpha Omega Publications. <u>Greek 1 Lifepacs</u>. Tempe, AZ: Alpha Omega Publications.

(Course description taken from Alpha Omega catalog.)

3. **Spanish 1** (JR)   1 year course - 10 credits

The student will learn over 3,000 words and will understand conversations in Spanish. The focus of the course is to learn Spanish through hearing it spoken. Once the student has been introduced to the language, through hearing it only, he will begin to work with reading and writing.

Winitz, Harry. <u>The Learnables</u>, Levels 1-5. Kansas City, MO: International Linguistics Corporation, 1993.

4. **Spanish 1** (SR)   1 year course - 10 credits   (courtesy of the Knighton family)

A text and a vocabulary manual will be used in the course, along with cassette tapes to help the student's pronunciation of proper Spanish. Grammar and conversational skills will be taught. Student will join a Spanish Club that meets once a month with other first-year students for memorization skills and learning about the Spanish culture (foods, dance, traditions, etc.)

<u>Por Todo El Mundo I</u>. Pensacola, FL: A Beka Book Publications. With test packet.

<u>Vocabulary Manual I</u>. Pensacola, FL: A Beka Books Publications. With 2 cassette tapes.

Geography

1. **Geography** (SR)   1 year course - 10 credits

"*The Geography of Nature* (1st semester)
The Earth: in the universe, in the solar system, and the terrestrial globe
The Constituents of the Globe: land, water, atmosphere
Organic Life: vegetable, animal
Provisions and Providence: food, raiment, shelter; metals, minerals, gems

The Geography of Man (2nd semester)
The Human Family: races, cultures
The Continents of Nature: Australia, Africa, South America
The Continents of History: Asia, Europe, North America

State Geography: physical structure, products, industry and commerce, civil government"

Dang, Katherine. "Geography: An American Christian Approach" from A Guide to American Christian Education for the Home and School by James B. Rose. Camarillo, CA: American Christian History Institute, 1987. pp. 257-275.

Guyot, Arnold. Physical Geography. New York: Ivison, Blakeman and Company, 1885. Facsimile reprint available from American Christian History Institute, P.O. Box 648, Palo Cedro, CA 96073.

American Christian History Institute. Physical Geography Map Outlines. Palo Cedro, CA.

(Geography Overview by Katherine Dang, from "Geography: An American Christian Approach" in A Guide to American Christian Education for the Home and School by James B. Rose. P. 261.)

2. **Geography** (JR)   1 semester course - 5 credits

An introduction to geography emphasizing map skills, identifying the nations of the world, and understanding the diversity of cultural contributions of modern civilizations.

Bigham, Dane, et al. Where in the World is Carmen Sandiego? San Rafael, CA: Broderbund Software, 1989.

Birdsall, Stephen S. "Geography," World Book Encyclopedia. 1988.

Cheyney, Arnold B. and Donald L. Capone. The Map Corner. Glenview, IL: Scott, Foresman, and Company, 1983.

Haycock, Ruth C. Bible Truth for School Subjects, Vol I. Social Studies. Whittier, CA: Association of Christian Schools International, 1982. pp. 17-22.

Maps, Charts & Graphs: The World. Cleveland: Modern Curriculum Press, 1990.

Government and Civics

1. **United States Government and Civics** (SR)   1 semester course - 5 credits

The form of our government and qualities for good citizenship are covered in this course. The purpose and function of each of the three branches of government are discussed. California's state and local governments are covered also. In particular, the principle of self-government is stressed. Ways of preserving America's republican form of government and the Constitution are emphasized. Community involvement, understanding of current issues, and privileges and duties of citizenship are included.

Foster, Marshall and Elaine Swanson. The American Covenant: The Untold Story. Thousand Oaks, CA: Mayflower Institute, 1983.

Hall, Verna M. Christian History of the Constitution. Ed. Joseph Allan Montgomery. San Francisco: Foundation for American Christian Education, 1966.

Slater, Rosalie J. and Verna M. Hall. Rudiments of America's Christian History and Government. San Francisco: Foundation for American Christian Education, 1968.

Slater, Rosalie J. Teaching and Learning America's Christian History. San Francisco: Foundation for American Christian Education, 1965.

2. **American Government** (SR)   Semester course - 5 credits

The principles and the mechanics of our constitutional republic are examined underscoring the responsibilities of Christian citizenship within our society. Areas of emphasis include biblical and governmental principles, the Constitution, political parties, elections, pressure groups, citizenship, the branches of government, and economics.

American Government for Christian Schools Greenville, SC: Bob Jones University Press.

(Course description taken from Bob Jones University Press catalog.)

Health & Driver Education

1. **Driver Education and Driver Training** (SR)   ½ semester course - 2 credits

    ABC Driving School (555 Main Street, Yourtown) private course including 30 hours of class work and 10 hours driving.

2. **Health and Driver Education** (SR)   1 semester course - 5 credits

    Driver Education will cover the information needed to help the student become a safe, efficient driver. Topics covered include driving maneuvers and decisions, traffic laws, vehicle control, and the highway systems. The student will read the text and will complete 28 project assignments which coordinate with the chapters of the book, and are designed to give a practical, hands-on application of the driving concepts presented.

    Health will include a ten-hour basic CPR course through our local hospital, which will provide American Heart Association certification. The course will also include a study of Scriptural principles related to health, and basic concepts for good health, including exercise, diet and nutrition; the effect of unhealthy habits; preventive medicine; and natural health methods like herbal remedies, homeopathic medicines, fasting, aromatherapy, hydrotherapy, and other natural home remedies.

    American Automobile Association. Sportsmanlike Driving. New York: McGraw-Hill, 1980.

    Department of Motor Vehicles. California Driver Handbook. Sacramento: DMV, 2004.

    Fries, James F., M.D. and Donald M. Vickery, M.D. Take Care of Yourself: Your Personal Guide to Self-Care & Preventing Illness. 4th ed. Reading, MA: Addison-Wesley, 1990

    Rector-Page, Linda G., N.D., Ph.D. Healthy Healing: An Alternative Healing Reference. California: Healthy Healing Publications, 1992.

    Thrash, Agatha, M.D. and Calvin Thrash, M.D. Home Remedies: Hydrotherapy, Massage, Charcoal and Other Simple Therapies. Seale, AL: Thrash Publications, 1981.

    (Course description taken from introductions and tables of contents of the books listed.)

3. **Health** (JR)   ½ semester course - 2½ credits

    This course is designed to help the student understand the normal changes which take place in his body during the adolescent years. In-depth studies of the following systems are included: the endocrine system and how it affects mental and emotional health; the skeletal system and skin and how they affect personal appearance; and the nervous system and how it is affected by drugs, including a look at the worldwide tragedy of drug abuse. Students will learn to maintain physical fitness and make healthful, responsible decisions, knowing that the choices they make during their teenage years will have long-term effects on their health.

    A Beka Books. Let's Be Healthy. Pensacola, Fl: A Beka Books.

    (Course description taken from the A Beka Books catalog.)

4. **Health** (JR or SR)   1 semester course - 5 credits (health)
   Spiritual Health (JR or SR)   1 semester course - 5 credits (Bible)

   (This course could be counted as both health and Bible)

   The course is designed to inspire the student as it teaches practical principles of good health, including physical mental, social, and spiritual aspects. Included in the text are four units. Unit One, Physical Health, includes chapters on the human body and its systems, nutrition, fitness and exercise, infectious disease, and noninfectious disease. Unit Two, Mental Health, includes chapters on stress and anxiety, lifestyle management, and proper self image. Unit Three, Social Health, includes chapters on hygiene, safety and first aid, attitudes and responsibilities, physical maturity, and relationships. Unit Four, Spiritual Health, includes chapters on spiritual fitness, consistency in spiritual growth, and Christian maturity.

   Boe, Susan. Total Health: Choices for a Winning Lifestyle. West Linn, OR: RiversEdge Publishing Co., 1995.

History

1. **U.S. History** (SR)   1 year course - 10 credits

   The hand of God in the founding and maintaining of the United States is emphasized. Great Patriots and their influence on our country is covered in depth. How our past affects us today as a nation and particularly what the Constitution means today are covered extensively. A survey of American history, from God's preparation for the development of the American continent through the modern day, will be included, with special focus on the character of great men and women used by God throughout our nation's history.

   Foster, Marshall and Elaine Swanson. The American Covenant: The Untold Story. Thousand Oaks, CA: Mayflower Institute, 1983.

   Hall, Verna M. Christian History of the Constitution. Ed. Joseph Allan Montgomery. San Francisco: Foundation for American Christian Education, 1966.

   Slater, Rosalie J. and Verna M. Hall. Rudiments of America's Christian History and Government. San Francisco: Foundation for American Christian Education, 1968.

   Slater, Rosalie J. Teaching and Learning America's Christian History. San Francisco: Foundation for American Christian Education, 1965.

   Thayer, William M. Gaining Favor with God and Man. Portland, OR: Mantle Ministries, 1989.

2. **Modern U.S. & World History** (JR or SR)   1 year course - 10 credits
   Modern U.S. & World Literature (JR or SR)   1 semester course - 5 credits

   This study features the span of American and World History from the 1860's to the 1970's. Divided into distinct periods, essential events, political figures, inventions and technological advances will be listed with corresponding literature which features theses important aspects. In addition, classic literature of the corresponding time period will be read and studied. A full list of books read is attached.

   Berg, Rea C. Modern History Through Literature: From the Civil War to Vietnam. Sandwich, MA: Beautiful Feet Books, 1997.

   Slater, Rosalie. A Family Program for Reading Aloud. San Francisco, CA: Foundation for American Christian Education, 1991.

   Greenleaf Press Catalog, 1570 Old Laguardo Road, Lebanon, TN 37087.

3. **World History** (SR)   1 year course - 10 credits

A comprehensive survey of world history from Creation to the present. History is presented as being part of God's plan, with the emphasis on the Biblical truth that God is in control of the affairs of men and nations, both of the godly and the ungodly. Although the focus is on our Western, Judeo-Christian heritage, the contributions of the Asian, African, and Latin American cultures are included.

The political and economic history of past civilizations is covered, as well as the influence of God's people on the world and the influence of the world on God's people. Major topics studied include the earliest civilizations, the Greek Civilization, the Roman Empire, the Byzantine and Islamic Empires, the civilizations of Asia, the Medieval world, the Renaissance, the Reformation, the Age of Reason, the Industrial Revolution, the Great Awakening, the World Wars, and the modern world.

Outside reading of literature selections from major time periods will be assigned.

Fisher, David A. World History for Christian Schools. Greenville, SC: Bob Jones University Press, 1984.

Haycock, Ruth C. Bible Truth for School Subjects, Vol I. Social Studies. Whittier, CA: Association of Christian Schools International, 1982.

(Course description taken from the introduction to World History for Christian Schools, Teacher's Manual, and from the Table of Contents.)

Sample course design on page 126.

Mathematics

1. **Math 7** (JR)   1 year course - 10 credits

See the sample course description form on page 69.

2. **Logic and Critical Thinking** (JR or SR)   1 semester course - 5 credits

See the sample course description form on page 72.

3. **Algebra I** (SR)   1 year course - 10 credits

The course covers the standard topics of first year algebra, plus introductory geometry, including: signed numbers, integer exponents, scientific notation, linear equations, graphs and equations of linear functions, ratio problems, percents, variation problems, unit conversions, perimeter, area, and volume.

Saxon, John H., Jr. Algebra 1: An Incremental Development. Norman, OK: Saxon Publishers Inc., 1990. 2nd Ed.

Sample course standards are on pages 148-149.

4. **Consumer Mathematics** (SR)   1 year course - 10 credits

Topics covered include buying a car, budgeting, banking, investing, keeping tax records, and purchasing food, clothing and a home. A Scriptural view is presented of working, tithing, saving, paying taxes, and budgeting time and money. An introduction is given to the American free-enterprise system. Analytical skills will be developed as the student works on practical problems.

Consumer Mathematics in Christian Perspective. Pensacola FL: A Beka Books.

Sample course standard is on page 150 — Sample 1.

5. **Consumer Math** (SR)   1 semester course - 5 credits

The focus will be on improving basic arithmetic skills necessary to function in the adult world. Daily drills will be done in arithmetic facts, a part-time job will be held, money earned will be budgeted. The student will learn to handle his own finances through tithing, keeping a savings account, and monitoring his spending. He will buy parts for his car, find and pay for auto insurance, and pay for gas and any other car repairs.

Sample course standard is on page 150-151 — Sample 2.

6. **Consumer Math** (JR or SR)   1 year course - 10 credits

Jane will completely take over our home budget for this school year. She will work with her dad to develop a year-long budget. Jane will deposit all paychecks into the family account and handle all bills. She will learn about insurance policies, home loans, bank accounts, interest, investments, etc.

Sample course standard is on page 151 — Sample 3.

Physical Education

1. **Advanced Ballet and Performance** (JR or SR)

See course description under Fine Arts on page 77, example 6.

2. **Soccer / Swimming / Racquetball / Weight Training** (JR or SR)   1 year course - 10 credits

Student will take a four-week course in basic swimming strokes, including the crawl, back crawl, elementary back stroke, and breast stroke, plus diving, including basic front dive, inward dive, and simple flips. The course will be taught by staff at the Diamond Springs Racquetball and Fitness Club. During the remainder of the summer quarter, the student will swim laps to develop endurance and to practice the strokes learned.

Introduction to Racquetball fundamentals and Beginner's Weight Lifting will be covered, also at the Diamond Springs Club. The student will play racquetball regularly to build skill and to become familiar with basic rules. Weight lifting will be under the supervision of the gym staff, with a basic program designed to strengthen the different muscle groups of the body.

During the fall quarter, the student will play soccer on a team. Emphasis will be on improving soccer skills developed in previous years, plus working with other team members and learning to exhibit a sportsmanlike attitude. The student will participate in regular practice sessions and games.

Diamond Springs Racquetball and Fitness Club, including weight rooms, racquetball courts, and pool. Four-month summer membership.

El Dorado Youth Soccer League will provide an opportunity to play soccer on a team, with regular practice sessions and games supervised by the league's coach.

Sample course standard is on page 158.

3. **Physical Education** (SR)   2 year course - 20 credits

Student will participate in a minimum of eight different sports or fitness activity units, each unit consisting of at least ten 40-minute sessions. His exercise program will include three 40-minute exercise sessions per week throughout high school. The eight required activities may be chosen by the student, with instructor's approval, and will include a study of the techniques, rules, and safety standards for each activity studied.

Sample course design is on pages 119-120.

Science

1. **Biology I** (SR) or **Life Science** (JR)   1 year course - 10 credits

   The first part of this course covers science and its relationship to the Word of God, examining the attributes of life, classification, cells, and biblical creation. The second half covers subjects such as the life processes of organisms, plant and animal reproduction, genetics, and biological evolution. A unit on ecology looks at ecosystems, interrelationships among organisms, and a biblical perspective of man's stewardship of the earth. The study concludes with a discussion of the human body and its basic structure and function.

   Pinkston, William S., Jr. Life Science for Christian Schools. Greenville, SC: Bob Jones University Press, 1984.

   Pinkston, William S., Jr. Student Activities in Life Science for Christian Schools. Greenville, SC: Bob Jones University Press, 1984.

   (Course description taken from the Bob Jones University Press Catalog.)

2. **Field Biology** (SR)   1 year course - 10 credits

   Included in this laboratory course are field studies of different biospheres and the plant and animal life found in each. The student will create collections of samples, photographs, and drawings of plants, insects, birds, reptiles, mammals. Also included are reports on the various life forms and geographic zones.

   1 year course - 10 credits

   Sample course design is on pages 105-108. Sample course standard is on page 154.

3. **Botany** (JR or SR)   1 semester course - 5 credits

   Jane will work at Descanso Gardens in La Cañada as a volunteer. The course will include the docent training program at Descanso Gardens. She will learn to identify the varieties of plants and will learn how to care for and propagate them.

   Sunset Books and Sunset Magazine. Western Garden Book. Menlo Park, CA: Lane Publishing Co., 1988.

   Sample course standard is on page 150.

4. **Creation Science** (SR)   1 Semester course - 5 credits

   This course will compare the Theory of Evolution with Biblical Creationism. Scientific procedures will be identified as the student learns to distinguish between theory and proven fact.
   Four basic units will cover:

   > A. The old earth vs. the young earth theories: Big Bang Theory, geometric dating, geochronometers, climactic changes since earth's beginning, catastrophic events, 2nd law of thermodynamics, mutations, Darwinism.

   > B. Evolution of all life from a single cell vs. each species created fully developed: Fossil records, spontaneous generation theory, complexity of cells, geologic chart, relationships among species, extinct species, dinosaurs.

   > C. Evolution's idea of man evolving from apes vs. the Bible's creation story: Missing links, fossil record of men: Ramapithecus, Australopithecus, "Lucy," Skull 1470, Peking Man, et al.

D. Primitive ancient civilizations vs. advanced ancient civilizations: Ancient "mysteries," cave men, ancient technologies, ancient life spans, Mayans, Chinese, Mesopotamians and other ancient cultures.

Petersen, Dennis R., B.S., M.A. Unlocking the Mysteries of Creation. South Lake Tahoe: Christian Equippers International, 1987.

----------. Unlocking the Mysteries of Creation Seminar. Placerville, CA. May 28-30, 1992.

Richards. Lawrence, It Couldn't Just Happen. Dallas: Word Publishing, 1987.

Taylor, Paul. The Great Dinosaur Mystery and the Bible. San Diego: Master Books, 1987.

(Course description taken from seminar materials by Dennis Petersen.)

5. **Herbology and Natural Healing** (Advanced Placement)   1½ year course - 15 credits

This course is being taken through the School of Natural Healing, founded in 1953 by Dr. John R. Christopher M.H., N.D. The course includes instruction and training in the prudent, safe, and effective use of herbs, within the confines of natural healing. Topics covered include: herbal home health care; fundamentals of Herbology; assimilation and elimination; the role of and care for the blood stream, glandular system, stomach, pancreas, and urinary system; wholistic incurables; central nervous system; herb identification, including learning to identity over 135 herbs, their look-alikes, medicinal qualities, edibility; poisonous plants; regenerative diets; herbal formulas; case histories; harvesting herbs. After the study program has been completed, the student will attend a final intensive seminar and earn the Master Herbalist certificate. Study materials, reference books, texts and exams provided by The School of Natural Healing, P.O. Box 412, Springville, UT, 84663.

(Course description taken from information packet by The School of Natural Healing.)

6. **Master Gardening / Horticulture** (SR) (Advanced Placement)   1 year course - 10 credits

Student will complete the Master Gardener's course through the University of California Extension Program. The course consists of 25 hours of training classes, followed by 75 hours of service to the community as part of the Master Gardener's program. The course is taught by university professors following the standards set by the University of California.

7. **Animal Husbandry** (JR or SR)   1 year course - 10 credits

The student will participate in the 4-H Club, dairy goat project. After attending introductory classes and completing the textbook and research portion of the course, the student will purchase two dairy goat kids, raise them himself, breed them, and use them for milk production.

Belanger, Jerry. Raising Milk Goats the Modern Way. Charlotte, VT: Garden Way Publishing, 1975.

8. **Beekeeping** (JR or SR)   1 year course - 10 credits

The student will keep a hive of bees throughout a full year, including starting a colony in the spring, maintaining the bees through harvest of honey, and caring for the hive through the winter season. Background material on the habits and care of bees will be covered.

Adams, John F. Beekeeping, The Gentle Craft. New York: Avon Books, 1974.

Dadant, C. P. First Lessons in Beekeeping. Hamilton, IL: American Bee Journal, 1957.

9. **Organic Gardening** (SR)   1 year course - 10 credits

This course covers the fundamentals of organic gardening, including preparation of the garden, composting, selection of seeds, planting, watering systems, weed and pest control, and harvesting of vegetables and fruits.

The main vehicle of study is the student's garden project, a 200 square foot garden, over which he will take responsibility.

Jeavons, John. How to Grow More Vegetables* -- *than You Ever Thought Possible on Less Land Than You Can Imagine. Berkeley, CA: Ten Speed Press, 1982.

Philbrick, Helen and Richard Gregg. Companion Plants and How to Use Them. Old Greenwich, CT: Devin-Adair, 1966.

Yepsen, Roger B., Jr. ed. The Encyclopedia of Natural Insect & Disease Control. Emmaus, PA: Rodale, 1984.

Sample course design for this course is on page 118.

10. **General Science 7-8** (JR)   2 year course - 20 credits

A two-year study, including twelve units:

What is Science?, Fundamentals of God's World, The Starry Heavens, The Force of Gravity, Heat Energy, Weather, The Planet Earth, Life on the Earth, Fire, Parasitic Diseases, Food and Digestion, Agriculture.

Investigating God's Orderly World. Crockett, KY: Rod and Staff, 1994.

11. **General Science** (SR)   1 year course - 10 credits

This is a basic science course covering the following areas:

- Science and the Bible
- The Scientific Method
- Description of Matter:
  Measurement,
  Properties,
  Classification
- Structure of Matter:
  Models of Atoms
  Families of Atoms
- Forces Between Atoms
- Chemistry of Matter:
  Reactions, Solutions,
  Acids, Bases, Salts
- Motion of Matter:
  Machines, Mechanics,
  Energy
- Energy of Matter:
  Heat, Electricity,
- Magnetism
- Energy of Waves:
  Vibrations
  Sound
  Light
- Matters of Technology:
  Engineering
  Electronics

Jenkins, John E. and George Mulfinger, Jr. Basic Science for Christian Schools. Greenville, SC: Bob Jones University Press, 1983.

Sample course outline for this course is on page 97.

Electives

1. **Auto Mechanics** (SR)   1 semester course - 5 credits

John and his father will spend three months rebuilding the engine of the used car John purchased. The owner's manual, the local auto parts store manager, and library books will be sources of information. John will work for and budget the money for parts, which will also be a part of his Consumer Mathematics course.

Sample course standard is on page 150.

2. **Christian Missions Work/Building Construction** (SR)

5 credits - Christian Missions
5 credits - Building Construction

John will work with our church on an outreach program this summer. He will go through a training and planning session and then spend three weeks in Mexico helping to build a church and establishing home Bible studies.

Home Economics

1. **Home Economics and Family Living** (JR or SR)   1 year course - 10 credits

This course will include six units:

Basic Living Skills, including manners, personal organizers and time management, grooming and hygiene, and household or job organization;

Cooking, including basic terminology and skills, shopping, menu planning and kitchen organization;

Sewing, including mending, fabric care, basic operation of a sewing machine, and how to follow a simple pattern;

Home Repair and Maintenance, including household cleaning materials and tools, basic repair of house structural elements like roofs, plumbing, and electrical systems, and furniture and appliance care and maintenance;

Car Maintenance, including oil changes, tune-ups, tire changing, and basic care of automobiles; and

Family Living Skills, including dating vs. courtship studies, marriage principles, respect and consideration of others' needs, care giving for children, the elderly, and the ill, family problem-solving, and leading a home.

(Ideas for organization of this course adapted from High School: A Home Designed Form+U+La by Barbara Shelton.)

2. **Sewing 1-2** (JR or SR)   1 year course - 10 credits.

Student will learn the basic skills of sewing while making clothes for herself. Three garments will be made each semester, and the student will cover the following skills: hemming (by hand and machine), selecting patterns, fabrics, and notions, care of fabrics, layout of pattern and cutting, casings, facings, buttonholes and buttons, top-stitching, zippers, gathering, pockets, collars, sleeves, darts, matching plaids or stripes, and simple alterations of patterns.

Sample course design is on page 123. Sample course standard is on page 157.

3. **Gourmet Cooking / Foreign Foods** (SR)   1 semester course - 5 credits

Students will become aware of the influence of geography and culture on foods of an ethnic group; develop skill in budgeting for, buying, and preparing gourmet foreign foods; develop skill in time and energy management for foreign gourmet foods, be aware of the different ways that foreign foods meet the basic nutritional needs; and develop an appreciation for foods derived from a variety of cultures.

(Course description taken from Crescenta Valley High School Registration Manual.)

Typing and Computers

1. **Typing, Word Processing and Computing Skills** (SR)   1 year course - 10 credits

    The student will learn the basics of our computer by first learning correct keyboarding skills, through a computer typing course. He will be expected to practice typing until he is familiar enough and fast enough to be able to use the computer for home and school projects.

    Once the student has mastered the keyboard, he will advance to basic computer literacy skills by learning and working in word processing, spreadsheet, database, and home accounting programs.

    Mavis Beacon Teaches Typing! Chatsworth, CA: The Software Toolworks, 1987.

    Online Training Solutions and Curtis Frye. Understanding Microsoft Office 2003. Redmond, WA.: Microsoft Publications, 2004.

    Quicken Deluxe 2003. Mountain View, CA: Intuit, 1996

    Sample course design is on page 125.

2. **Typing** (JR or SR)   1 semester course - 5 credits

    The student will learn the typing keyboard and will practice proper form for business letters, essays, reports, outlines, and tables.

    Sample course standard is on page 151.

Vocational Education

1. **Work Experience** (SR)   1 year course - 10 credits

    Robin studied job-hunting techniques, including business attire, interviewing, applications and resumes. She filled out applications and interviewed for several local businesses, and was offered a job by three of them. She will work at her present job at a local restaurant throughout the school year, arranging her school schedule to fit with her work schedule, learning to get along with co-workers and to take direction from a supervisor, working with customers, handling money, learning food preparation, serving and cleanup. Her employer will be asked to evaluate her performance as part of her grade.

2. **Office Skills** (SR)   1 year course - 10 credits

    The student will work in our home business office one afternoon per week. He will learn how to handle telephone calls from clients; file and organize paperwork; type business letters; receive and sort incoming mail, and prepare outgoing mail of various types; operate basic office machines, including computer, printer, copier, adding machine, telephone system and facsimile machine.

3. **Vocational Education** (JR or SR)   1 semester course - 5 credits

    The student will complete four units:

    Work experience will require him to find jobs for a minimum of 30 hours total, through avenues other than home. He may work for neighbors, local businesses, or church, as long as the job is a hired, paying job.

    Carpentry and Construction will require the student to complete at least five different carpentry or construction projects of a minimum of three hours each. These jobs do not have to be paid employment.

Service/Ministry will require him to design and complete a service or ministry project of at least 20 hours total. The project may be a one-time event requiring some of the hours to be used in planning, preparation, and cleanup. Or it may be a continuing project, with time spent daily, weekly, or monthly until completed. The student will choose one project only; combining several short projects will not count toward credit.

Career Opportunities will require the student to research at least ten different occupations, filling out a report form on each.

(The Career Opportunities unit is taken from High School: A Home Designed Form+U+La by Barbara Shelton. It includes an interview sheet for use in the unit.)

High School Course Description

Student's Name:	

Grade:	**Credits:**	_____ Semester Course _____ Full Year Course

Start Date:	**End Date:**

Course Title:

Course Description:

Curriculum:

❖ 6 Designing Courses

Before actually buying books or deciding what assignments to include in each course, take time to assess your student's level of learning. Particularly if you are new to homeschooling, a time of assessment will be vital, even if it seems to delay your start of "real school." Assessment is part of real school, and taking the time to evaluate your student will actually help prevent delays when you realize he is not at the level you thought he was.

If you are new to home education, and there were problems in your last school (whether related to discipline or academic success) you may want to consider having your student tested for learning disabilities. Often learning disabilities are undetected for years. If you suspect that this may be the case for your own child, it could be well worth the expense of a diagnostic test.

Whether you have homeschooled for years or only for a couple of days, take time during the planning of each year's courses to prayerfully assess your student. Often, in the day to day work of homeschooling, we don't get a chance to step back a bit and take an honest, objective look. Ask your student how he feels about his studies. Is he bored? Why? Is he struggling and often frustrated? Again, ask why.

You make the decision of what to include in your courses. Even among your own children, you will find that you vary the content of the same subjects according to each one's needs. You do not need to do every assignment listed in the books you purchase, and you are free to add assignments and projects as you like.

A course plan or outline will help you and your student know what to expect of each other. For example, are you planning to have your student read a history textbook, write answers to end-of-chapter questions, and take a test after each unit? Or are you planning to have him read each chapter, discuss the questions with you over breakfast, and complete several projects to demonstrate he has learned the material? Or are you planning to have him read the book independently, and write a summary of what he learned in each chapter, with a final exam at the end?

There is no need at this point to write out a daily assignment chart setting dates for every project due, nor to map out which days will be spent on a particular chapter. What needs to be done now is just to decide which projects and assignments you want to include in each course; don't worry about when. In Chapter 7: Scheduling & Lesson Planning, we'll work on when the assignments and projects will be done.

The sample course designs in this book are presented to give you ideas. Please do not feel you must study all the courses included here, or in the same way they are shown, or in the same way they are taught by other families you know. Use the ideas that will fit your family's goals and adapt or completely discard the rest.

Begin your assessment and course designing with Bible. It is amazing how much easier the other courses come together when you first make a definite plan for studying the Lord's Word. Time and time again I have seen that He honors this commitment to put Him first by blessing the rest of the work.

For if the firstfruit be holy, the lump is also holy: and if the root be holy, so are the branches. Romans 11:16

❖ Five Areas of Emphasis in Every Course

The content of each course will vary, of course, depending on the subject. However, there are five areas of emphasis in learning which apply to any course. Each of these areas is an important part of learning. But understanding what area a particular assignment fits into can make your work much less stressful. Students will be able to avoid spending a lot of time trying to memorize trivial facts and will instead be able to focus their efforts on the more relevant parts of each subject. As parents, you will be more relaxed since you will be able to identify which parts of each subject are most important and which don't matter as much. You will be confident in making choices about what assignments to require, without being fearful of leaving "gaps."

When we began homeschooling our niece, she needed help in many mastery areas, having done poorly in school for years. Our biology course included a semester-long project—an insect collection. After beginning the project, it was clear she had absolutely no interest in insects (in fact, she was rather squeamish about the whole idea.) Should we have insisted she spend ten to twenty hours during the semester on the insect collection? There were worthwhile skills and concepts involved: research, organization, patience, etc. Or should we have allowed her to drop the insect collection and devote her time to learning the multiplication facts she never mastered in elementary school? We went for the multiplication and have never felt it was a mistake.

1 Mastery Areas

My son, forget not my law; but let thine heart keep my commandments:
For length of days, and long life, and peace, shall they add to thee.
Let not mercy and truth forsake thee:
Bind them about thy neck; write them upon the table of thine heart:
So shalt thou find favour and good understanding in the sight of God and man. Proverbs 3:1-4

Mastery areas are the concepts or parts of a subject that everyone should master. They are the ideas or facts which will be used again and again throughout life. These are the areas that, if not learned, would hinder a student when he becomes an adult.

For example, in the subject of Bible, mastery areas would be the basic doctrines of historical Christianity: that Jesus Christ is the only begotten Son of God; that He was born of a virgin; that He died as atonement for the sins of every man; that He rose bodily from the grave after three days; that the Bible is inerrant; that salvation comes by grace, as a free gift from God through Christ alone, etc. Without knowledge and full understanding of concepts like these, a student could either not understand his need for salvation at all, or would be subject to false teachings throughout his life.

In the subject of science, one concept that would be part of a mastery area is that there is a difference between scientific fact and scientific theory. Mastering the concept of scientific method to be able to make an educated guess about something, and then design a test or experiment using the skills of observation, measurement, recording of data, and analysis of facts to arrive at a correct conclusion—this is a part of science that everyone would benefit from knowing. The lessons learned would apply to later life problems.

Another mastery area in science would be learning that the more one studies the world around him, the more he learns of God—that all nature points to the God who created and upholds His creation.

2 Exposure Areas

Every man that striveth for the mastery is temperate in all things. 1 Corinthians 9:25

There are some parts to every subject or course that would be of benefit to most students if the students were simply exposed to the ideas or topics, without necessarily spending hours and hours trying to master them.

In Bible, most students would benefit from studying about the intricate design used in the building of the tabernacle, described in the book of Exodus. Reading the description of the beautiful details impresses the student with the Lord's care for the smallest details, with the artistry that He ordained, and with the specific instructions he gives to those He commands to carry out His plans.

However, the vast majority of students do not need to memorize all of the detailed facts about the tabernacle. Most adults do not remember that the boards were of acacia, ten cubits in length, with two tenons in each board and two sockets of silver for each. Most adults are not hampered in their daily life for lack of such knowledge. Yet the *exposure* to the detailed description is of value, and students would benefit from reading it.

In science, an exposure area might be the study of the classification system of living organisms. Latin names for every kingdom, phylum, class, etc. are well worth being exposed to for the concept of orderliness and for the understanding of the differences among the various types of creatures. However, most adults cannot recite all the kingdoms, nor can they remember that there are seven levels of classification. The lack of this knowledge does not hinder them.

The important part for most of us is understanding that there is a classification system in place so that, should we ever need to identify some creature scientifically, we can look up the necessary information to do so. The exposure to the classification system was good; however, devoting hours and hours to memorizing every detail of it should not be the emphasis of a course.

3 Gifts

Neglect not the gift that is in thee. 1 Timothy 4:14

For each of the exposure areas listed above, there is likely someone who thought it very worthwhile to memorize all the details that I mentioned as not being worth a lot of hours. A zoologist, for example, would shudder at the very thought that the full knowledge of the classification system might not be vital. Obviously, this is because the zoologist has a gift (or at least a vested interest) in this area, so he needs to have more information than the rest of us.

Consider a boy who, while in junior high, reads five different books about Robert E. Lee. Now, most of us would consider learning some facts about Robert E. Lee to be important; we may even require our students to read a biography about him. But five different ones? Why would any boy read so many different books about the same man?

To a person with a love of history (or at least the Civil War), the answer is obvious. A biography written by a Southerner would have an entirely different perspective than one written by a Northerner. A book by a family member would be different than one by a soldier who served under Lee. A historian might say that to even *begin* to get a true picture of Robert E. Lee, the reading of five different books would be minimal.

Gift areas are fun because they are unique to each person. In planning your courses, give special consideration to your student's gift areas if you are aware of them. Many students think that if they are good at a subject, it will be an "easy A." They assume they will need to put more effort into subjects in which they are not as gifted. Contrast this with the Word of God:

For unto whomsoever much is given, of him shall be much required:
and to whom men have committed much, of him they will ask the more. Luke 12:48

The areas in which your student has a gift will require extra time and harder work to fully develop that gift. You may have to cut back on some of the exposure areas you hoped to cover, but this will prove worthwhile. Usually the gift areas are what lead to a lifelong hobby or career, so the studies here are among the most important.

4 Interests

To every thing there is a season, and a time to every purpose under the heaven. Ecclesiastes 3:1

At first, it may be difficult to tell the difference between interests and gifts. This is because often a gift will first show up as an interest. A student will say he might like to try playing piano, the parents have no idea he has a gift for the instrument, then the student blossoms into an accomplished musician.

The difference between an interest and a gift (at least in school subjects) is that an interest may crop up for a short time, provide worthwhile studies, and then fade away. For example, during a trip my family took across the country, we became very interested in historical buildings, architecture and decorating styles. We studied buildings, went out of our way to travel to some we wished to see, and talked about methods of reproducing historic furnishings. We learned a lot from our study and benefitted from the extra time spent on what would normally be an exposure area. But once we got home, the interest faded and we turned to other things.

If there is a particular topic in one of your courses that grabs your student's interest, take time to delve into it deeper than you had planned. Another exposure area can be shortened to make time, if necessary. Taking time to study topics that interest your family will give life to your studies, and the interest may continue to develop if the student has a gift for it.

5 Continuing Learning Areas

Give instruction to a wise man, and he will be yet wiser:
teach a just man, and he will increase in learning. Proverbs 9:9

There are some areas of study in which we all need to continue learning and growing. Growing in godly character is a lifelong pursuit because we can never attain a perfect character. Whether it be patience, compassion, mercy or other traits, the Lord will continue to teach us and stretch us throughout our lives.

Other areas require continuing learning because the facts change. In government, for example, adults find it important to continue paying attention to who is currently running for office and who is doing a good job as an elected official. We are asked to vote for president e0very four years, so keeping up with current political events is important.

Continuing learning areas are those parts of a subject that we all must continue to study. These areas can be worked on together, in family studies, in breakfast discussions, or even on field trips. Or, in areas in which your student will work independently, do not expect him to grasp all of it in one or two semesters. If it has taken you much of your life to learn, it will likely take some effort throughout all the years from junior to senior high school and beyond.

❖ What Do You Want Your Student to Learn?

For each subject, whether the study materials arrive in a neatly bound, all-laid-out package, or whether you put them together yourself at the library, it will be important to take time at the beginning to decide what you want your student to learn. Why are you studying this subject anyway? Are there parts to the subject which are mastery areas? Is the purpose of the entire course primarily exposure? If some parts need to be mastered, which parts are there only for exposure? Are there any areas that you could use to tie in with a gift your student has?

Most pre-packaged courses come with a variety of suggested assignments and projects. There are always more than anyone could complete because the writers know that some teachers like one kind of ideas and other teachers have different preferences. Some students work slower than others, so there are extra ideas to keep the faster students busy. But you won't need to give your faster student busywork to keep him quiet till the rest of the class catches up. You also won't need to assign the extras to your slower student or the course will drag on forever.

If you have trouble weeding out the fluff in your pre-packaged courses, it may be that you haven't decided what you want to get out of the course. If you are including a project in your studies "because it's required," without any real interest, you or your student will feel forced and possibly resentful of the time spent. Mary Pride's book, Schoolproof[6] , gives excellent tips for deciding what is worthwhile and what is a time-waster. After reading Schoolproof, you should feel comfortable circling the ideas you like, and putting a big "x" over ones you don't want to use. Do use a pencil, though, so you can erase some of those marks and resell your curriculum at the end of the year.

Designing your own course can mean marking up a pre-packaged one, using a pre-packaged one for part of the course, or starting from scratch with your own plan. We have successfully planned courses all three ways, and have also used a couple that we kept as-is.

❖ Using a Pre-packaged Course As Is

If you have found a text that you are happy with as is, your planning may take less time, but is still necessary. An example in our house is math. We have used the same publisher's math books for years with good success. But we must still do some planning. We want our students to know from the beginning that we expect all assignments completed and corrected until every answer is right. Their diligence in completing and correcting all assignments is counted as part of their grade. We give the tests that come with the book and also count these as part of the grade. We did need to decide, however, how much of the grade to base on the tests, and how much to base on daily work. This is discussed in Chapter 8: Evaluating Progress and Setting Standards.

You must decide how much of the material in your pre-packaged course must be completed in order to pass the course. For us, with our math program, this was easy. The student had to complete the whole book to pass the course. We began by counting up the lessons and tests, dividing them in half. When the student finished half the book, he earned a semester's credit.

---

[6]   Pride, Mary. Schoolproof: How to Help Your Family Beat the System and Learn to Love Learning — The Easy, Natural Way. Westchester, IL: Crossway, 1988.

We once used a general science course that we purchased as a fully designed, all-inclusive course. But what a lot of work I had in laying it out! For the course, I received a student textbook, a teacher's textbook, a student activity manual, and a teacher's activity manual. The text included the reading material, vocabulary, and end-of-chapter questions. The activity manual included written exercises and science experiments. The teacher's versions gave the answers to questions, lists of needed lab materials, and ideas for presenting topics of study.

For this kind of a course, I have found that we have an easier time during the year if I take some time at the beginning to map out our course in some detail. I usually begin by looking at a chapter and estimating how long it might take my student to read it. Assume, for example, that it looks like a chapter would take about three hours to read. For an older student, I might write "Read Chapter One" on my weekly lesson plan; however, for a younger student, I would probably need to break the week's reading assignments into smaller chunks and list them by daily assignments.

I have found that if I list specific page numbers on my weekly plans, I can't plan very far ahead. Within about three weeks, we would be off whatever lofty schedule I had envisioned. So I make a separate sheet with the course design, on which I leave out dates, but make a list of the assignments I plan to include. It is worthwhile to take an hour or two to go through the course materials before we start it will save me hours of extra work once we begin. In addition to breaking down reading assignments, I will go through the activity book and decide which written assignments I want to use, which extra projects I like, and which experiments I can figure out and buy materials for without blowing up the house.

The first page of my sample course design for the Basic Science course is on page 97. Since this course design would be too cumbersome for a portfolio, I would also fill out course description sheet. You can see that even though I avoided designing my own course by purchasing a whole packaged program, and even though I used all the program materials and didn't add any extra books, I still had quite a bit of work to do in planning how to use the course.

The text has 22 chapters, so first semester will be chapters 1-11.

Basic Science for Christian Schools
1st Semester - Chapters 1-11

Unit 1: What Matters to the Christian

Chapter 1

☐ Read pages vii-ix in textbook
look at table of contents, appendices on pages 566-570, glossary, and index
Read pages vi-viii in activities book

☐ Read pages 1-6 + facet on pages 6-7

☐ Experiment 1B

☐ Read pages 7-14

☐ Read pages 14-18
Written Assignment 1A

☐ Chapter 1 Test

Experiments are in the Activity Book. I must decide how far we should be in the text when we do the experiment. In this case, the experiment illustrates the material covered in pages 1-6 of the text.

Chapter 2

☐ Read pages 20-26

☐ Experiment 2B

☐ Read pages 26-30
Research Project 2G

☐ Experiment 2C
Discuss results of 2G
Read Pages 31-33
Written Assignment 2E

☐ Experiment 2D

☐ Read pages 33-38
Written Assignment 2A

☐ Chapter 2 Test

Written assignments are in the Activity Book. I must decide which ones to do, and how far we should be in the text. In this case, the assignment uses material covered in pages 14-18 of the text.

No dates are on the outline. It simply tells what assignment we do next, not what day. The check box helps track what we have completed so far. Another benefit of having no dates on the outline is that I can photo copy the page before marking any boxes and use it again with another student.

Unit 2: A Description of Matter

Chapter 3

☐ Read pages 41-46
Research Project 3B

☐ Read pages 47-55
Written Assignment 3C

☐ Experiment 3D

☐ Read pages 56-61

☐ Experiment 3E

☐ Read pages 61-63
Read discuss Experiment 3F

☐ Written Assignment 3A

☐ Chapter 3 Test

In this case, we won't be *doing* the experiment, just reading and discussing it.

Chapter 4

☐ Read pages 65-72

☐ Experiment 4B
Read pages 72-77 and 80-82

☐ Read pages 78-79

☐ Experiment 4D

☐ Experiment 4E
Read pages 82-86

☐ Research Project 4G
Experiment 4C

☐ Read pages 86-89 and 90-91

☐ Written Assignment 4A & 4F

☐ Chapter 4 Test

This course outline is based upon the textbook, <u>Basic Science for Christian Schools</u>, 1983 ed., by John E. Jenkins and George Mulfinger, Jr., published by Bob Jones University Press, Greenville, SC.

❖ Altering a Pre-packaged Course

Some courses require a lot changes to fit your goals and your family. Others require just a few. Don't feel like you are wasting your money by not teaching a whole course or book. If there are parts you'd rather do differently, it will be more of a waste to follow someone else's plan. Our family has run the full gamut making just a teeny alteration in one course, and using only one or two ideas out of another one.

For example, we made just a minor change in our seventh grader's math program. It included a daily timed drill to be done before the lesson. The purpose of the drill was to make sure the student knew his basic addition, subtraction, multiplication and division facts inside and out. We wanted our student to know the facts that well, too, but he hated the drills. We decided to give him the choice of doing the drill with the book, spending twenty minutes on Math-It, or going through all the math Wrap-Ups. A minor change, but we had to consider our goals and decide what changes were needed to make the course work for us.

Another example was the Life Science course we did. The text book we used was good, but we wanted to do anatomy first and it came at the end of book. Since the book was arranged in separate units, that part was easy to fix. But I had some materials I had collected through the years that I really wanted to use. We ended up reading the book, Skin and Bones aloud together, cutting out and using a felt body model, and having my oldest son read some of the text book as background. For the most part, we ignored all the assignments suggested in the anatomy chapter of our text.

The life science book included so many assignments and experiments that no one could do them all. We had to decide which projects we wanted to include, and we had to make the decision in advance so we could make sure to have the needed experiment materials on hand. So during an evening before we began the course, I looked through all the experiments and found that for every chapter in the book, there were two to five experiments offered. Of these, there was nearly always one which used materials that wouldn't be too hard to find. So we did one experiment with each chapter and skipped the rest.

We made plenty of other changes along the way, but learned a lot and enjoyed the study. We went much more quickly through some chapters than was recommended, and much slower through others. I was able to use many resources that I already had. Our study was successful because we adapted it to fit our family and our goals.

❖ Designing Your Own Courses

In some subjects, we may use a standard text or pre-packaged resource for *part* of the course, pulling together many different resources for the rest. This allows us to pick and choose what we want to include. Some publishers don't like this and have begun to warn prospective customers that if they don't buy the whole pre-packaged unit, they will have serious "gaps" in their student's education. The course is so thoughtfully designed and well-constructed that it will work for everyone, they say. "Trust us, we're the experts."

The publishers and writers of textbooks, no doubt, have more expertise in their fields than you or I do. But you and I have much more expertise in our field (our own children) than they do. Do not be intimidated by the experts in the publishing industry any more than you allowed yourself to be intimidated by the challenges of "experts" in the education industry when you made the decision to homeschool. Parents, as well as other teachers, are perfectly capable of deciding which books or parts of books they want to use.

Many campus schools use a books and resources from a variety of sources. Textbook salesmen also try to convince these schools to buy all their materials from one company. This is not unethical—a good salesman works for a company in whose product he believes, and his job is to get you to believe in it, too. But don't be intimidated; choose what you decide will work best for you.

We have used standard textbooks for reference only, or as background reading, without using any end-of-chapter questions or other assignments. We have also used one chapter out of a whole book if we found that the book included the information we wanted to study. We borrow books from friends if we only want to use it for a short time, and we borrow books from the library if we find what we want there.

Sometimes I have no idea what to include in a course we want to cover. I can't seem to plan the course myself because I don't remember enough about the basics of the subject to get started. To get ideas for units or components of this kind of course, I sometimes photocopy the table of contents from a textbook at the library, then use that as an outline. I can then use a wide range of materials, methods and assignments to fill in the outline. Another good source of outlines is the encyclopedia. Nearly every subject is covered in the encyclopedia, and at the end of the article will often be an outline.

For other courses, particularly those which relate to a hobby or special interest of mine, I may collect everything I already own about a subject and design most of my course according to what I have available. Since I love to collect books, I have a lot sitting on the shelf that we haven't taken full advantage of yet. Our computer course was designed this way. I already had lots of software. I want my children to learn to use the computer as a tool, doing real-life applications with it rather than only being able to play submarine or fighter jet games. Since every program comes with a whole book, I already have a shelf full of computer materials. I also know I'm not getting full use of these expensive texts, since I only look at them when I'm in trouble.

Looking at my computer course on page 125, you'll see that I used the basic programs I had, along with the books that came with them. An extra benefit is that my son now knows how to use the programs we have, and he can help me. He enjoys doing all the family bookkeeping on the computer, so I no longer have to balance my own checkbook. He can also type letters or print out an extra copy of a document I need. Sometimes he can even answer my questions about my own programs.

For still other courses, I plan the course around my own ideas of what I want to cover. I may not have the materials yet, but I have an idea of what I want. For example, I may know that my seventh grade son needs more handwriting practice in a daily worksheet format. He also needs a basic spelling program. But he is ready to move into a strong, upper-level literature and analysis program. He hates writing, so I want something to spark his interest, giving a lot of flexibility in subject matter. We have not covered parts of speech formally at all, so I need a self-paced program which starts from the beginning, but doesn't look like a second grade program.

By working out my course on paper first, I know exactly what I am looking for before I hit the curriculum sales. I write down the different things I want to incorporate in my course and then find materials that will cover the subjects I have chosen. My Bible and English courses are often covered in this way.

To decide which of these methods of planning to use for a course, simply ask yourself what it is you want the student to learn. If you have little expertise in a subject which you want to teach, you may not have any idea what you want your student to learn. In this situation, an outline may help. If looking at an outline or table of contents in a library book on the subject doesn't spark any ideas, then a pre-packaged course may be the best choice.

On the other hand, if you do have some ideas about what you want the student to learn, you will want to do more of the designing yourself. If you are planning a course in a subject about which you have studied recently, or have an interest in, or have purchased materials over the years because you have been planning to study it, you probably have some materials on your own shelf. Pull them out and see if they generate any ideas without your needing to spend more money on additional books.

If you don't have materials available for your subject, but you do have some ideas about what needs to be covered, jot down a list of ideas to include. Perhaps you don't have the specific materials available yet, but you may have enough ideas to write your course description. Your list of ideas or your course description will serve as a guide in putting together materials for your course.

Following are examples of courses designed by outline, by materials available, and by my own list of sub-topics or components I want included. Beginning on page 112 are additional sample course designs for many different subjects.

❖ Designing a Course from an Outline

Sample Journalism Course

Consider the following outline for Journalism, taken from the <u>World Book Encyclopedia</u>:

"I. Fields of journalism

    A. Newspapers
    B. News Services
    C. Magazines
    D. Radio
    E. Television

II. The Role of U.S. Journalism

    A. Informing the public
    B. Protecting the public interest
    C. Influencing public opinion
    D. Entertaining the public

III. Major issues in U.S. Journalism

    A. Restrictions on freedom of the press
    B. Protecting identity of news sources
    C. The Fairness Doctrine
    D. Criticism of the Press

IV. Journalism in other countries

    A. In free societies
    B. In government-controlled societies

V. History

VI. Careers in journalism"

In designing a semester-long journalism course, I would consider that the *mastery* areas, the parts of the subject that I want my student to remember throughout his life, are:

- Freedom of the press is vital

- Don't believe everything you read or see

- Learn to look beyond the writer's own slant to pick out the facts

- Be aware of the powerful influence the press has on the populace.

- Learn to use the "5 'W's & an 'H'" (who, what, where, when, why & how) to write an interesting article without leaving out any important facts

In this course, let's assume my student doesn't have an obvious gift in communication skills. Interests haven't been expressed, but may pop up as we work through the course. Continuing learning areas are the new developments in communications technology, and reinforcing the mastery areas listed above. Most of the rest is for exposure only, unless an interest or gift is uncovered. The parts of the course that apply to English class (writing, speaking, analyzing others' work) would include some mastery areas, but not for the sake of journalism; rather for the English skills themselves.

In considering the outline, there are six major topics, with the first one, Fields of Journalism, being the obvious place to include fun projects and field trips to study each of the fields. The last topic, Careers in Journalism, could be included as we study each field.

Item V, History, could be studied independently, with an essay assigned. Since it is only an exposure area, I won't assign a full research paper; a couple of hours of research at the library with an essay will suffice. My student can complete this assignment whenever he likes, as long as he knows the course is not completed until he does it.

Items II and III have some concepts which I include as mastery, but since they are *concepts*, not simple facts to be memorized, I want to stress them throughout the course. It doesn't make sense to wait until after our studies of each of the fields of journalism to introduce the importance of freedom of the press. So I will rearrange the outline, putting an introduction to key concepts first, and referring back to them throughout the study.

Item IV, Journalism in other countries is an exposure area, except that it provides a good opportunity to study what happens when the key concept of freedom of the press does not exist. I decide to put it last, allowing me to use it as a wrap-up for the rest of the study.

Since this is a semester course, I need to break the course into about 75 points (which will take about 75 hours to complete.) I write my new outline, leaving space to add in field trip ideas and assignments. I may also add books and resources that I already own and want to use. Or if I don't have any books covering the topics, we will use the library to research background information.

I don't know what the Fairness Doctrine (item III, C) is, so I will look that up in the encyclopedia article. Oh. The Fairness Doctrine is the law that requires equal time be given to opposing views on controversial issues. Having looked it up, I decide this will be a good place to discuss Rush Limbaugh and similar programs, since Mr. Limbaugh claims his program is part of the fulfillment of the Fairness Doctrine for the rest of the media.

On the next page is a copy of my new outline, with most of the designing process completed. Remember, you are seeing the completed design. In actual practice, there is a lot of erasing and rewriting as you determine what projects to include, the exact number of points you will award for each project and the order of assignments.

The assignments on the outline are generalized as a guide for the teacher. As the course progresses and assignments are made, more specifics would be included. Obviously, as projects are begun, there would be more information discussed than what is listed here.

Journalism
1 semester (75 pts) — 5 credits on completion

	Points
I. The role of U.S. journalism	
A. Character of a godly journalist - discuss traits	1
B. Assign paper on the history of journalism	5
C. Informing the public	
1) Freedom of press - look at Constitution (4-R[7] what it means)	3
2) Watch & discuss TV news, get 4 or 5 news magazines, plus two or three newspapers - compare editorials, news, etc.	4
D. Protecting the public interest	
1) Investigative reporting - watch "60 minutes" & discuss	1
2) Look up articles on Watergate at library	1
3) Listen to part of a Rush Limbaugh show	1
4) Ask several adults if they think the media protects the public interest. Ask what could be done for improvement.	2
E. Influencing public opinion	
1) Choose one recent news topic. Compare the coverage by all sources gathered for A-2 above.	1
2) Write a persuasive essay on a current issue.	1
F. Entertaining the public	
1) Find several articles meant as entertainment	1
II. Major issues in U.S. journalism	
A. Restrictions on freedom of the press	
1) Interview a writer from the local paper and ask what limitations he has on printing information.	1
2) Look up libel, slander, and other prohibitions & restrictions. 4-R[8] Scriptural restrictions	2

— Continued on next page —

---

[7]   A brief definition of "4-R" is in the footnote on page 5.

Points

B. Protecting the identity of news sources

    1) Discuss why this might be necessary. Find an example in a magazine or newspaper of an unnamed source.   1

C. The Fairness Doctrine

    1) What is it? Is it followed in today's media?
    Do you agree with Rush's opinion on this? What does the Bible say?   3

D. Criticism of the press

    1) Find a letter to editor, editorial, or article which includes a criticism of the press. How would the criticized reporter respond? Write a letter to the editor about an article which was biased.   3

III. Fields of journalism (including careers)

A. Newspapers

    1) Field trip to local newspaper   2

    2) Write a two-page newsletter (for relatives, church, homeschool children, etc.) include a news story, editorial, events, and as many newspaper components as possible.   6

B. News services

    1) Identify at least three news stories that came from a news service.   1

    2) Ask the local paper what percentage of their stories come from a service.   1

C. Magazines

    1) Compare at least three different news magazines' coverage of the same event. Notice where the story was printed and the slant of the reporter.   2

    2) Count how many pages are used by ads & how many by news stories.
    Compare the kinds of ads in the different magazines.   1

    3) Compare the coverage of an issue between newspapers and magazines.   2

D. Radio

    1) Field trip to radio station.   2

    2) Listen to news broadcasts on at least three different stations.
    Count the amount of time spent on each story.   2

    3) Write a 5-minute radio news report and deliver it (using a tape recorder.) Include weather, news and human interest stories.   5

— Continued on next page —

Points

E. Television

   1) Field trip to local TV station.   2

   2) Watch three different newscasts over several days. Chart the amount of time given to each story, and the place featured in the newscast.   5

   3) Write a news report on one issue and deliver it. (Try to borrow a video camera & record it.)   5

IV. Journalism in other countries

  A. In free societies

   1) What are some countries which have freedom of the press? Try to find an article from a foreign country about one of the news stories studied during this course.   2

  B. In government-controlled societies

   1) What are some countries which have no freedom of the press? Try to find an example of a news story covered in one of these countries.   2

   2) Find out what news programs are run on short-wave radio. Try to arrange to hear one. (Call local ham operators group.)   3

V. Wrap up

  A. Write a report comparing the ways the different media cover the news. Include examples which show the weaknesses and strengths of each.   5

———————————

Total Points   79

At this point, I'm not too worried that I have 79 points instead of 75. The points are based on my ball-park figures for write-ups and research. It could vary quite a bit once we actually start the class. If everything seems to be taking a lot longer than I figured, I can cut back on some areas by having a discussion rather than having my student write a paper. Or I can award more credits. Or I won't worry about it if all my field trip ideas don't work out.

❖ Designing a Course from What You Have on Hand

I have found that for subject areas in which someone in our family is already interested, if we design our own course, we are usually more successful than if we purchase one from someone else. This is because we already know quite a lot about our interests or hobbies. Among just my own family members, we have a variety of interests, with accompanying books and magazines loaded with information about them. On our shelves, there are plenty of books about history, photography, raising and training Labrador Retrievers, natural cooking, and several other hobby-related topics.

You probably have plenty of materials related to your family's hobbies, too. For these kinds of subjects, it isn't usually necessary to go out and buy a textbook to teach from, unless of course, that is a handy excuse to cover the "necessity" of the next hobby book you just "have" to have!

Sample Field Biology Course

I took Field Biology in college. It was a semester-long course for which I earned *five college credits*. The average academic courses met three times a week and netted only three credits. It has been years since I took that course, and I don't remember most of what I learned, but I did learn that it is fun to be able to identify the different trees, flowers, and animals. It's still a hobby of mine to take pictures of the local flora, both around our home and when we travel. Many homeschoolers have done a lot of nature studies throughout elementary school, so there is a tendency to think nature studies are for little children. What I remember as being different in the college course from our family's nature walks is that, for the college course, we visited several different ecosystems and we were a little more technical in our terminology.

I still have the book we used in college. It is a paperback field guide called <u>Sierra Nevada Natural History: An Illustrated Handbook</u> by Tracy I. Storer and Robert L. Usinger. The book is still available at any store in the west which sells science or nature study books or backpacking and camping books. Through the years, I have collected a lot of nature study books. Including the one from college, here are the ones I could grab off my shelf in just a couple of minutes:

Books to Identify Plants:

<u>Pacific Coast Tree Finder</u> by Tom Watts. Berkeley, CA: Nature Study Guild, 1973.

<u>Pacific States Wildflowers</u>, <u>Peterson Field Guides</u> by Theodore F. Niehaus. Boston: Houghton Mifflin Company, 1976.

<u>Sierra Flower Finder: A Guide to Sierra Nevada Wildflowers</u> by Glenn Keator, Ph.D. Berkeley, CA: Nature Study Guild, 1980.

<u>The Time Life Encyclopedia of Gardening</u>, 30 volumes! Alexandria, VA: Time-Life Books, 1978.

<u>Tree Finder, a Manual for the Identification of Trees by Their Leaves</u> by May Theilgaard Watts. Berkeley, CA: Nature Study Guild, 1986.

<u>Trees of North America</u> by Frank C. Brockman. Racine, WI: Golden Press, Western Publishing Company Inc., 1986.

Western Garden Book by the editors of Sunset Books and Sunset Magazine. Menlo Park, CA: Lane Publishing, 1990.

Books to Identify Insects:

The Bug Book by Dr. Hugh Danks. New York: Workman Publishing, 1987.

A Field Guide to the Insects of America North of Mexico, Peterson Field Guide Series. by Donald J. Borror and Richard E. White. Boston: Houghton Mifflin, 1970.

Books to Identify Birds and Mammals:

Birds of North America by Chandler S. Robbins, et al. Racine, WI: Golden Press division of Western Publishing Company. 1983.

Familiar Mammals, North America, Audubon Society Pocket Guides by Chanticleer Press. New York: Alfred A. Knopf Inc., 1988.

Pacific Coast Bird Finder by Roger J. Lederer. Berkeley, CA: Nature Study Guild, 1977.

General Field Guides and Naturalist Books:

The Amateur Naturalist's Handbook by Vinson Brown. New York: Prentice Hall Press, 1980.

Investigating Nature through Outdoor Projects by Vinson Brown. Harrisburg, PA: Stackpole Books, 1983.

A Sierra Club Naturalist's Guide by Stephen Whitney. San Francisco: Sierra Club Books, 1979.

Sierra Nevada Natural History by Tracy I. Storer and Robert L. Usinger. Berkeley, CA: University of California Press, 1963.

Plus the World Book encyclopedia and a stack of other gardening books and articles.

It would be downright embarrassing to buy another book to teach a field biology class, so I design my course using the materials I already own. To plan my course, I will categorize our studies as I have our books. We will include studies of plants, insects, birds, reptiles and mammals. I also want to include habitats for the various creatures we study, so I will plan trips to various locales. The trips will make it a true "field" biology course, but will add some expense and time constraints.

Because of the travel involved, I may not be able to fit the whole field biology course into a one-year time period. I am not even sure it would be wise to *require* too many specific geographic locations. For example, I'm not sure at this point if we'll be able to drive to the coast to study plants and birds. Instead, I will list as many areas as I think may be possible to study, and will *require* only a percentage of them to be visited. If we don't get to the beach, perhaps we can go to the desert.

Looking in my old college field guide, I find the following zones or regions in our state:

1) Great Central Valley

2) Foothill Digger Pine—Chaparral Belt
    a. Brushlands—Chaparral

b. Pine—Oak Woodland (This is where we live.)

3) Yellow Pine Belt

4) Lodgepole Pine—Red Fir Belt

5) Subalpine Belt

6) Alpine Belt (above timberline)

7) Jeffrey Pine Belt (eastern side of Sierras)

8) Sagebrush Belt

9) Southeast Desert

10) Northwest Humid Coast

Among these elevation/plant zones, there are further divisions, for example, marshes, meadows, etc.

Since we live in the Sierras and have easy access to at least six or seven ecosystems, I will require a study of at least eight. This will force us to study a little outside our own area. In each study, I will require either a sample, photograph or a sketch of the specimen, to be kept in some sort of pleasing arrangement—an album, scrapbook, shadow box, etc. Each specimen must be identified by its correct scientific name, and must be labeled with the date and specific location where seen.

In addition, I will require a written report on each of the five units: plants, insects, birds, reptiles and mammals, plus a written description of each of the eight areas studied. My outline would be simple. The 10 credits will be awarded upon completion. I have tried to make the assignments total about 150 hours, but it may take two or three years to complete because of the traveling and because little work on this course can be done in the winter.

Field Biology

1 year (150 pts) — 10 credits on completion

date
completed[8]

Independent study and written report on:

    Characteristics of plants   5 points _____

    Characteristics of insects   5 points _____

    Characteristics of birds   5 points _____

    Characteristics of reptiles   5 points _____

    Characteristics of mammals   5 points _____

    (These are about five hours of work each.)

Report on the difference between the various geographic zones   15 points _____
       (Include diagrams or drawings or models)

Collection, identification and display of plants (50 required)   50 points _____
       Must have samples from eight areas.

Identification and display of insects (25 required)   25 points _____

Identification and display of birds (25 required)   25 points _____

Identification and display of mammals (10 required)   10 points _____

                                             _____

Total   150 points

---

[8]   Once a course is designed, I like to put the major assignments on a checklist. My student can keep this in his own notebook to follow and record completion dates. He can easily see at a glance how much more work needs to be finished in each course, and if a busy day comes along, he can even choose assignments which need little help from me, saving those which must be done together for a time when I am available. On this course sheet, I have added a space for dates.

❖ Designing a Course from What You Want to Study

Sample Bible Course

In designing a Bible study, we must first take time to consider what we want out of the study. I desire my students to be well-grounded in the Word, not shaky in their beliefs. I hope they will be committed Christians. They must develop their own independent relationships with the Lord. It would be nice if, over the course of high school, each read through the entire Bible. They need to know how to use the various types of Bible study tools available, and they should be familiar with the writings of great Christians.

The main areas I want to include in the Bible course are:

Instruction in the Word — by someone with greater understanding than the student, to help him learn the ways of the Lord. This could be a time of family reading aloud from the Bible, with explanation and discussion led by the parents, or it could be done using a Bible study book with explanations and research directed by a knowledgeable author. If a study book is used, it may be done as a family study, or it could be done independently.

Hear counsel, and receive instruction, that thou mayest be wise in thy latter end. Proverbs 19:20

Scripture Memorization — We have used short, separate verses like those in *The Four Spiritual Laws* or similar tracts, and also lengthier sections of Scripture. We don't necessarily choose all the memorization selections at the start; but you do need to decide how much to require. A verse a day could be memorized, but probably not remembered long-term. A verse a week would give more time for it to really sink in, but may also be easily forgotten unless previously memorized verses are practiced during the year.

Thy word have I hid in mine heart, that I might not sin against thee. Psalm 119:11

Prayer and Worship — Years ago our friend, Linda Beeson, introduced us to the idea of a prayer calendar, and we have used one ever since. A prayer journal also works well for teens. A calendar helps them remember others that need prayer, and a prayer journal gives a visual lesson in how God answers prayers. Worship is also an important part of Bible study, but is sometimes overlooked in non-musical families. Purchasing a couple of hymnals for home use is a worthwhile investment if you don't already have them.

I will bless the Lord at all times: his praise shall continually be in my mouth. Psalm 34:1

Ministry Work or Service — Giving teens a chance to serve the Lord through service to others in their own projects can help develop a heart of servanthood. How different than the world's system of serving one's self first! One caution: In order for a ministry to *be* a ministry, it involves some sacrifice for the Lord. Usually when a new ministry is first begun, the vision is fresh and there is some excitement. But once the work has continued, it is easy to get bored or disillusioned. Yet working past this time of "let down" is an important part of ministry. I hope you will require a fairly long term commitment from your teen, so that he will not get in the habit of jumping from job to job for "spiritual highs" while forgetting that his own *feelings* about the work are not the issue.

We then that are strong ought to bear the infirmities of the weak, and not to please ourselves. Romans 15:1

Some ministry suggestions that are workable for teens are:

Missionary box and letter: Send a package monthly or bi-monthly, including American foods which may be hard to find overseas, a book, toiletries, etc., plus a letter.

Food closet: Many churches have a food closet and would allow a teen to take over keeping of inventory and organization.

Church care: Make a commitment to keep a specified part of the grounds kept up, repairing of worn hymnals, help in Sunday School or nursery.

Meals on Wheels: Deliveries of meals to shut-ins may require the parents to do the driving, but the teen can deliver the meal and be the one to build a relationship with those on his route.

Newsletter mailing: Churches and homeschool groups often have newsletters. What a blessing it has been for me to be finished with mine when it goes to print! My sons have done the labeling, stamping, sealing, etc. to get it ready to mail.

Neighbors: Do you have elderly or shut-in neighbors who would appreciate having their trash taken out to the curb, or their lawn mowed, or their yard tidied? How about a mom with lots of young children who would appreciate a weekly story hour in her home?

Event Set Up, Clean Up, or Coordinating: An afternoon or short-term ministry would be to volunteer at a church or homeschool group event. If tables need to be set up, teens could volunteer to help, or even volunteer to recruit helpers for set up and tear down.

Based on these components, I put together my Bible course, setting the points for each assignment based on roughly the amount of time or on the percentage of the overall course I feel the assignment should use. The following page shows the process of laying out this course, including notes regarding the purpose and points of each component. Page 112 shows the finished course design, which includes spaces for recording completion dates. This sheet will go into my student's notebook. The *student* does most of the record keeping.

Bible 9

1 semester (75 pts) — 5 credits on completion
[It will take a full year to complete this course at about ½ hour per day.]

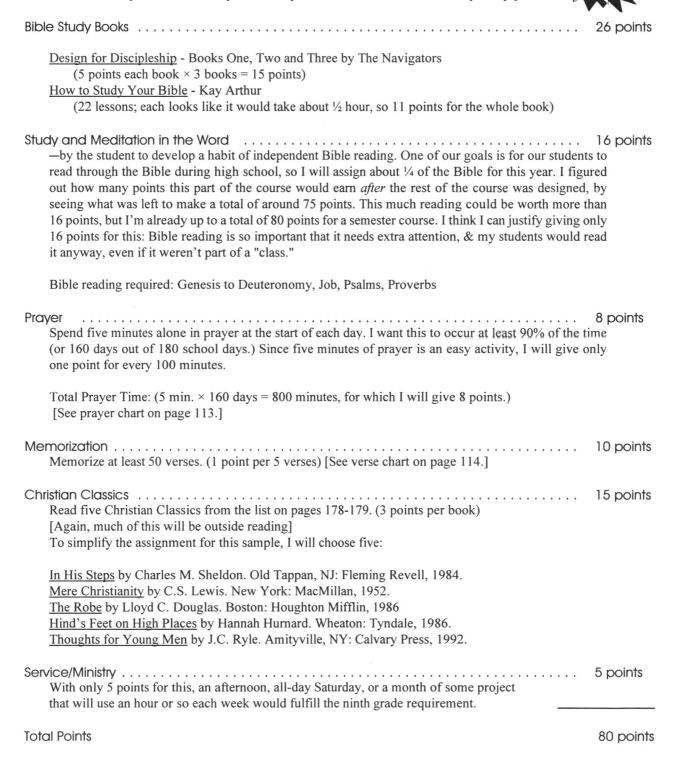

Bible Study Books . . . . 26 points

> Design for Discipleship - Books One, Two and Three by The Navigators
> (5 points each book × 3 books = 15 points)
> How to Study Your Bible - Kay Arthur
> (22 lessons; each looks like it would take about ½ hour, so 11 points for the whole book)

Study and Meditation in the Word . . . . 16 points
—by the student to develop a habit of independent Bible reading. One of our goals is for our students to read through the Bible during high school, so I will assign about ¼ of the Bible for this year. I figured out how many points this part of the course would earn *after* the rest of the course was designed, by seeing what was left to make a total of around 75 points. This much reading could be worth more than 16 points, but I'm already up to a total of 80 points for a semester course. I think I can justify giving only 16 points for this: Bible reading is so important that it needs extra attention, & my students would read it anyway, even if it weren't part of a "class."

Bible reading required: Genesis to Deuteronomy, Job, Psalms, Proverbs

Prayer . . . . 8 points
Spend five minutes alone in prayer at the start of each day. I want this to occur at least 90% of the time (or 160 days out of 180 school days.) Since five minutes of prayer is an easy activity, I will give only one point for every 100 minutes.

Total Prayer Time: (5 min. × 160 days = 800 minutes, for which I will give 8 points.)
[See prayer chart on page 113.]

Memorization . . . . 10 points
Memorize at least 50 verses. (1 point per 5 verses) [See verse chart on page 114.]

Christian Classics . . . . 15 points
Read five Christian Classics from the list on pages 178-179. (3 points per book)
[Again, much of this will be outside reading]
To simplify the assignment for this sample, I will choose five:

In His Steps by Charles M. Sheldon. Old Tappan, NJ: Fleming Revell, 1984.
Mere Christianity by C.S. Lewis. New York: MacMillan, 1952.
The Robe by Lloyd C. Douglas. Boston: Houghton Mifflin, 1986
Hind's Feet on High Places by Hannah Hurnard. Wheaton: Tyndale, 1986.
Thoughts for Young Men by J.C. Ryle. Amityville, NY: Calvary Press, 1992.

Service/Ministry . . . . 5 points
With only 5 points for this, an afternoon, all-day Saturday, or a month of some project that will use an hour or so each week would fulfill the ninth grade requirement.
_____

Total Points   80 points

Bible 9

Assignment	Date Completed	Points

Bible Study Books:

Design for Discipleship Book One	_____	 5
Design for Discipleship Book Two	_____	 5
Design for Discipleship Book Three	_____	 5
How To Study Your Bible	_____	 11

Independent Bible Reading with Reports: 16

Genesis	_____
Exodus	_____
Leviticus	_____
Numbers	_____
Deuteronomy	_____
Job	_____
Psalms	_____
Proverbs	_____

Prayer Chart: (each box = 100 minutes. Record date completed in each box) 8

Scripture Memorization Chart: (Each box = 5 verses. Record date in each box) 10

Christian Classics: 15

In His Steps	_____
Mere Christianity	_____
The Robe	_____
Hind's Feet on High Places	_____
Thoughts for Young Men	_____

Service/Ministry Project: 5

_____

_____

Date service project completed: _____

Bible 9 — Continued

Prayer Record [9]

Each Box = 5 minutes (Write date in box)

100 minutes = 1 point
8 points required

---

[9]   The inspiration for this chart and many of the other fill-in-the-box charts in this Designing Courses chapter came from Barbara Shelton's book High School: A Home Designed Form+U+La.

Bible 9 — Continued

Scripture Memorization Sheet

Verse:	Date:	Verse:	Date:
Verse:	Date:	Verse:	Date:
Verse:	Date:	Verse:	Date:
Verse:	Date:	Verse:	Date:
Verse:	Date:	Verse:	Date:
Verse:	Date:	Verse:	Date:
Verse:	Date:	Verse:	Date:
Verse:	Date:	Verse:	Date:
Verse:	Date:	Verse:	Date:
Verse:	Date:	Verse:	Date:
Verse:	Date:	Verse:	Date:
Verse:	Date:	Verse:	Date:
Verse:	Date:	Verse:	Date:
Verse:	Date:	Verse:	Date:
Verse:	Date:	Verse:	Date:
Verse:	Date:	Verse:	Date:
Verse:	Date:	Verse:	Date:
Verse:	Date:	Verse:	Date:
Verse:	Date:	Verse:	Date:
Verse:	Date:	Verse:	Date:
Verse:	Date:	Verse:	Date:
Verse:	Date:	Verse:	Date:
Verse:	Date:	Verse:	Date:
Verse:	Date:	Verse:	Date:
Verse:	Date:	Verse:	Date:

Careers/Vocational Education
-- 1 semester course = 5 credits --

[This course was designed by starting with the outline for the article on careers in the World Book Encyclopedia.]

I.   Choosing and Planning a Career

    A.   Learning about oneself
        --   study of spiritual gifts   5
        --   skill assessment
        -- *Finding the Career that Fits You* by Lee Ellis & Larry Birkett   30

    B.   Discovering the world of work
        --   work habits
        --   interview 3 employers (what is valuable in an employee?)   1.5

    C.   Exploring career fields
        --   read World Book article on fields   1
        --   library book on jobs and fields   1.5
        --   6 interviews with people working in areas of possible interest   6

    D.   Preparing for a career
        --   training needed in interest area   5
        --   how to get training (college, apprenticeship, entry-level job?)   2
        --   3 goals (dream job, good living, something to fall back on)   3

II.   Getting a Job

    A.   Finding job opportunities
        --   want ads   2
        --   government employment office (field trip)   2
        --   private employment agency   2
        --   networking, chambers of commerce, etc.   2

    B.   Writing a résumé
        --   assignment   2

    D.   Completing application forms
        --   application from stationers   2

    E.   Being interviewed
        --   interview skills (dress, attitude, speech)   1
        --   practice interview   1

    F.   Contacting employers
        --   set up the 6 interviews for exploring career fields   3

                                      73

7th Grade English

150 points = 10 credits

McGuffey Reader (30 stories read aloud with questions answered in writing)   -- 30 points

Lesson Read	Q & A	Lesson Read	Q & A	Lesson Read	Q & A	Lesson Read	Q & A	Lesson Read	Q & A

Classics: (Three read and reported on)   -- 15 points
- ☐ *Treasure Island* - Stevenson   date completed: _____
- ☐ *Old Yeller* - Gipson   date completed: _____
- ☐ *Men of Iron* - Pyle   date completed: _____

Winston Grammar: -- 30 points

1	2	3	4	5	6	7	8	9	10	11	12	13	14	15
16	17	18	19	20	21	22	23	24	25	26	27	28	29	30

Handwriting: *Writing with Power* (Christian Liberty Academy)   -- 14 points
   (I figured about 15 minutes per page, so gave 1 point for every 4 pages)

4-8 ___   9-12 ___   13-16 ___   17-20 ___   21-24 ___   25-28 ___   29-32 ___
33-36 ___   37-40 ___   41-44 ___   45-48 ___   49-52 ___   53-56 ___   57-60 ___

Spelling: (30 weekly lessons)   -- 30 points

1	2	3	4	5	6	7	8	9	10
11	12	13	14	15	16	17	18	19	20
21	22	23	24	25	26	27	28	29	30

Composition: Understanding Writing — Bradrick Family Enterprises   -- 30 points
   (3 times per week [about 20 min. each] = 60 minutes per week)

☐☐☐	☐☐☐	☐☐☐	☐☐☐	☐☐☐	☐☐☐
☐☐☐	☐☐☐	☐☐☐	☐☐☐	☐☐☐	☐☐☐
☐☐☐	☐☐☐	☐☐☐	☐☐☐	☐☐☐	☐☐☐
☐☐☐	☐☐☐	☐☐☐	☐☐☐	☐☐☐	☐☐☐
☐☐☐	☐☐☐	☐☐☐	☐☐☐	☐☐☐	☐☐☐

English 9: Fundamentals of Literature and Composition

1 year course — 10 credits

Fundamentals of Literature -- BJU text   Date Completed: _____   75 points

Five Additional Books Read & Reported On:

Date	Title	
_____	_____	3 points
_____	_____	3 points
_____	_____	3 points
_____	_____	3 points
_____	_____	3 points

<u>**Format Writing**</u> - by Frode Jensen   Date Completed: _____   30 points

Correspondence:

Date	Letter to	
_____	_____	1 point
_____	_____	1 point
_____	_____	1 point
_____	_____	1 point
_____	_____	1 point
_____	_____	1 point
_____	_____	1 point
_____	_____	1 point
_____	_____	1 point
_____	_____	1 point

4-R Project: Obedience   Date Completed: _____   25 points

Organic Gardening
1 year course = 10 credits

Composting
Build compost pile in fall & maintain thru winter for spring use.

Garden preparation & Soil
Map out garden, till, test soil, add compost, prepare beds.

Garden Logs
Begin log book in fall, keep through harvest.

Buying Seeds
Order seeds in winter.

Planting
Plant seeds in spring.

Watering, pruning, growing
Maintain garden. (Extra points for aesthetics.)

Weed and pest control
Create scrapbook of weeds found. Identify and label.
Collect insect samples found. Identify and label.

Harvesting & Storage
Canning (also counts toward Home Ec.)
Drying (also counts toward Home Ec.)
Freezing (also counts toward Home Ec.)

Materials Needed

Put my garden books all on one shelf for easy accessibility during course.
Garden Log Book
Materials to build compost pile
Gardening supplies (row markers, tomato cages, etc. -- have student make list and check our supplies.)
Scrapbook for weeds.
Canning supplies
Dehydrator

Physical Education [10]

2 year course — 20 credits

- 40 minutes of exercise × 3 times per week = 120 minutes (2 hours) per week.

- 2 hours per week × 36 school weeks recorded = 72 hours = 1 semester of credit

- 3 workout sessions of at least 40 minutes per week will be required, for 36 weeks, for a total of 108 workout sessions required for each 5 credits. 20 credits required for graduation.

- 1 exercise/sports session of at least 40 minutes = 1 point

- 108 points per year × 4 years = 432 points required upon graduation.

At least 8 different activities required for 10 times each.

Activity Dates (10 dates per activity)

This sheet =   80 points. Two of the following sheets must also be completed for graduation.
Sheet 2   =   176
Sheet 3   =   176
Total Points   432

---

[10]   Our goal for physical education is to develop a habit of fitness and exercise in our students. In addition to regular exercise (3 times per week), we would like them to try several sports or activities, with the hope that they may enjoy one or two enough to continue through their adult years. We decided to require them to try an average of at least two different activities per year, for a total of eight. We figured that if they try an activity ten times, they should have learned enough of the basics to know if it is something they would like to continue. So this sheet is to record ten points in each of eight different activities. The eleventh time they do the same activity, it is recorded on the following sheet. The following sheet also can have activities which were tried just a few times, as well as "household" exercise, like wood cutting.

Physical Education — Continued

List Activity & Date

This sheet = 176 points
(2 sheets like this one required for graduation)

Piano — Advanced

10 credits = 150 points

Lessons: Attended weekly & practiced daily - list lesson date (3 points each)   108 points

Music/Composer Reports: Completed - list date and topic (2 pts each)   14 points

Performances: (7 points each)   28 points

Date, Occasion and Location   _____

                                _____

    Selections   _____

                                _____

Date, Occasion and Location   _____

                                _____

    Selections   _____

                                _____

Date, Occasion and Location   _____

                                _____

    Selections   _____

                                _____

Date, Occasion and Location   _____

                                _____

    Selections   _____

                                _____

Practical Photography
1 semester — 5 credits

Six two-hour class sessions, held monthly, plus photography assignments for each which will be shot and developed by the students between the class sessions.

Session # 1

Open with prayer & introduction to the arts from the Bible.

Definition of basic photography terms.

Parts of a camera. Parts common to all cameras & how to use each part on your own camera.

Special features of some cameras.

Caring for a camera.

Manners for photographers.

Uses of photography.

What makes a picture good?

Recording your work.

Experiment: Taking pictures without a camera.

Portraits.

- Portrait Assignments for next class:
  □ Child □ Adult
  □ Candid □ animal
  □ group portrait

Session # 2

Open with prayer & principle related to the arts from the Bible.

How to display photos for class discussion.

Critique of portrait assignments.

Lighting.

Buildings, Monuments, etc.

- Architecture Assignments for next class:
  □ Home □ Sightseeing
  □ Building □ Portrait
  □ Historical Landmark

Session # 3

Open with prayer & principle related to the arts from the Bible.

Critique of Portrait review photos.

Critique of Architecture assignments.

Special events & holidays photography.

Being prepared ahead when you have to shoot quickly.

Documentation and Editorializing.

Ethics in photography.

Photojournalism.

Telling a story.

Action.

- Special Events/Photojournalism assignments for next class:
  □ Holiday □ Action
  □ Mood □ Documentary
  □ Architecture

Session # 4

Open with prayer & principle related to the arts from the Bible.

Critique of architecture photos.

Critique of special events/ photojournalism assignments.

Framing your subject.

Perspective & Depth of field.

Foreground & background.

Landscapes.

- Landscape Assignments for next class:
  □ Sunset □ Trees
  □ No sign of man □ City
  □ Action/Holiday/Documentary

Session # 5

Open with prayer & principle related to the arts from the Bible.

Critique of Action/Holiday/ Photojournalism assignment.

Critique of Landscapes assignments.

Tripods or tripod substitutes.

Lighting angles and availability.

Focus.

Close Ups & Stills.

- Close-Ups/Stills Assignments for next class:
  □ Texture □ Flower
  □ Still life □ Landscape
  □ Lighting experiment

Session # 6

Critique of landscape & Critique of Close Ups/Stills assignments.

Field Trip to photo lab: Bring one roll of TRI-X black and white prints which you have shot. We will develop the negatives and print photos.

Sewing 1

1 semester — 5 credits

Three projects must be completed to pass the course, but a fourth must be completed in order to receive an A.

Basic skills listed below must each be used in at least one of the projects.

____ Hand hemming	____ Machine hemming	____ Darts
____ Basting	____ Buttons & button holes	____ Zipper
____ Casing & elastic	____ Gathering	____ Waistband
____ Sleeves	____ Matching plaids or print	____ Collar
____ Pockets	____ Top stitching	____ Facings

Projects will be graded on:

    1. Finished appearance.
    2. Selection of pattern & fabric and layout & cutting.
    3. Work attitude and habits, care of equipment and following instructions.
    4. The basic skills from the above list which were used in the project.

Projects and grade:

Project	Finished Appearance	Pattern, fabric, layout, cutting	attitude, habits	basic skills used	Project Grade
1.					
2.					
3.					
4.					
Total Points					

Survey of Fine Arts [11] -- 10 credits = 150 points

- **Concerts:** Attended and evaluation sheet completed - list date and event

- **Plays:** Attended and evaluation sheet completed - list date and event

- **Music Styles:** Evaluation sheets completed - list date and style

- **Movies/TV:** Viewed and evaluation sheet completed - list date and title

- **Museums:** Visited and evaluation sheet completed - list date and place

- **Vocal or Radio Projects:** Completed - list date and project

- **Architecture:** Assignment completed - list date and assignment

- **Crafts:** At least 2 points each on 6 different crafts - list date and project

- **Photography:** Assignment completed - list date and assignment

- **Drawing/Painting:** Completed - list date and project

- **Miscellaneous:** Extra assignments from the above categories or others - list date and project

---

[11]   Ideas for this course are from Barbara Shelton's <u>Form+U+La</u>, which also includes report sheets for critiques on plays, concerts, films, etc. Note that this course will be worked on throughout high school, not all in one year. The student receives 1 year's worth of credits (10) when all the work is completed.

Typing
Word Processing
Computers

1 year course — 10 credits

● **Typing Speed Test:** (Take when ready) .... 40 points

Date: _____   Speed: _____
Date: _____   Speed: _____
Date: _____   Speed: _____

Overall Average Speed: _____   (40 wpm = A, 35 wpm = B, 30 wpm = C)

● **Business Letters Typed:** .... 6 points

Date: _____ Letter To: _____

Date: _____ Letter To: _____

Date: _____ Letter To: _____

● **Report with Footnotes & Bibliography:** .... 4 points

The report may be used to meet the requirements of any other class.
For this class, typing and layout are considered for the grade.

Date: _____ Report On: _____

● **Computer Programs:** .... 100 points

Complete the tutorial or workbook and demonstrate ability to operate each program:

Word Perfect 7.0   Date: _____ (20 points)

Quicken   Date: _____ (20 points)

Windows 95   Date: _____ (20 points)

Quattro Pro   Date: _____ (20 points)

Paradox   Date: _____ (20 points)

World History - 150 points = 10 credits

World History text assignments read   Date Completed: _____   50 points

15 Historical Books Read or Heard: (3 points each)   45 points

Title: _____ Author: _____ Date: _____
Title: _____ Author: _____ Date: _____
Title: _____ Author: _____ Date: _____
Title: _____ Author: _____ Date: _____
Title: _____ Author: _____ Date: _____
Title: _____ Author: _____ Date: _____
Title: _____ Author: _____ Date: _____
Title: _____ Author: _____ Date: _____
Title: _____ Author: _____ Date: _____
Title: _____ Author: _____ Date: _____
Title: _____ Author: _____ Date: _____
Title: _____ Author: _____ Date: _____
Title: _____ Author: _____ Date: _____
Title: _____ Author: _____ Date: _____
Title: _____ Author: _____ Date: _____

Research Project   Date completed: _____   15 points

Short Essays/Maps/Written Assignments = ½ to 1 point each   15 points

Time Line & Explanation   Date completed: _____   10 points

Museums/Field Trips/Travel or Bio Videos   15 points
     (Movie = 1 point, Field Trip or Museum = 2 points)

❖ 7 Scheduling & Lesson Plans

School scheduling is an abstract subject for many homeschool families. Many of us desire to avoid following the government schools' pattern and, instead allow learning to become an on-going part of our lives. We tell our children that life is school and school is life, so they should always be learning something. We try to teach them that school is more than sitting in a classroom for 50 minutes each day. The line between school and hobby or pleasure activities becomes blurred for most homeschoolers.

I began homeschooling with a schedule that was supposed to dictate the precise time at which we would get up, do chores, have breakfast, do a Bible study, and begin each academic assignment. I quickly left that type of schedule, mostly because of my aversion to some piece of paper on the refrigerator dictating my day. I did need to plan to have reading, writing and arithmetic in the mornings while we were fresh, but I began to focus on simply finishing the tasks and moving on. If math took 70 minutes instead of 50, that no longer made us feel like we were "behind" 20 minutes in our day. Our plan was to do arithmetic in the morning, then move on to the next assignment for the day.

I have found that my students like this approach to their work. They like to have a list of tasks so they know when they have done enough "academics," or "table time" or "study" for the day. Listing the assignments I expect them to complete each day, as opposed to listing the times they need to begin and finish each task, helps them become self-motivated. School is more than just "doing time." If my student chooses to waste time staring out the window or doodling, his math may take longer. If he focuses diligently on his work, he will be finished sooner—his decisions affect his day.

One of our family's goals during junior and senior high is to make a transition from the parent being fully responsible for the education of the student to the student taking the responsibility for educating himself. This is not usually a natural transition—the student must be taught to be responsible and diligent. The progression for a student to begin to take the responsibility for his work will usually look something like this:

1. Teacher makes assignments, keeps lesson plans, monitors progress, and tells the student what to do next.

2. Student chooses what to do next. Teacher makes assignments, keeps lesson plan, and monitors progress.

3. Student chooses what to do next and keeps the lesson plan. Teacher makes assignments and monitors progress.

4. Student chooses what to do next, keeps the lesson plan, helps make assignments and monitors his own progress. Teacher directs assignments and verifies the student's progress.

By junior high school, unless you are brand new to homeschooling, your student is likely already past the first stage. If not, be patient and move ahead slowly. You could start at stage one, spend a full year or two working to move to the next level, and still be comfortably working at stage four by the end of high school.

In order to progress to the point at which the student becomes responsible for his education, he must have something for which to be responsible. If you have not used lesson plans or course outlines in the earlier years, I encourage you to try them now. A course outline will tell the student what he needs to do to earn credit for completing a course by showing him the overall or long-term goal. On the course design or course outline, he can see what needs to be done over the entire course. A lesson plan can also give the student a tangible way to demonstrate responsibility and initiative—on a day-to-day basis.

Before you can make an effective lesson plan, however, you must decide when the lessons you are planning must be done. Not only do you need to know when "school" will happen, but you must decide how long of a session you will plan lessons for at a time. Planning for too short a term (like for each week at a time) will hinder you from viewing the course as a whole, plus your planning will become tedious because there is so much repetition in each plan. But planning for too long a term (like for a whole semester) will hinder you from the flexibility you need to be able both to manage a home and teach your children.

❖ Setting Your School Calendar

I suggest deciding the basic calendar of your whole year before beginning lesson plans. You can, of course, be flexible during the year and change things around as needed, but laying out a general idea of the year beforehand will help you to have the "big picture" in mind as you work.

We have used many different school schedules. We began by following the schedule of the public schools in our area. Then when I began working with new homeschool families, I delayed the start of our own family's school until October because I was so busy during September. Later, we moved to a four-day school week, leaving Fridays for errands. Next I used a six-weeks-on, two-weeks-off schedule. Finally, I modified that to a six-weeks-on, one-week-off schedule, which we followed for the final five or six years of homeschooling high school.

You will need to assess your own family's lifestyle in determining the schedule that will work for you. Does your husband have "minor" holidays off of work? At our house, Washington's Birthday, Veterans Day, etc. are school days because my husband is usually working. But if your husband is home, you'll probably want to take school off, too.

Do you want a semester break? If so, when? Our family likes to take a two-week semester break at Christmas. While we do need to start our school year a little earlier than the public schools in our area, the payoff is that at Christmas, we are halfway done with our school year. Also, we are always finished by Memorial Day weekend. I find I have more energy in the fall for school, when the school year is new. By late spring, I am ready for a break and ready to finish the main books we have been studying. So starting a little earlier and finishing a little earlier works well for me.

Ask yourself how many weeks or days you can maintain academic lessons without a break. For me, the six-weeks-on, one-week-off schedule works well. After three weeks of school, I know we are halfway to a week-long vacation. During that week off, I will be able to catch up on household projects and prepare lesson plans for the next six weeks.

I know of some who have successfully used a modified four-day-week schedule. They have school Monday through Friday, then the next week just Monday through Thursday. This gives a three-day weekend every other week. On the Friday off, lesson plans are prepared for the next two weeks. Others I know, especially those with large families, find that a four-day week works well, giving one day off of school each week. Still others plan academic subjects needing Mom on four days each week with Friday being a totally independent learning day. This gives Mom a chance to do household projects without being called upon to answer a lot of Algebra questions on Fridays, but still counts as a five-day school week.

Whatever schedule you are contemplating, the first part of lesson planning is to pull out a calendar and mark out your basic school year. I start by working backward from Christmas, because having that as our semester break is important to me. I circle the Monday of each school week and write the number of the school week.

Just so you know, we do take Thanksgiving and the day after it as holidays. This means that our actual number of school days will total 178, not 180 as recommended for our state. We rarely miss any other days, so I figure two excused absences will not be too bad. We don't take a week off at Easter as many schools do, preferring to keep to our consistent six-weeks-on, one-week-off schedule. Finally, as I mentioned earlier, we don't take any "minor" holidays off.

On the following page is a blank calendar on which you can mark any school year. On the one I use, I start with August, since that is our first month of a new school year. Our family's sample calendar is shown on page 131. Use that as a starting place and modify it to fit your needs, or start from scratch on the blank calendar.

Calendar for _____

Schofield 1998-99 Calendar

36 5-day weeks divided into 6 week sessions (180 school days)
(1 week breaks after each 6 week session & 2 weeks semester break at Christmas)

August 1998

						1
2	3 (1)	4	5	6	7	8
9	10 (2)	11	12	13	14	15
16	17 (3)	18	19	20	21	22
23 / 30	24 (4) 31	25	26	27	28	29

September 1998

Aug 31 (5)	1	2	3	4	5	
6	7 (6)	8	9	10	11	12
13	14 week off	15	16	17	18	19
20	21 (7)	22	23	24	25	26
27	28 (8)	29	30			

October 1998

				1	2	3
4	5 (9)	6	7	8	9	10
11	12 (10)	13	14	15	16	17
18	19 (11)	20	21	22	23	24
25	26 (12)	27	28	29	30	31

November 1998

1	2 week off	3	4	5	6	7
8	9 (13)	10	11	12	13	14
15	16 (14)	17	18	19	20	21
22	23 (15)	24	25	26	27	28
29	30 (16)					

December 1998

		1	2	3	4	5
6	7 (17)	8	9	10	11	12
13	14 (18)	15	16	17	18	19
20	21 week off	22 week off	23	24	25	26
27	28 week off	29 week off	30	31		

January 1999

					1	2
3	4 (19)	5	6	7	8	9
10	11 (20)	12	13	14	15	16
17	18 (21)	19	20	21	22	23
24 / 31	25 (22)	26	27	28	29	30

February 1999

1 (23)	2	3	4	5	6	
7	8 (24)	9	10	11	12	13
14	15 (16) week off	16	17	18	19	20
21	22 (25)	23	24	25	26	27
28						

March 1999

1 (26)	2	3	4	5	6	
7	8 (27)	9	10	11	12	13
14	15 (28)	16	17	18	19	20
21	22 (29)	23	24	25	26	27
28	29 (30)	30	31			

April 1999

				1	2	3
4	5 week off	6 week off	7	8	9	10
11	12 (31)	13	14	15	16	17
18	19 (32)	20	21	22	23	24
25	26 (33)	27	28	29	30	

May 1999

						1
2	3 (34)	4	5	6	7	8
9	10 (35)	11	12	13	14	15
16	17 (36)	18	19	20	21	22
23 / 30	24 / 31	25 off for summer	26	27	28	29

June 1999

		1	2	3	4	5
6	7	8	9	10	11	12
13	14	15	16	17	18	19
20	21	22	23	24	25	26
27	28	29	30			

July 1999

				1	2	3
4	5	6	7	8	9	10
11	12	13	14	15	16	17
18	19	20	21	22	23	24
25	26	27	28	29	30	31

❖ Making Lesson Plans

You will need to leave some room in your schedule for lesson planning. This is important!! Make planning ahead a priority and you can enjoy the whole year. I know it is difficult to set aside time just for making lesson plans with a house full of children. But if you can't find time to figure out what your lessons are and when to do them, how do you plan to find time to complete them?

During the first year of writing out your course designs or outlines for junior or senior high school, plan a whole weekend (or the equivalent) to write the courses descriptions and course outlines. This will include most of the 4-year courses, plus the ones you plan to complete entirely during the school year. Then figure another whole day to lay out your first batch of lesson plans. Know that you will be able to write lesson plans faster as you gain experience.

My biggest mistake in the beginning was putting detailed lesson and page numbers on my lesson plans, rendering them useless within three or four weeks, because I had crossed out so much that my plans were practically unrecognizable. I have since learned to put the page numbers on my course outlines, and leave them off my lesson plans as much as possible.

You may need to "buy" time for lesson planning at the start of your year. Crockpot meals, frozen 30-day meals, barbeque meals, or having your student cook dinners for a week (counting as Home Economics, of course) can all help you find the time you will need. Pay your older children to babysit or plan something else for little ones each afternoon for a week if you must. If you can set aside a weekend, a week of evenings, or a week of afternoons, you'll find that you make progress faster than you think. Once the task is finished, the rest of the year will go much more smoothly.

If you have a computer, the work is very fast, but it can be done by hand if necessary. I start by opening a document in my word processor and immediately paging down six times, creating one page for each week that I am planning. (Since our family's school schedule is six weeks on, then one week off, I do lesson planning in six-week chunks.) Your school year may be divided into sessions which are smaller or larger, so adjust accordingly. Be aware, however, that it probably isn't a good idea to plan less than two weeks or more than eight or ten. Too few weeks mean too many lesson planning sessions, and it doesn't take much longer to plan four weeks than it does two. Too many weeks increases the likelihood that halfway through you will be hopelessly off schedule.

At the top of each of my six pages, I put the dates for the week. I like to fit a whole week's lessons on one sheet so my student can learn to look at the week's work as a whole and see how I have broken it down into daily parts. Starting with Bible, I write in the items from our Bible course outline that need to be done every day, for example, prayer and Scripture memorization. I know that prayer and memorization together will use up about ten minutes each day. Since I want to plan about 30 minutes per day of our Bible course, that will leave me 20 minutes to work with.

From my course outline (on page 112) I choose to start the year with the Bible study, <u>How to Study Your Bible</u>. I have already decided that each lesson in the book will probably take about half an hour, which is more than the 20 minutes I need to add to my lesson plan. However, I don't see a good way to divide the Bible study book further, so I will go ahead and assign four lessons per week. This means my student will spend about 40 minutes on four days a week, including prayer, memorization, and Bible study. But on the fifth day, he will only have prayer and memorization, for about 10 minutes of work. It all works out about the same in the end.

Back to that Scripture memorization assignment. I want to choose verses for the entire six weeks I'm planning. I can look through the Bible study book we will be using, to see if there are any ideas for Scripture memorization. Yes. Looking there, I see 2 Timothy 3:16-17, 2 Peter 1:20-21, Luke 24:45, and James 1:22-25. I decide to use these nine verses for our first six weeks of study, so I put them on the appropriate weeks' lesson plans. At this point, my first sheet of lesson plans might look like the sample shown on the following page.

Steven   August 3-7, 1998
School Week 1

<u>Bible:</u> 5 minutes each day of quiet prayer: (record in your prayer journal)
☐ Monday   ☐ Tuesday   ☐ Wednesday   ☐ Thursday   ☐ Friday

Scripture Memorization: (2 Timothy 3:16-17)
☐ Monday   ☐ Tuesday   ☐ Wednesday   ☐ Thursday   ☐ Friday
Recite 2 Tim: 3:16   Recite 2 Tim: 3:16   Recite 2 Tim: 3:16-17   Recite 2 Tim: 3:16-17   Recite 2 Tim: 3:16-17

Bible Study: <u>How to Study Your Bible</u> by Kay Arthur
☐ Monday   ☐ Tuesday   ☐ Wednesday   ☐ Thursday
Introduction   Lesson 1   Lesson 2   Lesson 3

I will use the same format for each of the other five pages of my six-week lesson plan, simply changing the memorization assignment and the lesson numbers for the Bible study.

I have found that lesson planning always goes more smoothly when I start with Bible. Once my assignments for our Bible course are laid out for the session I'm working on, I put away all the Bible materials and begin on English or math. I continue with each subject, one at a time, using my course descriptions and outlines as a guide to remind me what projects I want to include.

Remember that younger students need more details on their lesson plans. As they mature, they will know what is required to complete each assignment, so you will not have to put as many notes on your lesson plan. Once finished, the lesson plans can go into the student's notebook. It is then his responsibility to work from the lesson plan each day; your job is to check that he has finished enough each day to complete all the assignments at the end of the week.

By high school, it is reasonable to expect your student to plan his time well enough over the course of the week that he does not fall behind. If something special comes up for one day, he can adjust by doing a little extra on the other days and finishing up on the weekend. Of course, you, as teacher, can waive assignments if you need to. Also, if you find that you have over-estimated, you can cut back. I have found that few students mind when their parents cut back; however, there is a tendency to complain when their parents add work. With that in mind, I would err on the side of optimism when planning how much you can do in a week, knowing you can cut back if necessary.

You can, of course lay out your lesson plans any way you like. I prefer to use the computer so that I can type in the name of a book just once—I just copy it to the rest of the pages. When I used to do lesson plans by hand , I did them a similar way by making a master sheet for each student, then photocopying them and just filling in dates and pages as needed.

My student is usually free to choose the order of his assignments. If he regularly puts off math until late in the day, then struggles through it because he is too tired, I would probably step in and tell him he must do math first for a while. But barring that kind of problem, he will have a great deal of freedom in arranging his own day. I help him learn to plan his time by adding regular family activities to his lesson plan so that he won't save all his history reading for a day when I planned to finish early and go out. At our house, my students will regularly take Fridays off by working hard during the beginning of the week to finish all their assignments. When they do this, I still count Friday as a school day. After all, they completed Friday's assignments.

The following three pages show samples of three different students' weekly lesson plans. The first sample is for a younger student, so it includes more detail and is arranged into daily assignments. It also is done as a template which would be photocopied and filled in for each week. I would make six copies (for a six-week session) and fill them in all at one sitting. Then, after the current six-week session is finished, I would adjust the form and make six more copies to use in our next six-week session. This would give me a chance to change book titles or main projects.

The second plan is for a student a couple of years older. Although it doesn't have columns drawn in, you will notice that most of the assignments are laid out in columns. This makes it easy for the student to see how much work he should do each day.

Sample Lesson Plan 1

Sample

Seventh Grader John Brown　　　　　　　**Week of** August 3-7, 1998

	Monday	Tuesday	Wednesday	Thursday	Friday
	☐ Chores	☐ Chores	☐ Chores	☐ Chores	☐ Chores
Bible	☐ 5 min quiet prayer ☐ Memorization: _Psalm 1:1_ ☐ Read in The Cross & the Switchblade _Chapter 1_	☐ 5 min quiet prayer ☐ Memorization: _Psalm 1:1_ ☐ Read in The Cross & the Switchblade _Chapter 2_	☐ 5 min quiet prayer ☐ Memorization: _Psalm 1:1-2_ ☐ Read in The Cross & the Switchblade _Chapter 3_	☐ 5 min quiet prayer ☐ Memorization: _Psalm 1:1-2_ ☐ Read in The Cross & the Switchblade _Chapter 4_	☐ 5 min quiet prayer ☐ Memorization: _Psalm 1:1-2_ ☐ Read in The Cross & the Switchblade _Chapter 5_
Arithmetic	☐ Arithmetic Drill ☐ Lesson	☐ Arithmetic Drill ☐ Lesson	☐ Arithmetic Drill ☐ Lesson	☐ Arithmetic Drill ☐ Lesson	☐ Arithmetic Drill ☐ Lesson
English	☐ Spelling Lesson _1_ _page 8 - ex. A_ ☐ Cursive pg _4_ ☐ Winston Grammar Wksht _1_ Sent _1-2_ ☐ _Understanding Writing_ w/Mom	☐ Spelling Lesson _1_ _page 8 - ex. B_ ☐ Cursive pg _5_ ☐ Winston Grammar Wksht _1_ Sent _3-4_ ☐ _Understanding Writing_ w/Mom	☐ Spelling Lesson _1_ _page 8 - ex. C_ ☐ Cursive pg _6_ ☐ Winston Grammar Wksht _1_ Sent _5-6_ ☐ _Understanding Writing_ w/Mom	☐ Spelling Lesson _1_ _page 8 - ex. D_ ☐ Cursive pg _7_ ☐ Winston Grammar Wksht _1_ Sent _7-8_ ☐ _Understanding Writing_ w/Mom	☐ Spelling Lesson _1_ _Test_ ☐ Cursive pg _8_ ☐ Winston Grammar Wksht _1_ Sent _9-10_ ☐ _Understanding Writing_ w/Mom
History	☐ _Light & the Glory_ (read by Mom)	☐ _Light & the Glory_ (read by Mom)	☐ _Light & the Glory_ (read by Mom)	☐ _Light & the Glory_ (read by Mom)	☐ _Light & the Glory_ (read by Mom)
P.E. (write in if done)	☐ _____	☐ _____	☐ _____	☐ _____	☐ _____
Fine Arts	☐ Practice Guitar	☐ Practice Guitar	☐ Practice Guitar	☐ Practice Guitar	☐ Practice Guitar
Typing	☐ 20 minutes	☐ 20 minutes	☐ 20 minutes	☐ 20 minutes	☐ 20 minutes
Miscellaneous	☐	☐ _Guitar Lesson_	☐ _Bible Study at Church_	☐	☐

Sample Lesson Plan 2

<u>**Sophomore Jane Brown**</u>   <u>**Week 19**: Jan. 6 - 10</u>

Bible: 10 min of prayer -- ***record in journal***

☐ Mon	☐ Tues	☐ Wed	☐ Thurs	☐ Fri

Read I Thessalonians & II Thessalonians

☐ Read I Thess.	☐ Report	☐ Read II Thess.	☐ Report	

Memorize: Ephesians 6:11-18
Each day, read section aloud 3 times:

☐ Read aloud	☐ Read aloud	☐ Read aloud	☐ Read aloud	☐ Read aloud
☐ Recite vs. 11	☐ Recite 11-12	☐ Recite 11-12	☐ Recite 11-13	☐ Recite 11-13

Math: Saxon lesson every day

☐ Mon	☐ Tues	☐ Wed	☐ Thurs	☐ Fri

English: **Grammar:** *Winston Grammar*: Worksheet 28

☐ Sentences 1-2	☐ Sentences 3-4	☐ Sentences 5-6	☐ Sentences 7-8	☐ Sent. 9-10

Spelling:

☐ Mon	☐ Tues	☐ Wed	☐ Thurs	☐ Test

Literature: *Great Expectations*

☐ Chapter 7	☐ Chapter 8	☐ Chapter 9	☐ Chapter 10	☐ Chapter 11

Composition: *Format Writing*

☐ Write an analogy paragraph	☐ Write another analogy paragraph paragraphs w/Mom write a cause & effect paragraph	☐ Read about cause & effect paragraph	☐ Write another cause & effect paragraph	☐ Write another cause & effect

Fine Arts: **Photography**
☐ Shoot your roll of portraits (review the class handout on portrait photos first)
☐ Take the film to Long's for developing (need them for class next Tuesday)

Science: **Organic Gardening:**
☐ Order your seeds this week
☐ Don't forget to record what you ordered in the <u>Garden Log Book</u>
  ☐ Recorded under seed types
  ☐ Recorded amount of order in budget section

Animal Husbandry: *4-H Rabbit Project*

☐ Clean & Disinfect Cages	☐ Meeting on Tuesday	☐ Record Meeting Info in your log book		

Sample Lesson Plan 3

Senior Jim Brown   **May 13-17**

Bible: Memorization:
☐ Be ready to recite I Cor. 13 on Friday.

Bible Reading:
☐ Finish Revelation & write report

Read <u>Liberating the Nations</u>:
☐ Intro.   ☐ Ch. 1   ☐ Ch. 2   ☐ Ch. 3   ☐ Ch. 4

English:

☐ Finish Reading *Hamlet*
☐ Winston Grammar: *Worksheet 56*
☐ Write a letter to the newspaper editor

Calculus: Complete at least 3 lessons
☐ ☐ ☐

American Government:
☐ Begin Part II of <u>*Rudiments*</u> (due Fri May 31)

Field Biology:
☐ Finish your Field Biology project (due to Mom on Friday)

Vocational Education:
Line up three interviews for next week
☐ ☐ ☐

❖ Checking Your Lesson Plans

When you have finished adding each of your main or daily subjects to your lesson plans, it will help to stop and assess the amount of time you have already planned. Look back to your list of graduation requirements. When you finished that list, did you jot down the approximate number of hours needed each day on the back? Multiply that figure by five (assuming you are planning five days per week of school) and use this as a general guide of the amount of work needed for each week.

For example, if your total number of credits required for graduation, as shown on your list of graduation requirements, is 220, and if you are planning about 150 hours of work for each full-year, 10 credit course, figure your weekly work like this:

220 credits ÷ 4 years = 55 credits per year,

55 credits per year × 15 hours per credit = 825 hours per year,

825 hours per year ÷ 36 weeks = 22.92 hours per week.

You can see that the student will need to complete about 23 hours of work per week. If he does so consistently throughout the year, he should be on track for completing his graduation requirements within four years.

Using 23 hours as my ballpark figure for the amount of work to require each week, I would quickly estimate my weekly lesson plan assignments before I printed them out, to make sure that I had assigned a reasonable amount of work for the week.

For example, consider the sample lesson plan for Jane Brown on page 136:

For Bible, there are 10 minutes of prayer each day, totaling 50 minutes or about . . . . 1 hour
there is memorization each day; figure 10 minutes per day or about . . . . 1 hour
reading I & II Thessalonians & writing a brief report will total about . . . . 2 ½ hrs

For Math, there is one lesson per day, at around an hour (maybe a little more) each day . . . . 5 hrs

For English, there are 10-15 minutes for grammar, and for spelling, so I'll figure about
an hour for each for the week . . . . 2 hrs
There is also about half an hour a day of reading for Literature . . . . 2½ hrs
For Composition, there are also about 20 minutes per day . . . . 2 hrs

For Photography, there are about 2 hours for the week . . . . 2 hrs

For Organic Gardening, I'll figure about 2 hours . . . . 2 hrs

For Animal Husbandry, I'll figure about 4 hours . . . . 4 hrs
----
My rough estimate for Jane's weekly lesson plan is . . . . 24 hrs

I know that math may take longer, but photography and animal husbandry may take less time, so I decide that my estimated total for the week is close enough to my estimate of 23 hours needed per week. By quickly tallying the work on each of my six weekly sheets, I can tell if we are on track.

With a little practice, you will be able to estimate the number of hours on your week's lesson plan. If you are stuck, have your student read a page of the text you are working with, and time him. If he can read a page in 5 minutes, you will know to figure about 12 pages per hour for that book. You may even need to time his math lesson once or twice to see about how long it takes him to complete it. Then, knowing that some lessons will take a little more time and others a little less, you will be able to estimate your lessons with reasonable accuracy.

As you begin lesson planning for your next session, first get out the lesson plans that have just been completed. Then pull out your course outline or course design sheet for Bible. Before you write in the new assignments to be done in the upcoming session, look over the just-completed lesson plan sheets. Record completed projects on your Bible course design sheet so that as the year progresses, you will be able to see at a glance which projects have already been completed for your Bible course, and which projects still need to be done. Follow the same pattern for each course, again working through one subject at a time.

❖ 8 Evaluating Progress & Setting Standards

There are two parts to evaluating progress: *how much* work toward promotion to the next grade or toward graduation has been completed, and *how well* has the student done the work?

If you have set up courses using the credit system, your student can check his progress toward graduation or promotion very easily. Although you will likely be working on many courses throughout the year, simply adding up the points listed on each sheet will show how the student is progressing toward completion of his requirements during the year. Remember that although your student may have points earned in a lot of different courses, he will not necessarily complete all those courses in one year.

I expect my students to complete whole courses in the basic subjects like Bible, English and Math each year. If they didn't, they could end up with three years worth of English to complete during twelfth grade. However, I don't expect that they will finish courses like Home Economics, Fine Arts or Auto Mechanics all in one term. In our school, classes like these are spread out over the entire four years of high school (or two years of junior high.)

Since our progress is spread out over so many different subjects, I encourage my students to check their overall progress occasionally. If we are doing a good job of lesson planning, we should finish about the right number of credits each year, and we should be able to meet our graduation requirements at the end of junior or senior high. Even though we may be working on different subjects each day, week, month, or even each semester, all those hours should add up at the end.

It is easy enough to figure out that if I assign about an hour a day of English work from my course outline, by late spring, we should be nearly finished with the course. But what about those odds and ends that will fit together to make one course—but not till the end of high school? I don't really want to wait until the end of twelfth grade to see whether we completed all the fine arts and home economics projects.

At least at the end of each semester (and more often if I suspect we have been lagging) I will add up all the points completed. Since my courses were designed by figuring that each credit would take somewhere around 15 hours to complete, I can add all the points completed in all the courses, then divide by 15, and see how many credits have been completed so far.

Since our family's graduation requirements list 225 credits, I have figured that my student needs to complete 55 credits each year. At the end of the first semester, as I am getting ready to do lesson planning for second semester, we might sit down together and go through my student's notebook, adding up the points recorded on each course description. Assume that at the end of first semester of ninth grade, his course descriptions show the following:

Bible	(Completed <u>How to Study Your Bible</u>; earned 4 points on prayer chart; memorized 28 verses; read 5 books of the Bible; & completed 2 Christian classics)	37 points
Algebra 1	(Completed 65 lessons and 16 tests, which is about a half of the book.)	75 points
English 9	(Completed <u>Format Writing</u>; 3 classics; and we are about ⅔ through the literature text.)	84 points
Field Biology	(Completed 2 reports; identified 10 plants, 8 insects, 3 birds, 2 mammals)	33 points
World History	(About 1/4 through text; read 3 historical books; completed 3 maps & 2 essays; visited 1 museum; watched 2 historical videos)	27.5 points
Fine Arts	(Attended 2 concerts; completed 12 points in crafts; completed 6 points in photography; plus 1 museum)	21 points
P. E.	(Completed 65 sessions)	65 points
Home Ec.	(Changed car oil for 1 point; organized school records for 2 hours into new file cabinet; completed 15 hours of cooking)	18 points
Typing/ Computers	(Did speed test 3 times; typed 1 business letter; ½ way through WordPerfect workbook)	52 points
Adv. Piano	(Attended 9 lessons; performed once)	34 points
Vocational Ed.	(Completed 1 carpentry project)	3 points

- - - - - - - - - - - -

Total points earned so far: 449.5 points

449.5 points ÷ 15 for each credit = 29.96 credits earned so far.

With 55 points needed to move into the next grade and about 30 completed so far, he has 25 left to go. At halfway through the year, we are right on track.

❖ Grading

In addition to knowing what work will be required to earn credits toward graduation, you will also need to decide how to award grades. Some courses have just one main project or unit. For these courses, it will be easiest to grade by setting a simple standard of work for the whole course. Other courses are composed of a number of projects and assignments which are graded individually. For these courses, you may want to award the overall course grade based on the total of the individually graded projects.

Whether the course is graded as one project, or whether the grade is based on many different projects, in order to grade fairly, you must decide what the standard for each grade will be. A "C" is recognized as average. What would be a minimum amount that the "average" student would learn? What extra effort would constitute "above-average" (B)? What would be "excellent"?

I started out thinking I would use a hard scale, in which 95% equaled an "A." But the purpose for awarding grades is to communicate how well my student has learned. If he ever needs to show a transcript, the grades should show a true assessment of what he has accomplished. If all the other students who scored a 93% in math received an "A," but my student's 93% only earned a "B," I haven't really showed an accurate appraisal of my student's mastery of the subject. The scale below is commonly used and works well for most courses where there are specific assignments that can be individually graded (like math papers, tests, essays, etc.)

A	=	90 - 100%
B	=	80 - 90%
C	=	70 - 79%
D	=	60 - 69%
F	=	0 - 59%

Some homeschools choose not to award any grade lower than a C. If a student has not mastered at least 70% of the material, he spends whatever time is necessary to repeat the material until he has mastered it (a semester course may take a year). Or the class may be discontinued to be taken later when the student has matured a bit more.

90% of What?

Does 90% of daily work make an A? Or an average score of 90% on all chapter tests? Usually a combination of daily work plus tests is used, but what combination? Each course and each student (and each teacher) will likely have different requirements.

You will probably have fewer misunderstandings during the year if at the beginning of each course you decide how to determine the grade. A course standard will show clearly how a course grade is to be assigned.

Grading Individual Assignments

Assignments like math papers or multiple choice tests are easy to grade because the answer is either right or wrong. You simply need to figure out what percentage of the answers were right. Some individual assignments, however, are more subjective, like essays, reports or artistic projects. For these, you will need to set your grade standard based on what was expected from the student for each assignment. Some teachers grade essay assignments in two parts: half the grade for grammar, spelling and other mechanics, and half the grade for content and composition. Some teachers may mark down an essay one percentage point for each spelling, punctuation or glaring grammatical error. Some mark down for work that is not neatly written. This part is fairly easy, since if a word is misspelled or if a paper is crumpled with peanut butter splotches on it, the teacher can objectively point it out.

However, the artistic or composition part of the grade may be more difficult to assess. In an essay, consider whether the student composed his thoughts well and whether he has communicated his ideas. If the essay was on an assigned topic, did he stick to that topic? Is each paragraph well thought out, with a beginning and ending statement and with relevant supporting statements in the middle? Or do the student's points wander off the topic, lack logical thinking, or lack good supporting examples? Does he sound like he knows his topic? Does he have clear ideas to share?

For grading written assignments, a good English handbook is indispensable. Most of the major curriculum publishers carry one. They also should be available at any large bookstore. Ruth Beechick's book, You _Can_ Teach Your Child Successfully, has a great section on writing which can help you learn to assess your student's written work if you find this area challenging. Another excellent tool for grading composition assignments is Frode Jensen's book, Format Writing. In it, he includes a grading chart which lists all the key components to a good essay. Points are awarded or subtracted based upon an objective standard for each area.

For written assignments with a particular goal, of course, the grade should be awarded based primarily on how well the student has met that goal. For example, if the student has been studying the use of meter in a poetry course or unit, the related assignment may be graded based mostly upon whether the student's poem uses the correct rhythm or meter, not on his use of metaphors. However, if he has been studying imaginative comparisons, the grade should be based on his use of metaphors, even though his use of meter may be ineffective or inconsistent.

Do keep in mind that grading of written essays or artistic expression is always somewhat subjective, whether the grade is awarded by you or by an institutional classroom teacher. There is no single correct way to grade students' work.

❖ Setting Course Standards

A course standard will answer the question of what overall grade to award for each class. Your student may think that if he simply checks off all the assignments on your course outline and hands in a stack of papers, he should receive an "A" for completing 100% of the work.

But finishing the 150 hours or 150 points required to receive course credit does not tell what grade was earned in the course. Merely completing 100% of the assigned 150 points worth of work does not guarantee that each individual project received a _grade_ of 100%. What if all the work is messy, disorganized, and handed in late? What if your student griped and moaned through every project? What if the well-thought out, profound essay you expected is merely a review of the facts as listed in his textbook, rather than his own opinions, supported by Scripture?

Three items are useful for any course.

1. A _course description_ tells the purpose and overview of the course, in summary form for quick review. Course descriptions were covered in Chapter 5.

2 A _course design_ or _course outline_ maps out your course, listing projects and assignments so you will know when the course is done. On the course design, you may list the number of points or amount of

time you expect each assignment to take. For example, a research paper may be estimated at 15 hours, or $^1/_{10}$ of a 150 point course. When the assignment is completed, it is checked off on the course design sheet or assignment chart, and the points *toward completion* of the course are awarded. Course designs were covered in Chapter 6.

3. A *course standard* is needed to tell how the grade will be assigned. Once all the work is done, does the student receive an "A" or a "B"? A well-defined course standard will let everyone know what is expected to earn a particular grade.

It is easy to use some of the same point charts from your course designs to figure out the grade on the course standard. For example, on a research paper which is set at 15 points on the course description, the parent must decide what grade the paper earned. The 15 points are counted on the course design sheet toward course completion, but not necessarily toward the grade. If the paper received a grade of 75%, it would be counted *on the course standard* as only 11.25 out of a possible 15 points. (75% of 15 points = 11.25) When an assignment has been graded, the percentage of points earned toward the overall course grade can be figured out.

Each private homeschool will set its own standards. If any questions come up (like from a prospective university or employer, or in case of a future transfer to another high school) your course standards will show what the grades were based on. This is, indeed, a rare scenario, however. More likely, your course standards will be used to show your student what grade he earned, and to set up and grade similar courses in the future.

Setting up a course standard is easy when you have done the preliminary work of setting up your courses. Knowing the objective for the course (which you should have decided when writing a course description and course design) will help you determine how to set the course standard. Why is your student taking this class? What should he learn from it? How will he demonstrate to you that he has learned the subject matter?

If your student needs to improve writing skills, you will want the grade to be based heavily on regular written assignments. If he needs to improve study habits you may choose to weigh the daily work more heavily.

Some courses will require a more detailed standard than others, and some will be adjusted as you work through the course. You may make more assignments than planned and will then have to adjust your scale.

Even for pre-packaged courses, you will have to make the decision about what the grade will be based on. Do you want to rely heavily on tests? Or does your student do poorly on tests and you would prefer to use weekly assignments? Some courses (or students) may benefit from having the grade partially based on work habits and attitude.

The examples of course standards included in this manual are meant as a guide or idea source. The decision of what grade to award an assignment or a whole course is made by the teacher/parent. You may decide to award grades differently than the examples in this book show. That is, of course, fine. However, no matter how you set your grading policy, it will be important that both you and your student understand it at the *beginning* of each course.

❖ Sample Course Standards - Step By Step

These standards were set up with the courses from Chapters 5 and 6 in mind, so that you can see the designing of a course from beginning to end. If you have not already read through the sample course descriptions and designs, you may want to refer to them as you read the sample course standards in this section. The following course standards for Bible and Algebra are broken down to show how they were set up.

Bible 9 - 1 year class (Course description on page 70; course design on page 112.)

Using the same point value assigned to each project on the course design (which tells what assignments are required to complete the course), the total points can be added to arrive at the grade for the course.

<u>Design for Discipleship</u> Book 1	5 points
<u>Design for Discipleship</u> Book 2	5 points
<u>Design for Discipleship</u> Book 3	5 points
<u>How to Study Your Bible</u>	11 points
Five Christian Classics @ 3 points each	15 points
Prayer Chart	8 points
Scripture Memorization	10 points
Service/Ministry Project	5 points
Bible Reading and reports	16 points
Total points to complete the course	80 points

Note that the course is not completed until the student has finished all the assignments and has recorded 80 points on his course design form. The points he records there, however, are only used for the purpose of determining the completion of his work, not for determining the grade he will receive. (Remember that the ballpark figure I use in course planning is 75 points (about 75 hours) for a semester course. This course went a bit over that amount.)

For determining the grade, I used the grading scale on page 143 and set up the points required for each grade as follows:

72-80 points earned = A   (80 possible × 90% = 72.0)
64-71 points earned = B   (80 possible × 80% = 64.0)
56-63 points earned = C   (80 possible × 70% = 56.0)

As assignments are completed, each is graded. The graded assignments may be kept in a notebook or file until the course is finished. Or the grades may be immediately recorded on a course standard sheet or in a grade record book.

For this course, let's assume assignments were given the grades shown on the following page:

Assignment	Grade Points Awarded		Points Possible	Toward Grade
<u>Design for Discipleship</u> Book 1	95%	of	5 points =	4.75
<u>Design for Discipleship</u> Book 2	90%	of	5 points =	4.50
<u>Design for Discipleship</u> Book 3	89%	of	5 points =	4.45
<u>How to Study Your Bible</u>	100%	of	11 points =	11.00
Five Christian Classics at 3 points each				
<u>In His Steps</u>	90%	of	3 points =	2.70
<u>Mere Christianity</u>	95%	of	3 points =	2.85
<u>The Robe</u>	80%	of	3 points =	2.40
<u>Hind's Feet on High Places</u>	75%	of	3 points =	2.25
<u>Thoughts for Young Men</u>	85%	of	3 points =	2.55
Prayer Chart	100%	of	8 points =	8.00
Scripture Memorization	95%	of	10 points =	9.50
Service/Ministry Project	92%	of	5 points =	4.60
Bible Reading and reports				
Genesis	95%	of	2 points =	1.90
Exodus	90%	of	2 points =	1.80
Leviticus	94%	of	2 points =	1.88
Numbers	97%	of	2 points =	1.94
Deuteronomy	96%	of	2 points =	1.92
Job	86%	of	2 points =	1.72
Psalms	92%	of	2 points =	1.84
Proverbs	98%	of	2 point =	1.96

Total Points Earned Toward Grade   74.75

The grading scale for this course on the previous page shows that 72-80 points earns an "A." But since I like to list the actual percentage grade along with a letter grade on our transcript, I always figure out the exact percent grade:

74.75 points earned ÷ 80 points possible = 93.0% = A

Algebra 1 (Course description on page 82.)

Consider two different ways to award a grade for the same semester-long Algebra Course. Assume the course was laid out the same by each family, using the Saxon Algebra 1 book. There are 126 lessons and 32 tests in the book, so the student must complete 63 daily lessons (half the book) and 16 tests to be completed for the semester course. In the first sample, the grade is based heavily on daily assignments; in the second, the grade is based more on test scores.

Sample 1:

When half the book is completed and half the tests in the packet have been taken and passed, 5 credits will be awarded. Grade will be based on:

75%-daily work done on time and corrected; 25%-tests.

Formula = (Total of daily work points × 75%) + (Total of test points × 25%)

63 daily lessons were completed on time and corrected for full credit, so the grade for daily work is 100%.

16 tests were taken with grades as follows:

Test 1 .... 85%	Test 9 .... 70%
Test 2 .... 75%	Test 10 ... 75%
Test 3 .... 80%	Test 11 ... 75%
Test 4 .... 70%	Test 12 ... 80%
Test 5 .... 80%	Test 13 ... 85%
Test 6 .... 75%	Test 14 ... 85%
Test 7 .... 75%	Test 15 ... 80%
Test 8 .... 75%	Test 16 ... 75%

The total of all the test percentages = 1240. Divide this by 16 tests to get an overall average test score of 77.5%. So for the overall class grade:

Grade on Daily work of 100 × 75% of overall grade	=	75.00
Grade on Tests of 77.5 × 25% of overall grade	=	19.38
		————
The grade for this semester course would be		94.38 % or A

Sample 2: (Same Algebra course; same test scores; different grading method)

When half the book is completed and half the tests in the packet have been taken and passed, 5 credits will be awarded. Grade will be based on:

Each daily lesson counts as 1 point; each test counts as ten points.

Formula = (Total daily work points earned + Total test points earned) ÷ Total points possible.

Total points possible =   Daily Work   —   63 (1 point per lesson)
                           Tests   —   160 (10 points × 16 tests)
                           _____

                           223 points possible

63 daily lessons were completed on time and corrected for full credit, so the grade for daily work is 63 points.

16 tests were taken with the same grades received as in sample 1:

Test 1	85%	= 8.5 points	Test 9	70%	= 7	points
Test 2	75%	= 7.5 points	Test 10	75%	= 7.5	points
Test 3	80%	= 8 points	Test 11	75%	= 7.5	points
Test 4	70%	= 7 points	Test 12	80%	= 8	points
Test 5	80%	= 8 points	Test 13	85%	= 8.5	points
Test 6	75%	= 7.5 points	Test 14	85%	= 8.5	points
Test 7	75%	= 7.5 points	Test 15	80%	= 8	points
Test 8	75%	= 7.5 points	Test 16	75%	= 7.5	points

Grade on tests = 124 points total, so for the overall class grade:

	Grade on Daily work of	63
+	Grade on Tests of	124
		____
	Total Points earned	187

So the grade for this semester course is:

187 points earned ÷ 223 points possible = 83.85% or B

Note that this student had exactly the same test scores as the student in Sample 1. The different way of figuring the grade is what changed the final grade for the course.

❖ More Sample Course Standards

Again, some courses can be set up with much simpler course standards. If a course is designed with one main project or unit, or with only a couple of projects, you may want to simply describe what is expected to receive a particular grade. Some courses are designed primarily around "exposure areas" of learning, so the grade may reflect that by being based on time spent, attitude displayed or general understanding of a new subject.

Auto Mechanics (Course description on page 86.)

Grade will be mostly based on getting John's car to run. Estimated time = three months.

100 points possible as follows:

       70 - car runs great (considering its age)
       65 - car runs, needs refinement
       60 - problem verified, need more funds
       50 - call a tow truck!

additional points as follows:

       0-15 - attitude
       0-15 - work habits (i.e. clean-up and care of tools)

Note: In this course, John can pass with a "B" even if the car doesn't run. (50 points for car + 15 points for attitude + 15 points for work habits = 80 points or 80%) Also, the highest grade he could earn based on only the car running great is a "C-" (70 points). He must also have a good attitude and work habits to earn the points necessary for a higher grade.

Botany (Course description on page 84.)

In December, we will tour Descanso Gardens and test Jane's knowledge of the plants. We will also ask for an evaluation from Jane's boss.

    C =   Jane continued to volunteer through the whole semester.
    B =   She also demonstrates a knowledge of the field by being able to name and tell about the plants on our tour.
    A =   She also gets an excellent evaluation from her boss.

Consumer Math — Sample 1 (Course description 4 on page 82.)

Course using A Beka materials: Grade based on: 40% daily work - 60% tests
                                  Extra credit given for student's own budget

Consumer Math — Sample 2 (Course description 5 on page 83.)

Grade based on:

    Math-It   - 50 points (there are 5 sections)

Budget for Car Repair Job   - 50 points
General Budget   - 50 points (1 point taken off for every dollar that the budget doesn't balance)

Consumer Math — Sample 3 (Course description 6 on page 83.)

C = Jane demonstrates the ability to handle our home budget
B = Jane saved $100 during the semester (from last year's budget)
A = Jane saved over $100.00 during the semester.

Typing (Course description 2 on page 88.)

Student will learn the basic typing keyboard and will practice proper form for business letters, essays, reports, outlines and tables. To earn a "C", the student must demonstrate ability to type 35 wpm with 2 or less errors. 5 credits will be awarded upon completion.

Typing 40 wpm with 2 or less errors = B
Typing 45 wpm with 2 or less errors = A

❖ Using a Course Standard Form and Finalizing a Course

Additional course standards are shown on the following pages as they might be filled in on a course standard form. A blank form is on page 159.

Keeping the grades for each course on a separate sheet makes them easy to sort through and easy to find for reference if the course is taught again. While the course standards in this book are typeset and nicely aligned on the page, you should know that at home, I often just pencil in grades next to the assignment right on the course design. Or I make rude columns in pencil on the back of my course design sheet so I have everything together when the course is completed. Some families like to use a standard teacher's grade book, instead. A grade book works fine for course in which there are a lot of individual assignments, all averaged together for the overall grade.

Once a course is completed, I remove the paperwork from my teaching notebook (or from my student's notebook if he is at a point of responsibility to keep them there for me.) I staple the course description, course design, and course standard together (assuming my course needed all three) and keep them in a "Completed Courses" file. If my student wrote a few especially wonderful papers that I want to keep for posterity, I file them in a separate "school work" file, by subject. None of this is ever to be transferred to another school, as they are all part of my "teaching records," not the student's cum file.

Once a course is finished the grade should be added to the student's transcript, which is the formal record of grades commonly sent to colleges or other schools for admissions purposes. I often file the finished course paperwork in a temporary file and wait to record grades on the transcript at the end of the semester, when I can do several at once. Transcripts are covered in Chapter 9.

Course Standard

(Course description on page 75; course design on page 116.)

Course: **English 7**	Credits: 10
Student: Jim Brown	Grade: A - 92.6 %
Semester: Fall and Spring 1993-94	

Grade is based on:

30 points	McGuffey Reader (1 point each lesson)
15 points	3 Classics read and report completed (5 points each)
30 points	Winston Grammar (30 lessons @ .5 point each lesson + 1 test @ 15 points)
14 points	Handwriting
30 points	Spelling (one point each lesson)
30 points	Composition

149 points possible

Points Earned:

27	McGuffey Reader
4	Men of Iron
5	Old Yeller
4.5	Treasure Island
28	Winston Grammar (15 points for daily lessons) + (13 for 87% on test)
14	Handwriting assignments completed neatly, with much improvement shown over the course of the year.
30	Spelling — all words mastered during the course of the year.
25.5	Composition — total of scores from individual assignments

138.0 points earned = 92.62% = A

Course Standard

(Course description on page 71; course design on page 117.)

Course: **English 9: Fundamentals of Lit & Comp**	Credits: 10
Student: Jane Brown	Grade: A - 94.8 %
Semester: Fall and Spring 1992-93	

Course grade is based on:

600 points =	Classroom discussion of Literature
600 points =	Six Unit tests, based on the textbook
300 points =	Format Writing
100 points =	Correspondence
150 points =	Five novels
250 points =	9th grade "4-R" project

2,000 points possible

1800 - 2000 = A   1600 - 1799 = B   1400 - 1599 = C

Points Earned:

Classroom Discussion   600   Student participated willingly in discussions, showed an understanding of the concepts covered, added to the discussion with his own ideas and creativity.

Literature Study Exams:

Unit I - Conflict	92
Unit II - Character	84.4
Unit III - Theme	97
Unit IV - Structure	92
Unit V - Point of View	91
Unit VI - Moral Tone	86.5

Format Writing	280
Correspondence	95
Swiss Family Robinson	25
Kidnapped	28
The Black Arrow	28
Robinson Crusoe	30
The Greatest Story Ever Told	30
9th Grade "4-R" Project (Obedience)	237.5

Total Grade	1896.4 =	94.8 % =	A

Course Standard

(Course description on page 84; course design on pages 105-108.)

Course: **Field Biology**	Credits: 10
Student: John Brown	Grade: A - 91.4 %
Semester: Fall and Spring 1993-94	

Grade based on:

25 points	five written reports
15 points	research paper on geographic zones
50 points	plant collection
25 points	insect collection
25 points	bird display
10 points	mammal display

150 points possible

Points Earned:				
	A	95%	Characteristics of Plants Report	4.75 points
	B	84%	Characteristics of Insects Report	4.20 points
	A	100%	Characteristics of Birds Report	5.00 points
	C	78%	Characteristics of Reptiles Report	3.90 points
	A	94%	Characteristics of Mammals Report	4.70 points
	A	96%	Geographic Zones Report	14.40 points
	B	88%	Plant Collection	44.00 points
	A	93%	Insect Display	23.25 points
	A	100%	Bird Display	25.00 points
	C	79%	Mammal Display	7.90 points

Total Points Earned   137.10

137.10 points = 91.4% = A

Course Standard

(Course description on page 76; course design on pages 100-104.)

Course: **Journalism**	Credits: 5
Student: Jane Brown	Grade: A - 92.4 %
Semester: Spring 1992	

Grade based on:

5	History of Journalism paper
10	4-R work on Constitutional freedoms and Biblical restrictions
20	Class assignments (short essays, discussions, field trips, etc.)
15	Student's newsletter project
15	Student's radio project
15	Student's news report project
20	Wrap-up Report

100 points possible

Points earned:

A	95%	History of Journalism paper	4.75 points
A	100%	4-R work	10.00 points
B	86%	Class assignments (list on file)	17.20 points
B	82%	Newsletter project	12.30 points
A	100%	Radio project	15.00 points
A	98%	News report project	14.70 points
A	92%	Wrap-up report	18.40 points

Total points earned

92.35 = A

Course Standard

(Course description on page 72.)

Course: **Logic and Critical Thinking 1**	Credits: 5
Student: John Brown	Grade: A - 95 %
Semester: Fall 1992	

Course Grade is Based on:

200 points - daily work and discussion
 50 points - final debate
100 points - final written exam

350 points possible

315 - 350 points = A
280 - 314 points = B
245 - 279 points = C

Points Awarded:

Class Discussions/ Daily Work	200	Student willingly participated in all class work, thoughtfully considering responses to discussion questions and was well-able to apply concepts covered into the lessons.
Final Debate	48	Student ably participated in several practice debates before the final debate on "Should Christians watch TV?" Points supporting the student's side (he drew the "yes" side) were well thought out and logically presented. Rebuttal was concise and logical.
Final Written Exam	-	83	On file.

Total Points Awarded: 331

Final Grade: A 95%

Course Standard

(Course description on page 87; course design on page 123.)

Course: **Sewing**	Credits: 5
Student: Jane Brown	Grade: B - 83.5 %
Semester: Spring 1987	

Grade based on: Three projects required to pass, four for an A.
Basic skills listed below must each be used in at least one project.

Scoring as follows: 28 points per project:
       7 = finished appearance
       7 = pattern & fabric selection; layout & cutting
       7 = work attitude, habits, sewing methods, care of equipment
       7 = basic skills from list
   16 points for fourth project:
       7 = finished appearance
       3 = pattern & fabric selection; layout & cutting
       3 = work attitude, habits, methods, care of equipment
       3 = improvement on basic skills

Basic Skills Required: (list project which included it.)

1	Hand hemming	2	Machine hemming	3	Darts
1	Basting	3	Buttons & button holes	2	Zipper
1	Casing & elastic	2	Gathering	2	Waistband
3	Sleeves	2	Matching plaids or print	3	Collar
2	Pockets	3	Top stitching	3	Facings

Projects and grade:

Project	Finished Appearance	Pattern, fabric, layout, cutting	attitude, habits	basic skills used	Project Grade
1. Skirt	6	5	4	5	20 — 71.5%
2. Skirt	6.5	6	5	6	23.5 — 83.9%
3. Blouse	6	7	5.5	6	24.5 — 87.5%
4. Top	7	3	2.75	2.75	15.5 — 96.9%
Total Points	25.5 91.1%	21 87.5%	17.25 71.9%	19.75 82.3%	83.5 points 83.5% = B

Course Standard

(Course description on page 83.)

Course: **Physical Education:** Soccer/Racquetball/Swimming/Weight Training	Credits: 5
Student: Jim Brown	Grade: A
Semester: Summer & Fall 1992	

Course grade is based on:

1) Regular participation in scheduled activities listed in the course description,

2) Student's demonstration of knowledge of fundamental skills and proper use of equipment.

3) Student's attitude toward keeping a commitment to work and practice regularly, plus attitude on the playing field (soccer and racquetball) and attitude towards teacher/trainers.

Course Standard

Course:	Credits:
Student:	Grade:

Semester:

❖ 9 Transcripts

A transcript is simply a record of the courses taken during high school and the grade received for each. Colleges and universities will want a copy of a high school transcript to determine a student's eligibility for admission.

Although at first glance, students who are not heading to college don't need a transcript, it is usually worthwhile to make one. By providing a brief, easy-to-use overview of a student's high school education, the transcript is a useful permanent record. Perhaps a year or two after graduating from high school, your student will want to take a correspondence course from a university. Or, years in the future, when he is homeschooling your grandchildren, the transcript may be helpful for planning their high school course of study.

On the traditional transcript, there is usually a total of credits earned and the grade point average (GPA) for each semester. If your courses do not fit into neat semester divisions, you may omit the semester information, but you do need to include the cumulative total of credits and the cumulative GPA. To figure out the GPA, give grade points for each grade in each class (except Physical Education) as follows:

> A = 4 points
>
> B = 3 points
>
> C = 2 points
>
> D = 1 point
>
> F = 0 points

Some schools have changed the point schedule so that a B+ receives more than 3 points, or an A- receives less than 4 points. However, the points system shown in the box above is still the standard system used by most colleges and universities.

❖ Honors Courses

Honors courses are advanced courses, considered to be college-level, though taken during high school. If your student takes a very advanced course, you may count it as an honors course, but be prepared to justify the honors status of the course to a university admissions officer. Honors courses receive grade points as follows:

A = 5 points,   B = 4 points,   C = 3 points

Most colleges allow some leeway for high schools to assess their own courses as being honors level. However, some universities set specific requirements for courses which receive the honors designation. Check the catalog of the university your student is planning to attend before labeling courses as "honors." Here are some examples of courses which could be rated as honors courses:

- Your student takes an academic class at a community college while still in high school, and the course is a college-level (not remedial) course.

- Your student takes a college-level exam (AP, CLEP, etc.) and passes it after studying a subject at home. You could count the home course as honors level.

- Your student's educational activities are clearly at an adult level. For example, a sixteen-year-old in our local support group designs and publishes our group's newsletter. It is not a children's newsletter, it looks professional, and she does it all on her own. I would count it as an honors course.

Note that of these three examples, the first two will be unquestionably counted as honors level by nearly all universities; however, the third course has no official standing and thus could be downgraded by a prospective university. If you are confident that the course should be designated as honors, go ahead and label it as such; just be aware that individual colleges have their own standards.

❖ Preparing Your Transcript

Transcripts do not have to be fancy; usually they are mass-produced on public school computers. Just be sure yours has no typing errors, is clean, and is sent in a sealed envelope. There can be no corrections that look as if a student has tampered with his records. An official transcript sent to a university should be dated and signed by the school principal.

Include any extracurricular activities such as community service work, political campaign work, sports team participation, community or church choir, etc. But do not turn the transcript into an essay on the merits of your student. Extracurricular activities should be listed briefly and objectively at the bottom of the transcript.

Beginning on page 165, there are several sample transcripts followed by blank forms that can be used to make your own transcript. The first two samples are in the traditional format, which shows each semester of study separately. The third sample shows an alternate format, which is becoming more popular. In the alternate format, courses are grouped by subject area, rather than by semester. Course titles can be used to show the grade during which a course was taken, if desired.

❖ Figuring Out the Grade Point Average

- **For students taking courses which are broken into traditional semester-long courses of five credits each:**

  Calculate the GPA by adding the grade points earned for each course, and dividing the total number of points by the number of classes taken. This will be the GPA for the semester. Also figure a cumulative GPA: once for grades 9-12 and separately for grades 10-12, as many colleges do not look at the GPA for ninth grade. The GPA is recorded on the transcript with two decimal places.

  For example, Jane, grade ten, has the following record for fall semester:

Course Title	Credits	Grade	Grade Points toward GPA
English 10a	5	A	4
Algebra 1	5	B	3
U.S. Government	5	B	3
Tennis	5	A	(don't count P.E. for the GPA)
Journalism (honors)*	5	A	5 (honors)
Biology	5	B	3
French 1	5	A	4
Typing	5	A	4

Semester GPA = 3.71 (26 points ÷ 7 classes which count toward GPA)

Total Credits earned this semester = 40

- **For students taking courses which are NOT broken into traditional semester-long courses of five credits each:**

  Calculate the GPA by following these three steps.

  1. Multiply the grade points earned for each course by the number of credits awarded for the course. For example, a 5-credit science course which received a grade of B would receive 15 points (5 credits × 3 grade points = 15); a 3-credit health course which received a grade of A would receive 12 points (3 credits × 4 grade points = 12.)

  2. Add the number of points calculated for each course to get a total for all the courses. Do not include grade points for P.E.

  3. Divide the total number of grade points by for all the courses by the total number of credits. Do not include credits for P.E.

Because courses of this type are usually spread over several semesters or years, you probably will not want to record a GPA for each semester on the transcript. If your courses overlap years from grades 9-12 (like the courses shown on page 63), it may be difficult to figure a cumulative GPA separately for grades 10-12. Simply leave out courses which were clearly 9th grade level (like English), averaging all the rest for a cumulative 10th-12th GPA, and don't worry about trying to figure out which of the rest of the subjects should count for 10th grade or over. It is possible that some of the work done for your 10-12 GPA was from 9th grade, but the majority will be 10th-12th.

As an example of figuring the GPA for a student with courses which overlap and which have uneven numbers of credits, consider the following portion of completed courses—some worth 10 credits each, several worth 5, one worth only 2, and one worth 3:

Course Title	Credits	Grade	Grade Points toward GPA
English 10	10	A	40 (10 credits × 4 grade points)
Algebra 1	10	B	30 (10 credits × 3 grade points)
World History	5	B	15 (5 credits × 3 grade points)
Tennis	5	A	(don't count P.E.)
Journalism (honors)	5	A	25 (5 credits × 5 grade points)
Creation Science (honors)	5	B	20 (5 credits × 4 grade points)
Health	3	A	12 (3 credits × 4 grade points)
U.S. Constitution	2	A	8 (2 credits × 4 grade points)

Semester GPA = 3.75 (150 points ÷ 40 credits which count toward GPA)

Total Credits earned - 45

Planning chart for this student is on page 62.

School Transcript # 1

Brown Christian School • 22 Main St • Yourtown, CA 90000

Student: **BROWN, JANE**   Sex: **Female**   Birth Date: **08-06-78**
Parents: **M/M JOHN BROWN**   Address: **22 Main St., Yourtown, CA 900000**

Grade Level	School Year	---- 1st Semester ---- Course Title	Mark	Credits	---- 2nd Semester ---- Course Title	Mark	Credits
9	87/88	Bible - OT Survey	A	5	P.E. Soccer Team	B	5
		English 9a	B	5	English 9b	B	5
		Algebra 1	A	5	Algebra 2	A	5
		World History 1	B	5	World History 2	B	5
		Survey Fine Arts 1	B	5	Survey Fine Arts 2	B	5
		Typing/Computers 1	B	5	Typing/Computers 2	B	5
		Credits: 30 **GPA: 3.33**			**Credits: 60** **GPA: 3.20**		
		Cumulative GPA: 3.33			**Cumulative GPA: 3.27**		
10	88/89	Bible -Life of Christ 1	A	5	P.E. Soccer Team	A	5
		English 10a	A	5	English 10b	A	5
		Algebra 3	B	5	Algebra 4	B	5
		Biology 1	A	5	Biology 2	A	5
		US History 1	A	5	US History 2	A	5
		German 1	B	5	German 2	B	5
		Credits: 90 **GPA: 3.66**			**Credits: 120** **GPA: 3.60**		
		Cumulative GPA: 3.41			**Cumulative GPA: 3.45**		
10	89 Sum	Health & Driver Ed	A	5			
		Credits: 130 **GPA: 4.0**			**Cumulative GPA: 3.47**		
11	89/90	Bible -NT Church 1	A	5	P.E. Soccer & Coaching	A	5
		American Lit 1	B	5	American Lit 2	B	5
		Geometry/Trig. 1	A	5	Geometry/Trig. 2	A	5
		Chemistry 1	B	5	Chemistry 2	A	5
		State History	A	5	German 4	A	5
		German 3	B	5			
		Credits: 160 **GPA: 3.50**			**Credits: 185** **GPA: 3.75**		
		Cumulative GPA: 3.48			**Cumulative GPA: 3.51**		
12	90/91	Bible -World View	A	5	P.E. Soccer & Coaching	A	5
		English Lit 1	A	5	English Lit 2	A	5
		Calculus 1**	A	5	Calculus 2**	A	5
		Govt/Civics	B	5	Economics	A	5
		Carpentry 1	A	5	Carpentry 2	A	5
		Missions Outreach	A	5			
		Credits: 215 **GPA: 4.00**			**Credits: 240** **GPA: 4.25**		
		Cumulative GPA: 3.58			**Cumulative GPA: 3.65**		

Activities: Mexico Missionary Wk, Aug 95; German Club, 2 yrs; Preschool Aide Yourtown Bible Church, 2 yrs; Youth Soccer League Coach , 2 yrs

** Denotes honors class (college level course taken at Yourtown Community College)

Total Credits Completed: 240   **Academic GPA (9-12): 3.65**   **Academic GPA (10-12): 3.78**

School Transcript # 2

Note 8th grade course and early graduation.

Brown Christian School ● 22 Main Street ● Yourtown, CA 90000

Student: **BROWN, JOHN JR**   Sex: **Male**   Birth Date: **08-06-73**
Parents: **M/M JOHN BROWN**   Address: **22 Main St., Yourtown, CA 900000**

Grade Level	School Year	---------------1st Semester--------------- Course Title	Mark	Credits	--------------2nd Semester----------------- Course Title	Mark	Credits
9	87/8	Algebra 1 (8th)	A	5	Algebra 2 (8th)	A	5
		Latin 1-2 (Summer)	B	10			
9	87/8	Bible 9a	B	5	Bible 9b	A	5
		English 9a	B	5	English 9b	B	5
		Geometry 1	A	5	Geometry 2	A	5
		Biology 1	A	5	Biology 2	A	5
		World History 1	C	5	World History 2	C	5
		Latin 3	B	5	Latin 4	B	5
		P.E. Soccer Team	B	5	P.E. Basebl Team	B	5
		Credits: 55	**Total Cr: 55**		**Credits: 35**	**Total Cr: 90**	
		GPA: 3.30	**Cum. GPA: 3.30**		**GPA: 3.33**	**Cum. GPA: 3.31**	
10	87/8	Computer Sci (Sum)	A	10			
10	88/9	Bible 10a	B	5	Bible 10b	B	5
		English 10a	C	5	English 10b	C	5
		Algebra 3	A	5	Algebra 4	A	5
		Chemistry 1	A	5	Chemistry 2	A	5
		Greek 1	B	5	Greek 2	B	5
		Driver Ed	B	5	Health/CPR	B	5
		P.E. Soccer Team	B	5	P.E. Basebl Team	B	5
		Credits: 45	**Total Cr: 135**		**Credits: 35**	**Total Cr: 170**	
		GPA: 3.37	**Cum. GPA: 3.33**		**GPA: 3.16**	**Cum. GPA: 3.30**	
11	89/90	Bible 11a	B	5	Bible 11b	B	5
		American Lit 1	B	5	American Lit 2	C	5
		Calculus 1	A	5	Calculus 2	A	5
		Physics 1	B	5	Physics 2	B	5
		Amer Government	C	5	Economics	C	5
		Auto Mech 1	A	5	Auto Mech 2	B	5
		P.E. Soccer Team	A	5	P.E. Basebl Team	A	5
		Credits: 35	**Total Cr: 205**		**Credits: 30**	**Total Cr: 240**	
		GPA: 3.16	**Cum. GPA: 3.27**		**GPA: 2.83**	**Cum. GPA: 3.23**	

Activities: 4-H - 4 yrs; Church youth group - 4 yrs; Coached Church Baseball Team (8 yr olds)- 2 yrs

California High School Proficiency Exam: Passed, November 1989
SAT Scores: 6/90 Verbal -- R 650; Math -- R 680

Graduated June 15, 1990

High School Transcript # 3

Brown Christian School ✦ 22 Main Street ✦ Yourtown, CA 90000

Student: Brown, James Joseph
Address: 22 Main Street, Yourtown, CA 90000

Date of Birth: 07/01/76   Sex: Male
Parents: M/M John Brown

Subject Area	Req	Course Title	Grade	%	Credits
BIBLE	20	Fund. of Christian Faith	A	95.7%	5
		Christian Apologetics	B	83.6%	5
		Christian Living	A	94.2%	5
		Christian World View	B	87.5%	5
ENGLISH	40	Eng 9: Fund. Lit/Comp	A	94.8%	10
		Eng 10: Elem Lit/Comp	B	86.5%	10
		Eng 11: American Lit	B	83.2%	10
		Eng 12: English Lit	B	87.8%	10
MATH	20	Algebra 1-2 / Intr Geo	A	92.8%	10
		Algebra 3-4 / Intr Geo	A	93.3%	10
		Adv. Math / Geo / Trig	A	96.8%	10
		** Calculus	B	88.5%	10
		Logic & Crit. Thinking	A	95.0%	5
SCIENCE	20	Creation Science	B	89.4%	5
		Intro to Chemistry	B	85.4%	5
		Field Biology	A	98.7%	5
		Physics	A	96.8%	5
SOC. SCIENCE	10	** World Hist & Lit.	B	83.2%	10
	10	** US History	A	98.2%	10
	2	** State History	A	93.4%	2
	5	** Govt & Civics	A	99.6%	5

Subject Area	Req	Course Title	Grade	%	Credits
ECONOMICS	5	Economics	A	95.0%	5
BUSINESS	5	Typing/Keyboarding	B	84.9%	5
	10	Computer Science	A	98.2%	10
	5	Vocational Skills	B	88.2%	5
FOREIGN LANGUAGE	10	Latin 1-2	B	85.4%	10
PHYSICAL EDUCATION	20	Gen. Fitness & Sports	A	N/A	20
HOME ECONOMICS	10	Home Economics and Family Living	B	84.8%	10
FINE ARTS	10	Survey of Fine Arts	B	82.7%	10
		Piano - Intermediate	A	100%	10
		Piano - Advanced	B	89.4%	10
HEALTH & DRIVERS ED	5	Health & Safety/CPR	A	93.0%	3
		Driver Education	B	87.1%	2

ELECTIVES: Adv Math, Calculus, Logic, Int. Piano, Adv. Piano

Credits Required:	225	Grad Req. Met: 11/26/93	
Total Credits Earned:	252	CHSPE: 04/23/94 — Passed	
GPA: 3.63		SAT: 11/14/93: V650 M680	
Diplomas Awarded: 06/15/94		High School Diploma/College Prep	

Extra Curricular: Chr. Home Edrs Assoc. admin. help & volunteer - 4 yrs; Chr. Home Edrs. El Dorado Co. science fair - 3 yrs; California Youth Soccer League referee - 2 yrs; Republican Political Campaign volunteer - 1992

High School Transcript

School: _____

Student: _____ Date of Birth: _____ Sex: _____

Address: _____ Parents: _____

Grade Level	School Year	First Semester Course Title	Grade	Mark	Second Semester Course Title	Grade	Mark
9							
9th Credits:							
9th GPA:							
Cum. Credits:							
Cum. GPA:							
10							
10th Credits:							
10th GPA:							
Cum. Credits:							
Cum. GPA:							
11							
11th Credits:							
11th GPA:							
Cum. Credits:							
Cum. GPA:							
12							
12th Credits:							
12th GPA:							
Cum. Credits:							
Cum. GPA:							

Graduated:_____

High School Transcript

School: _____

Student: _____

Address: _____

Date of Birth: _____

Parents: _____

Sex: _____

Subject Area	Course Title	Grade	Credits

Subject Area	Course Title	Grade	Credits

	Grad Req. Met:
Credits Required:	
Total Credits Earned:	
GPA:	
Diplomas Awarded:	
Extra Curricular:	

❖ 10 Resources

This book is not designed to help you choose textbooks or workbooks for individual classes. There are two excellent curriculum guides available, one by Cathy Duffy and one by Mary Pride. Both are listed here. If you need help in choosing specific materials for your homeschool courses, I recommend purchasing one or both. I personally own both and have found them invaluable, not just for choosing textbooks, but for locating good supplementary materials to use in our courses.

The resources listed in this section were chosen because they are of the type or quality that should be useful to any family. A set of encyclopedias, even an older used one, will be used regularly enough by most teens to be worth the investment, as will some sturdy science equipment. In my family, most of our school budget is spent on resource items—the type of books that can be used again and again, year after year. We do purchase some texts, mostly used, if we can find them. But I have found that a good home library, well stocked with quality literature and reference books is far more useful than owning a textbook on every subject.

❖ Recommended Teaching Aids

American Dictionary of the English Language, 1828 facsimile edition by Noah Webster. San Francisco: Foundation for American Christian Education, 1985.

> This is an excellent resource for both parents and teens because it is written from a Christian perspective, with the view of language as a gift from God to man, not an evolutionary movement arising from prehistoric grunts and groans. Definitions and usage examples are biblically based. Available from FACE, P.O. Box 27035, San Francisco, CA 94127.

> Compare, for example, the definition of the verb "love" from Webster's 1828 and from "Webster's" New Twentieth Century:

> *American Dictionary of the English Language*, 1828 facsimile edition by Noah Webster:

>> "Love: 1) In a general sense to be pleased with; to regard with affection, on account of some qualities which excite pleasing sensations or desire of gratification. We *love* a friend, on account of some qualities which give us pleasure in his society. We *love* a man who has done us a favor; in which case, gratitude enters into the composition of our affection. We *love* our parents and our children, on account of their connection with us, and on account

of many qualities which please us. We *love* to retire to a cool shade in summer. We *love* a warm room in winter. We *love* to hear an eloquent advocate. The Christian *loves* his Bible. In short, we *love* whatever gives us pleasure and delight, whether animal or intellectual; and if our hearts are right, we *love* God above all things, as the sum of all excellence and all the attributes which can communicate happiness to intelligent beings. In other words, the Christian *loves* God with the love of complacency in his attributes, the love of benevolence towards the interests of his kingdom, and the love of gratitude for favors received.

Thou shalt *love* the Lord thy God with all thy heart, and with all thy soul, and with all thy mind—Thou shalt *love* thy neighbor as thyself. Matt. xxii.

2) To have benevolence or good will for. John iii."

Webster's New Twentieth Century Dictionary:

"Love: 1) To show love for by embracing, fondling, kissing, etc.

2) to delight in; to take pleasure in; as, she *loves* good music."

The Big Book of Home Learning by Mary Pride. Wheaton: Crossway, 1991.

This multi-volume set has been updated and should be available in 1997. Mary Pride includes reviews of all the big publishers' materials, plus innumerable smaller companies' products.

Available from Home Life, P.O. Box 1250, Fenton, MO, 63026.

Books Children Love by Elizabeth Wilson. Wheaton: Crossway.

This book lists literature by subject and age-level. Hundreds of books are listed, along with a brief description of each. An excellent source for finding out what quality books are available on different subjects. Available at Christian bookstores.

Books on Tape Inc. P.O. Box 7900, Newport Beach, CA 92658. (800) 252-6966.

Full-length, unabridged books on cassette, read by professional actors. The *Books on Tape* catalog includes classics, biographies, history books and modern best sellers. Our family has heard many of the classics and we are very impressed with the quality. Many families just beginning homeschooling teens have not read aloud to their children in years. *Books on Tape* is a great way to ease back into read-alouds, and is also great for families who love to read, but can't possibly finish all the great books available. The sets range from 6 to 15 hours and are great for trips in the car. Rental prices include return postage to *Books on Tape*.

Christian Home Educators' Curriculum Manual - Jr. & Sr. High Edition by Cathy Duffy. Garden Grove, CA: Home Run Enterprises, 1990.

This book is being updated for 1997. Contains subject-by-subject curriculum recommendations for junior high and high school, including where to buy materials. Also discusses learning styles to help you decide which type of materials will be best suited to your student.

Available from CHEA of California, P.O. Box 2009, Norwalk, CA 90651-2009.

Critique of Modern Youth Ministry by Christopher Schlect. Moscow, ID: Canon Press, 1995.

This booklet explores some of the problems with modern youth ministry, including the history of church youth groups and suggested solutions.

Available from Canon Press, P.O. Box 8741, Moscow, ID 83843.

<u>Encyclopedia of Bible Truth for School Subjects</u> by Ruth C. Haycock. Whittier, CA: Association of Christian Schools International, 1982.

> Originally four volumes, this excellent book has been republished by ACSI in a one-volume version. Organized by school subjects, the book lists the biblical principles for each subject with Scripture references. A must-have for high school.

> Available from ACSI, P.O. Box 4097, Whittier, CA 90607.

<u>Great Books of the Christian Tradition</u> by Terry W. Glaspey. Eugene, OR: Harvest House Publishers, 1996.

> This book lists more than 500 suggestions of books that have shaped the Christian faith. Glaspey also includes secular books which have had an important impact on our world.

> Available from Harvest House Publishers, 1075 Arrowsmith, Eugene, OR, 97402.

<u>A Guide to American Christian Education for the Home and School</u> by James B. Rose. Camarillo, CA: American Christian History Institute, 1987.

> Defines the Principle Approach and describes how to apply it at home. It teaches parents and teachers how to use the Principle Approach in over 12 subjects from mathematics and natural science to history, literature, geography, and economics.

> Available from American Christian History Institute, P.O. Box 648, Palo Cedro, CA 96073.

<u>Schoolproof: How to Help Your Family Beat the System and Learn to Love Learning — The Easy, Natural Way</u> by Mary Pride. Westchester, IL: Crossway, 1988.

> <u>Schoolproof</u> will help even the most institutionally-minded parents weed out the "educational clutter" that tries to work its way into every school. Ways to simplify pre-packaged materials, present lessons, evaluate you student's learning, and other practical ideas are shared.

> Available from Home Life, P.O. Box 1250, Fenton, MO, 63026.

<u>Senior High: A Home-Designed Form+U+La</u> by Barbara Edtl Shelton. Kelso, WA: Triune Biblical University Press, 1993.

> Contains step-by-step formula for setting up high school and high school courses. Also includes many report forms and planning sheets.

> Available from 182 North Columbia Heights Road, Longview, WA 98632.

<u>You Can Teach Your Child Successfully</u> by Ruth Beechick. Pollock Pines, CA: Arrow Press, 1988.

> Excellent resource designed for junior high, but also helpful for high school. Includes suggestions for teaching all subjects at home.

> Available through Arrow Press, P.O. Box 899, Pollock Pines, CA 95726.

<u>High School Manuals</u>

> Local public and private high schools usually have a manual which describes every course the school offers. These can be useful in choosing a title for a course or in checking to see what kinds of classes can be offered. Usually available free.

<u>Scope and Sequences</u>

Most major textbook publishers have a scope and sequence available that describes what is covered in each course offered. Sometimes the course description in the book catalog will be useful as an idea source of what to include in your course.

<u>College Manuals</u>

I can't stress enough that you should always consult the manual of the college you plan to attend when choosing high school courses. This is the only way to be sure you are taking the right courses to be eligible for college admission. College catalogs can have useful information for planning high school courses even if you are not planning to go to college. There are many courses listed that will give you ideas for high school classes.

❖ Graduation and Senior Year Supplies

If you are interested in a graduation ceremony complete with cap and gown, plan well ahead. Fall of the senior year is the right time to begin to check out suppliers, order catalogs, and ask about the appropriate time to make reservations. In addition to the companies listed here you may want to ask a local public or private campus high school where they get their caps and gowns. Finding a location close to where you live may save shipping costs and would allow you to make a selection in person.

Josten's (714) 879-4079 — caps and gowns for rent

Collegiate Cap and Gown (818) 781-1360 — caps and gowns for rent
P.O. Box 7074, Van Nuys, California 91409.

In addition to caps and gowns, some homeschoolers want to buy a senior class ring. The company listed below offers a generic class ring. Some families prefer to choose a special ring that doesn't look like a traditional class ring and have it engraved for graduation. Other families purchase a "promise" ring during high school as a symbol of a youth's commitment to remain pure until marriage. Your local jeweler may have some other ideas or be able to recommend you to a local jewelry designer who could design a one-of-a-kind ring for your student.

Lord's Fine Jewelry (405) 373-2877 — generic "Homeschool High School" class ring
P.O. Box 486, Piedmont, Oklahoma 73078-0486.

Many families like to send graduation announcements upon the graduation of their teens. Your local stationary store or printer should be able to order announcements for you, from a variety of designs. If you have a special logo you have used for your school, they will be able to include it in the design of the announcement. Order early—February or March. Allow 6-8 weeks to receive your order from the printer, and plan to send them to your friends and relatives in May.

Finally, a diploma in a nice case is available from Home School Legal Defense Association, (540) 338-8610, PO Box 3000, Purcellville, VA 20134.

❖ Ideas for Study

The following list has been included because of the course ideas contained. It is meant as a resource only, not as a requirement.

Art

Art Appreciation	Drawing	Oil Painting
Art History	General Art	Photography
Ceramics	Interior Design	Printmaking
Commercial Art	Introduction to Art	Sculpture
Design	Jewelry Making	Water Colors

Bible

Any Book of the Bible	Discipleship Training	New Testament Overview
Attributes of God	Life of Christ	Old Testament Heroes
Basic Doctrine	Major Prophets	Old Testament Overview
Biblical History	Minor Prophets	Paul and His Letters
Christian Apologetics	Missions	Prayer
Christian Lifestyle	New Testament Church	Witnessing

Business

Accounting	Computer Keyboarding	Management
Advertising	Computer Languages	Marketing
Bookkeeping	Computer Science	Record Keeping
Business Law	Data Programming	Shorthand
Business Math	Desktop Publishing	Typing
Clerical Training	Economics	Work Experience
Communications	Entrepreneurship	Word Processing

English/Language Arts — To include in a basic English course:

Composition	Literature	Reading Skills
Godly Use of Language	Listening Skills	Research Skills
Grammar	Oral Reports	Spelling
Library Skills	Poetry	Vocabulary

When basic skills are mastered, other English/Language Arts courses could be:

American Literature	Drama	Mythology
Children's Literature	English Literature	Poetry
Communications	Journalism	Public Speaking
Creative Writing	Library Science	Short Story Writing
Debating	Mass Media	Speed Reading

Fine Arts

Any Musical Instrument
Art - see above
Calligraphy
Ceramics
Choir
Dance

Design
Drama
Drawing/Painting
History of Music
Humanities
Interior Design

Music
Music Appreciation
Mime
Photography
Stage Arts
Survey of Fine Arts

Foreign Language

Chinese
French
German

Greek
Hebrew
Latin

Sign Language
Spanish
Any Other Language

Health and Safety

CPR
Driver Education
Driver Training

First Aid
Health
Hospital Work

Natural Healing   Nutrition
Life Guard Training

Home Economics

Child Development
Consumer Science
Cooking
Creative Stitchery
Family Living Skills

Fashion Design
Food Preserving
Gourmet Cooking
Handyman Skills
Home Maintenance

Home Management
Marriage & Parenting
Sewing
Tailoring
Textiles

Industrial Arts

Appliance Repair
Architecture
Auto Mechanics
Carpentry
Computer Repair
Drafting
Electricity

Electronic Assembly
Electronics
Engineering
Furniture Making
Graphic Arts
Layout/Paste Up Work
Leather Working

Machining
Masonry
Metals
Offset Printing
Plastic Fabrication
Television Repair
Woodwork

Mathematics

Accounting
Algebra
Business Math
Calculus

Computer Programming
Consumer Mathematics
Engineering
General Arithmetic

Geometry
Logic or Critical Thinking
Statistics
Trigonometry

Physical Education

Aerobics	Gymnastics	Soccer
Archery	Handball	Softball
Ballet	Hiking	Swimming
Baseball	Hockey	Tap Dancing
Basketball	Ice Skating	Tennis
Bicycling	Jogging	Track & Field
Bowling	Martial Arts	Volleyball
Dance	Mountain Climbing	Walking
Drill Team	Racquetball	Weight Training
Football	Roller Skating	Any other sport or
Golf	Running	physical training

Science

Agricultural Science	Earth Science	Master Gardeners
Anatomy	Ecology	Micro Biology
Animal Husbandry	Engineering	Natural Healing
Astronomy	General Science	Organic Gardening
Aviation & Aeronautics	Genetics	Robotics
Beekeeping	Geology	Rocketry
Biology	Gerontology	Physics
Botany	Herbology	Physiology
Chemistry	Horticulture	Taxonomy
Creation Science	Marine Biology	Zoology

Social Studies / History

Anthropology	Geography	Sociology
Archaeology	Government	State History
Civics	Law	U.S. History
Current Issues	Missions Work	U.S. Constitution
Economics	Philosophy	World History
Ethnic Studies	Political Science	World View

Vocational Education

Apprenticeship	Cosmetology	Journalism
4-H, FFA or Scouting	Education / Tutoring	Ministry / Missions
Career Planning	Entrepreneurship	Work Experience
Child Care	Event Planning &	Yearbook
Community Service	Coordination	

❖ Recommended Reading for Students

These lists offer suggestions for your consideration. Some are not really "classics," but are good books anyhow. There is such a wide difference in abilities and maturity between different students and between ages. Please use your own judgment on each of these suggestions. I have marked (JR) those selections which are generally considered suitable for either junior high or senior high students.

Christian Classics:

Ben Hur: A Tale of the Christ by Lew Wallace

Book of Martyrs by John Foxe

Born Again by Charles Colson

The Calvary Road by Roy Hession

Christy by Catherine Marshall

The Cross and The Switchblade by David Wilkerson (JR)

Essential Christianity by Walter Martin

Gaining Favor with God and Man by William M. Thayer

The Great Evangelical Disaster by Francis Schaeffer

The Hiding Place by Corrie ten Boom (JR)

Hind's Feet On High Places by Hannah Hurnard

How Should We Then Live? by Francis Schaeffer

How To Be Your Own Selfish Pig by Susan Schaeffer Macauley

Improving Your Serve by Charles Swindoll

In His Steps by Charles Sheldon (JR)

Joel: A Boy of Galilee by Annie Fellows Johnston (JR)

Joni by Joni Eareckson Tada (JR)

The Light and The Glory by Peter Marshall & David Manuel

Man In Demand or Christian Charm by Wayne & Emily Hunter

Mere Christianity by C.S. Lewis

Origins, Two Models: Creation/Evolution by Richard B. Bliss, Ed.D (JR)

Passion and Purity by Elisabeth Elliot

Peace Child by Don Richardson

Pilgrim's Progress by John Bunyan (JR)

The Practice of the Presence of God by Brother Lawrence

Prophet by Frank E. Peretti

The Pursuit of God by A.W. Tozer

Screwtape Letters by C.S. Lewis

So What's the Difference? by Fritz Ridenour

Stepping Heavenward by Elizabeth Prentiss

What's The Difference by Fritz Ridenour

This Present Darkness by Frank E. Peretti

Thoughts for Young Men by J.C. Ryle

Through Gates of Splendor by Elisabeth Elliott

A Time For Anger by Franky Schaeffer

Twice Pardoned by Harold Morris

Walk Across America by Peter Jenkins

A Walk West by Peter & Barbara Jenkins
Who Moved the Stone? by Frank Morrison
Why Wait? by Josh McDowell

Classic Literature:

The Adventures of Huckleberry Finn by Mark Twain
The Adventures of Tom Sawyer by Mark Twain
All Creatures Great and Small by James Herriot
Anne of Green Gables by Lucy Montgomery
Around the World in Eighty Days by Jules Verne
Autobiography by Benjamin Franklin
The Autobiography of Miss Jane Pittman by Ernest Gaines
The Bronze Bow by Elizabeth George Speare (JR)
The Brothers Karamazov by Fyodor Dostoevski
Carry On, Mr. Bowditch by Jean Lee Latham (JR)
Canterbury Tales by Geoffrey Chaucer
Captains Courageous by Rudyard Kipling (JR)
Daniel Boone by James Daugherty (JR)
David Copperfield by Charles Dickens
The Deerslayer by James Fenimore Cooper
Democracy in America by Alexis de Tocqueville
The Elements of Style by William Strunk & E.B. White
The Federalist Papers by James Madison & others
For Whom the Bell Tolls by Ernest Hemingway
Go Tell It On The Mountain by James Baldwin
The Grapes of Wrath by John Steinbeck
Great Expectations by Charles Dickens
Gulliver's Travels by Jonathan Swift
Hamlet by William Shakespeare (& other works)
Heidi by Johanna H. Spyri (JR)
The Hobbit by J. R. R. Tolkien (JR)
Idylls of the King by Alfred Lord Tennyson
The Iliad by Homer
The Incredible Journey by Sheila Burnford (JR)
Island of the Blue Dolphins by Scott O'Dell (JR)
Ivanhoe by Sir Walter Scott
Jane Eyre by Charlotte Bronte
Johnny Tremain by Esther Forbes
Kidnapped by Robert Louis Stevenson
Last of the Mohicans by James Fenimore Cooper
Little Britches by Ralph Moody (JR)
Little Women by Louisa May Alcott (JR)
The Lord of the Rings by J. R. R. Tolkien
Macbeth by William Shakespeare (& other works)
Men of Iron by Homer Pyle (JR)
The Miracle Worker by William Gibson

The Narnia Chronicles by C.S. Lewis (JR)
The Odyssey by Homer
Of Plimoth Plantation by William Bradford
Old Yeller by Frank Gipson (JR)
Our Town by Thornton Wilder
The Prince and the Pauper by Mark Twain (JR)
Old Man and the Sea by Ernest Hemingway
The Red Badge of Courage by Stephen Crane
The Robe by Lloyd C. Douglas
Robinson Crusoe by Daniel Defoe
Smoky by Will James
The Spirit of St. Louis by Charles A. Lindbergh
A Study in Scarlet (& other Sherlock Holmes stories) by Sir Arthur Conan Doyle
Swiss Family Robinson by Johann D. Wyss (JR)
A Tale of Two Cities by Charles Dickens
To Kill A Mockingbird by Harper Lee
Treasure Island by Robert Louis Stevenson (JR)
The Trilogy of the Ring by J. R. R. Tolkien
Twenty-One Balloons by William Pène du Buis (JR)
Up From Slavery by Booker T. Washington
Wuthering Heights by Emily Bronte
The Yearling by Marjorie K. Rawlings

Poets:

American

William Cullen Bryant
John Dickinson
Ralph Waldo Emerson
Eugene Field
Robert Frost
Oliver Wendell Holmes
Henry Wadsworth Longfellow
James Russell Lowell
Joaquin Miller
James Whitcomb Riley
John Greenleaf Whittier

English

William Blake
Elizabeth & Robert Browning
Lord Byron
John Keats
Rudyard Kipling
John Masefield
Christina Rossetti
Percy Bysshe Shelley
Sir Walter Scott
William Shakespeare
Robert Louis Stevenson
Alfred Lord Tennyson
Ann and Jane Taylor
Isaac Watts
William Wordsworth

❖ Ministry and Missions

Many teens are interested in a ministry on the mission field. Others do not want to be missionaries, but do want to be active Christians, participating in the Lord's work. Arranging for a ministry or mission to be a part of your high school program can be not only an excellent school course, but a life-changing experience for your family. While most missions opportunities are not available until your teens have matured enough to be out on their own, there are plenty of possibilities for short-term missions projects which can be undertaken as a family.

Whether at home or abroad, whether a part of your teen's regular school schedule or a special semester project, a focused, intensive service to the cause of Christ can draw your student closer to the Lord and give him a heart for service to others. Many teens who have participated in outreaches while still in high school have discovered a gift for missionary work. In addition to the ideas presented here, there are many other opportunities for short-term, beginning missions projects once your teens have reached age eighteen. These opportunities are discussed on pages 186-187 of Chapter 11: After High School.

On Your Own

"On your own" signifies a ministry or mission planned by your own family; it does not mean an unplanned or unorganized outreach. For an outreach to be successful (for the minister *and* the needy) goals must be set, a time-frame planned, materials gathered, and prayers offered.

Possibilities for outreaches you can do on your own are endless. To treat these as a high school course, you may want to plan to do related research, financial planning for your outreach, scheduled regular prayer for the needs you are trying to meet, a final write-up of the work, etc. Simply meeting needs as you come across them, without much forethought, may be a good lifestyle, but high school courses should be a bit more formal—you are *studying* ministry.

Here are a few ideas to consider:

Volunteer to work an afternoon a week for a semester at a local food closet, pregnancy hotline, Ronald McDonald house, church thrift shop, church building or grounds, church office, family in need (babysitting, housecleaning, etc.)

Organize a fundraiser for a worthwhile organization. Fundraisers could be bake sales, walk-a-thons, used curriculum sales, yard or garage sales, spelling bees, or baking or art contests. Or you could volunteer to help solicit funds from local businesses for annual projects like community Christmas baskets or gifts for a local orphanage or juvenile hall. A group of local teens and their families could sponsor an appreciation banquet for pastors.

Get involved with an existing ministry project, like your state's Christian homeschool convention, the Special Olympics, or helping out at a local homeschool group's park day or Mom's night. Or make a commitment to minister to a full-time missionary by sending a monthly box of special food items, a newspaper from their home town, a book, a letter, etc.

Through Your Church

Ministries arranged through your church will need to planned with approval (and sometimes active involvement) of your pastor or board. These may include on-going programs or one-time events. Many successful outreaches are being planned and carried out by teens, with guidance and supervision by their parents.

Ideas that may be arranged through your church are:

On-going: Prayer meetings, family potluck & game nights (organization, set-up & clean-up), regular church work days, monthly presentation for children or families, musical groups, Good News Clubs for children, street ministries.

One-time: Outreach (bringing in a special musical group or speaker or video), feeding the homeless on a holiday, church-wide banquet, inter-church prayer meeting, mayor's or prayer breakfast, retreat weekend, children's festival or party, church camping trip, Christmas outreach to a children's home or hospital, trip to work with a church-supported missionary.

Through Missions Organizations

Some organizations allow teens to participate in missionary outreaches while in high school. The programs range from a few days' trip to Mexico during a school holiday to a full summer outreach in a faraway country. Ask your pastor about missions organizations that your church supports. Be sure to do a full background check before signing up for a mission trip with any organization. Check with your church leadership and ask for recommendations from families of teens who have participated. Some of the organizations[12] from which I have received information about teen opportunities are:

International Family Missions arranges missions trips in which whole families can participate together. For information, call (303) 665-7635.

New Tribes Mission has an "Assist" program in which students age 15 or older, or families traveling together, may participate in a short term mission trip. Trips vary each year, depending on the needs of New Tribes' full-time missionaries. Trips range from two to four weeks.

Some examples of past mission opportunities are: a 15-person team building a guest house for missionaries in New Guinea, 18 people doing landscaping and construction for the Bible School/Missions Course/Language Center in Australia, or an 18-member team installing a water tank and building projects for Bible students in Bolivia. Most of the trips also include visiting the local people. For information, contact New Tribes Mission, 1000 East First Street, Sanford, FL 32771-1487. (407) 321-6196.

Students International offers two-week missions projects throughout the year for students age 16-20. Though this organization caters primarily to campus-based Christian high schools, they do offer at least five trips per year especially for homeschooled teens. Students International may also plan missions projects for whole families to participate together.

The opportunities offered by Students International are designed to work primarily with students who want to minister in an area that correlates with their academic interests. For example, opportunities are available in the fields of medicine, social work, agriculture, business, education, journalism, sports, and language. For information, write to Students International, 1438 North Ben Maddox Way, Visalia, CA 93292, (209) 627-8923.

---

[12]   My family has not personally participated in a program with any of these organizations. I neither endorse nor recommend sending teens on missionary trips (especially to foreign countries) without their parents. However, many families are interested in this kind of a program for their older teens so the information is provided as a place to begin checking available options for those families who are interested. Again, use discretion and check out the program fully before signing up.

Word of Life International has a "Youth Reachout" program each summer for teens (15 or older) and college-career age. Several month-long mission trips are offered each summer. Included in each trip is a week-long "boot camp" followed by about three weeks on the mission field. For information, write to Youth Reachout, Word of Life, Schroon Lake, NY, 12870.

Youth With a Mission has over 4,000 mission opportunities available. YWAM uses three methods of action: Evangelism, Training, and Mercy Ministries. Many opportunities are short-term (defined by YWAM as 2 weeks to 2 years.)

For overseas work, students must be at least 18 or a high school graduate. But for work here in the US, students may be only 16, and there are some opportunities for students as young as 13.

Youth With a Mission publishes a 200-page book, The GO Manual, which is an introduction to their missions programs, including all the opportunities, locations, and requirements. The GO Manual is available from YWAM, P.O. Box 55787, Seattle, WA 98155, (206) 771-1153.

❖ 11 After High School

Planning for after high school graduation can involve difficult choices for many families. Many of today's parents were brought up by a generation which held a college education as one of the primary goals in life. The decision was not whether or not to go to college, rather it was trying to decide which college to attend. Getting accepted into a top university was considered the first step to a prosperous and blessed future; staying home to attend a community college was second best.

If those ideas had died away, we might have an easier time in helping our students to make wise decisions for their futures. However, the idea that a college education is mandatory still looms large in today's society. One of the questions often asked of families who are homeschooling through high school is, "Will your children be able to get into college?" Everyone seems to recognize that there are many great Americans (even modern-day ones) who have done notably well in business without college. But those great businessmen are considered exceptions.

I am not saying that college is never a good choice for graduating high school students. It is simply not the only worthwhile choice. Before considering college or any of the other options available to our students, we must take time to pray, to study the alternatives, and to prudently assess each choice.

An inheritance may be gotten hastily at the beginning;
but the end thereof shall not be blessed. Proverbs 20:21

One obvious consideration is the condition of your child's heart. Is he sufficiently mature to make a wise decision? Is he following God's will or his own? Is his basic education complete? Consider again Webster's definition of education on page four:

- Are the "manners and habits formed?" Has your student developed an honorable character. Is he self-disciplined enough to follow God's leading on his own?

- Has the student's understanding "been enlightened?" Is there discernment of other people, of teachings and prophecies, and of who or what is in control of a given situation?

- Has the "temper been corrected?" Does your student have self-control? Is he kind, patient and respectful of others?

- Is your student "fit for usefulness in a future station?" Has a particular goal been set for a future station? If the Lord continues to lead in the direction the youth currently desires, what other preparation is needed? What other preparations would be prudent for the student, assuming the direction of the Lord changes?

Taking time to consider each student's path and readiness to follow it is vital. It is so easy today to simply figure that at the end of the month of June closest to the child's eighteenth birthday, he will suddenly blossom into maturity—with all the rights and responsibilities of adulthood. Under man's law, this may be so; the eighteen-year-old is considered an adult. But as Christians, we must follow God's law, which does not null our responsibilities as parents just because it is June and our children are eighteen.

More and more opportunities are becoming available each year, as families are desiring different options for post-secondary education. Apprenticeship is being hailed by some as the grand conclusion to home education. Others are excited by the trend in upscale colleges to actively seek out homeschooled students. College at home is gaining popularity among homeschoolers who have no intention of sending their children away to a university. Entrepreneurship is on the rise, even for teens. And although the world is still trying to destroy families, among many Christians, marriage and babies are once again considered worthwhile goals.

❖ Missionary Opportunities

Missions organizations are still growing and there are more each year offering opportunities for Christians who are eighteen or older. Many students participate in short-term projects to try missionary work before making a decision to apply for a full-time position. For students who are eighteen or older, opportunities range from very short (two to three weeks) to several months or longer.

Even for students who are not desiring a full-time missionary position, there are some good reasons to consider missions:

- Students who are desiring to leave home to attend college or begin a career can benefit from a summer missions project. Often these short-term assignments bring life-long changes of heart. Working to help the poor and needy, working with the full-time missionaries who have devoted their lives to Christian service, and working with other Christians on a project for God's glory can provide lessons that will carry over into the rest of the student's life, providing a good foundation on which to build. The student who has a fresh memory of such service may be less likely to fall prey to the many temptations that will likely strike once he is out of the home.

- Work on the mission field tends to build maturity and break down self-centeredness. A student who is unsure of his next path may find that a short-term missionary project will give him a good opportunity to seek God's will for his life. Since the fellow workers are Christians, and the focus of the project is on the Lord, the time spent is usually fruitful.

- Experiencing missionary work for even a short time will build an appreciation for those who work full time in the field. Involvement in a missions project will likely build a life-long commitment to support missionary work.

Some missionary organizations, like Youth With a Mission, operate a university or training program to prepare the student for work in the business community after he has spent time working in a mission field. YWAM's University of the Nations offers a college education in Christian Ministries, Communication, Counseling and Health Care, Education, Humanities and International Studies, Performing Arts, and Science and Technology. The university offers studies in over 70 countries and offers a multi-faceted program of degrees and diplomas.

Some organizations, like Wycliffe Bible Translators, offer an introductory missionary program. Wycliffe's "Discovery Program" is designed to provide you "with a chance to evaluate possible missionary service and assess your ability to adapt to another language and culture." The Discovery Program has team and individual trips that range from 4 to 10 weeks.

For more information about missionary opportunities, first talk to your own pastor. He will be able to help you find an organization whose mission and theology is consistent with your own. There are many organizations which offer opportunities to those eighteen or older. If you are interested in gathering information before beginning serious consideration, you may want to request information from the following organizations[13].

Campus Crusade for Christ International, Arrowhead Springs, San Bernardino, CA 92414.

Christian & Missionary Alliance, P.O. Box C, Nyack, NY 10960.

Evangelical Foreign Missions Association, Box 794, Wheaton, IL 60189-0395.

Interdenominational Foreign Mission Association, Box 395, Wheaton, IL 60189-0395.

International Family Missions, P.O. Box 309, Lafayette, CO 80026.

Mission Aviation Fellowship, P.O. Box 202, Redlands, CA 92373.

The Navigators, P.O. Box 6000, Colorado Springs, CO 80934.

Students International, 1438 North Ben Maddox Way # 226, Visalia, CA 93292.

New Tribes Mission, 1000 East First Street, Sanford, FL 32771-1487. (407) 321-6196.

Word of Life International, Schroon Lake, NY 12870.

World Vision International, 919 W. Huntington Drive, Monrovia, CA 91016.

Wycliffe Bible Translators, P.O. Box 2727, Huntington Beach, CA 92647.

Youth With A Mission, P.O. Box 55787, Seattle, WA 98155. (206) 771-1153.

❖ Apprenticeship

Many high school students are considering apprenticeship programs rather than college. Counting the high cost of college (not to mention many spiritual pitfalls), it may be a good idea for a student to apprentice in his chosen field. The idea of apprenticeship confuses many people because they think of apprenticeship in old-fashioned terms.

---

[13]   This listing does not imply an endorsement, as I am not familiar with all the mission statements or doctrines. In an effort to keep the list of reasonable length, I have tried to list the only larger organizations with good reputations for years of Christian service. There are many excellent organizations which are not listed here. Again, your best resource will likely be your own church.

The differences between historical and modern apprenticeship must be understood before considering apprenticeship today. Lack of understanding in this area has caused disappointment among some teens whose parents would prefer apprenticeship over college.

Historically, an apprentice was contracted to serve his master for several years, with the understanding that he would receive enough training that at the end of that time, he would be knowledgeable enough to earn wages as a journeyman. At the start of the apprenticeship, he began as little more than a go-fer, running errands, keeping the fire lit, sweeping up the shop, etc. During this period, which lasted a minimum of several months, and could last even longer, the apprentice observed the day-to-day business, without actually being much of an active participant.

As the apprenticeship progressed, *over the course of several years*, the apprentice gradually began to do more and more of the work of the master's particular trade. It took five to seven years to progress just to the level of a paid journeyman, several more to become a master of the trade if, in fact, he ever progressed that far.

Historically, children were typically apprenticed between 10 and 14 years of age, with the contract finishing at age 17 to 21, producing a well-trained journeyman, capable of earning a modest living.

How Has Historical Apprenticeship Changed?

Apprenticeship has, of course, changed from the days of indenturing children. Now, children are required to attend school full-time during their teen years in most states. Assuming that a full-time apprenticeship leading to a journey-level ability of the trade is not available until after high school, we now have a situation where 16 to 18 year olds may be interested in apprenticing in a trade, but do not want to spend five to seven years after high school just to reach journey-level.

Today's first-year apprentices have likely spent 4-6 years in secondary education. Today's youths are older and (hopefully) more mature when they consider an apprenticeship program, they are not bound by indenturement and they are legally able to leave the situation for greener pastures—so they are less willing to serve at the entry level of classic apprenticeship.

There are many government regulations today which were enacted to protect minors from dangerous working conditions. But, as is typical under the system of bureaucratic overkill, the regulations today make it difficult to find an apprenticeship program that is appealing to both the student and the master.

Indenturing of apprentices is no longer allowed. While most citizens would not want to see a return to some of the harsh conditions under the indenturement system, indenturing did make it

Historical Definitions

from Webster's 1828
American Dictionary of the English Language

Apprenticeship: "The term for which an apprentice is bound to serve his master. This term in England is by statute seven years. In Paris, the term is five years; after which, the person, before he is qualified to exercise the trade as a master, must serve five years as a journeyman; during which term, he is called the *companion* of his master, and the term is call his *companionship*."

Apprentice: "One who is bound by covenant to serve a mechanic, or other person, for a certain time, with a view to learn his art, mystery, or occupation, in which his master is bound to instruct him. Apprentices are regularly bound by indentures."

Journeyman: "Strictly, a man hired to work by the day, but in fact, any mechanic who is hired to work for another in his employment, whether by the month, year or other term. It is applied only to mechanics in their own occupations."

more appealing for the master to take in an apprentice. He knew that if he put in a few years of training, he would have a well-trained apprentice as an assistant.

Minimum wage laws now require apprentices to be paid, even though it costs the master/employer much valuable work time to train them. Along with minimum wage, employers must pay workers' compensation insurance and other required benefits which add a great deal to the cost of hiring. Businessmen today say that a rule of thumb is that all the extras that must be paid for each employee add 50% to his hourly wage. In other words, it costs an employer $7.50 per hour to pay an employee $5.00. This is a lot to pay for someone who is going to sweep up the shop, run errands, and observe the business for a year, especially considering that once he is trained, he may leave for a higher paying job.

Unions for most trades negotiate payment even at the apprentice level. Many trades are union-run, meaning that even though their apprenticeship programs are expensive for employers, the employers cannot hire apprentices without following the union contract. Under union contracts, apprentices typically are paid well over the minimum wage. But union control of apprenticeships also means that most modern-day apprentices in the trades will have to join the union.

Bureau of Apprenticeship and Training

Formal apprenticeship programs through the U.S. Department of Labor's Bureau of Apprenticeship and Training (BAT)[14] typically last about four years, but range from one to six years. Currently, over 800 occupations have registered apprenticeship programs with the BAT. These programs are sponsored jointly by employers and labor unions, or are operated by employers or employer associations. In order to be registered with the Federal Government, they must meet federally approved standards relating to job duties, instruction (a minimum of 144 hours a year is recommended), wages, and safety and health conditions.

Apprentices' pay usually starts out at about half the salary that trained craftsmen receive, and increases periodically throughout the apprenticeship. Apprenticeships are available for many careers. Each field is autonomous, setting its own requirements. Most will require a high school diploma or equivalent. Some have additional requirements, such as courses in algebra or geometry.

An apprenticeship covers all aspects of the trade and includes both on-the-job training and related instruction. The instruction usually takes place in a classroom and covers the techniques of the trade and also the theory behind the techniques. Apprentices who successfully complete registered programs receive certificates of completion from the U.S. Department of Labor or a federally approved State apprenticeship agency.

Information from the Bureau of Apprenticeship and Training is available online at the U.S. Department of Labor: www.doleta.gov. There are links on the site to state labor boards, as well as lots of information about apprenticeship programs.

Applications are often accepted only for fields that are currently hiring, but this will vary from office to office. There are no residency requirements, so you can take an apprenticeship in another city to which you're willing to move. Many offices publish lists of their programs and requirements, and many have orientation classes which provide general information on apprenticeships. Most public high school libraries or career centers have a copy of the lists of fields for their areas.

---

[14]   The Bureau of Apprenticeship and Training has several publications which list occupations with registered apprenticeship programs. These explain how to qualify and apply for apprenticeship programs, and how to set up a formal apprenticeship program. Information in this book about the Bureau of Apprenticeship and Training was taken from the BAT publications.

Many apprenticeship offices are willing to send a representative to speak to groups of interested students. This would be a worth-while presentation if you have a number of high school students in your support group.

Informal Apprenticeships

Informal apprenticeship programs are becoming more and more popular. An informal apprenticeship program differs from a formal one because it is not registered with the federal government, and is usually a self-designed program, set up by the employer, the apprentice, and his parents. You may be able to set up your own apprenticeship program through a local businessman in the field of your choice.

At the most simplified level, apprenticeship, as the term is being used among home educators, has come to mean going along with a swimming pool cleaner, a gardener, a midwife, an electrician, etc. It means learning the ropes of a job by being there, handing the boss his wrench, dumping the wheelbarrow load, etc. Many children going along with their fathers to work are actually filling the role of apprentices. They are learning the trade just by being there, observing a skilled worker, and getting some basic on-the-job training.

More than 80% of all apprentices* are in these occupations:

Airframe and power plant mechanic	Line erector
Automobile mechanic	Line maintainer
Boilermaker I	Machinist
Bricklayer (construction)	Maintenance mechanic
Car repairer (railroad)	Millwright
Carpenter	Operating engineer
Cement mason	Painter
Construction-equipment mechanic	Pipe fitter
Cook	Plumber
Correction officer	Police officer I
Diesel mechanic	Radio station operator
Electrician	Refrigeration mechanic
Electrician, airplane	Roofer
Electrician, maintenance	Sheet metal worker
Electronics mechanic	Stationary engineer
Environmental-control-system installer-servicer	Structural-steel worker
Fire medic	Telegraphic-typewriter operator
Firefighter	Tool maker
Insulation worker	Tool-and-die maker
	Welder, combination

* In formal apprenticeship programs registered with the U.S. Department of Labor.

Yet on-the-job training has continued to be a common way of learning and moving up within any company, while historical apprenticeship seems to have died out. Does the gaining popularity of the term "apprenticeship" among homeschoolers signal a comeback? Or have we simply taken an entry-level job and glorified it for our just-starting-out youths to bolster their confidence?

In some respects, apprenticeship today does seem like any other entry-level job. However, at least among homeschoolers, there is a key difference. The difference is what makes it so that while one youth is simply flipping burgers at MacDonalds, another is apprenticing in the fast-food industry.

Parents today are looking for godly role models who are currently working in a profession which interests their children. Having spent so many years carefully nurturing their children in the Lord, Christian homeschool parents desire that the first "real" job outside of the family will be under an employer who will recognize the specialness of their child, taking the time to really teach him a business.

He that walketh with wise men shall be wise: but a companion of fools shall be destroyed. Proverbs 13:20

Setting Up an Apprenticeship Situation for Your Student

Setting up your own apprenticeship program will take some time and will require you to do the groundwork. Sometimes the Lord simply provides an opportunity: a neighbor asks if he can hire your son part-time, and the part-time job opens doors to a whole industry. Or a friend who sews, paints, or builds agrees to teach your child. Often, however, parents and youths will actively search out an apprenticeship position.

Ten things to remember in setting up your own apprenticeship are:

1. Remember that the employer/master will become a role model for your youth. Godly character and the purist of business ethics must be a prerequisite. This means that, especially for a long-term or intensive apprenticeship, you will likely want to limit your search to those you know very well or at least to those who have a "blameless" reputation in your community.

2. Labor laws must be heeded or the apprenticeship situation could cause a lot of problems for the employer.

   First, the law requires that if an employer benefits from the required work or training of a worker, that worker must be paid at least the minimum wage. While it is possible to volunteer to work for free, if the volunteer position leads to a paying job, the employer is liable for past wages for the time in which the employee worked for free.

   It is not necessarily up to the employee to complain or file a suit; if the Department of Labor detects such a situation, they may decide to step in to investigate.

   To avoid problems, it is safest to try to set up a program in which the apprentice is paid minimum wage. This may close the door to some desirable apprenticeships, because the leading idea was to exchange training for labor. But an employee who is sincerely interested in the field, anxious to learn, and willing to do the low-level tasks with a helpful attitude, will certainly be an asset to the employer. One of your jobs will be to help the employer to recognize that you (the student) are such an employee.

   Second, if the employer benefits from classes or training courses being taken by his employee, the Department of Labor may hold the employer responsible to pay the employee by the hour for the time spent attending such classes or training. This may be a gray area—but if the employer *requires* the training, it is not a gray area; the employer must pay not only for the course, but for the hours spent there.

3. If the only way you can set up an apprenticeship in the desired field is on a volunteer basis, the situation should be limited to one in which, once the apprenticeship has been completed, the student will be self-employed or employed by someone other than the master. This way there will be no endangering of the business by making the owner liable for back wages.

4. Many students' and parents' expectations are too high. Some seem to want an apprenticeship which will guarantee a high-level, well-paying profession with only a year or two of commitment. This generation is so accustomed to immediate results, that the apprenticeship may not seem to be heading anywhere, especially during the first six to twelve months of adjustment. Expect that progress may seem slow at first. Plan to spend the first few months doing some outside research and study after work-hours if it will help the beginning phase seem more profitable.

   For technical or highly specialized jobs, you will need to commit to a longer period of time. Much of the work will be too difficult for the apprentice to perform at first, so progress will seem even slower. In businesses which operate at an extremely fast pace, expect that progress will also seem to take a long time, simply because there is too much work to do to for the employer to take a lot of time off for training the apprentice.

5. Make a commitment to the apprenticeship program. Both the employer and the employee will need to be committed to the long-term goal of the apprenticeship program in order for it to succeed. Both sides should agree to a specific length of time of apprenticeship.

The student/employee must understand that it will cost the master/employer a great deal of time, effort, and money to train him. Taking advantage of the first half of the apprenticeship, then leaving the job before the employer has had the opportunity to enjoy the fruits of his labor in training and supervision would be dishonorable.

The master/employer must understand that the apprentice he is getting is much more than an entry-level, minimum wage worker—the apprentice is expecting the master to help him to work his way up in the trade. The master/employer should be expected to commit to teaching specific skills, with the goals of accomplishment for the student clearly laid out. This will require a lot of work on his part—figuring out exactly what skills must be taught, how long each is estimated to take to learn, and what order to teach the skills.

6. Establish with the master/employer exactly what training will occur, and at what level the youth should expect to be working by the end of the specified time. If outside study is recommended, make a plan for what courses are to be taken and who is to pay for them. Remember, if the courses are *required*, the employer will have to pay.

7. Ask for periodic reviews of both the youth's work and his progress toward your stated goals. For some families, this can be as simple as asking (at the beginning of the program) if the employer will come to their home for dinner once each quarter to discuss the program. For others, a written evaluation at specific intervals will be more suitable.

8. You will need to make apprenticeship appealing to the prospective master/employer. Many professionals are unwilling to enter an apprenticeship situation simply because the time it would take to train a young person for two years would outweigh the benefits to the employer, even if the apprentice was working on a volunteer basis. Explain that you are willing to show up at the office each day just to answer phones, make coffee, sort mail, stuff envelopes, make copies, etc. Or tell the employer you *expect* to be the go-fer, hauling loads of materials, fetching tools or running errands.

Many businessmen fear that it will take too much effort to keep an apprentice busy. They don't want to pay someone even minimum wage unless they are sure it will be worthwhile. Your job will be to show how valuable an apprentice will be. Don't expect the already-busy employer to figure out if he can use you—you make a list of jobs you could do for him. In other words, parents, before your student approaches an employer with the idea of hiring him as an apprentice, he must do his homework. Be ready to answer any questions; be ready to dispel any uncertainty about the value of apprenticeship.

9. Prepare a resume. If experience in the field is lacking, show your interest by listing classes taken, books read, etc. Write a decent cover letter which clearly explains your apprenticeship goals: what you want to learn, what pay you expect, how much training you expect to receive, how long you are willing to commit. Stress that you are willing to just tag-along the first few months, if necessary.

10. Take the first step yourself. Rather than casually asking about apprenticeship possibilities, and waiting for a busy professional to sound interested or make an offer, you do as much of the groundwork as possible. Write a full proposal and present it to the employer seriously and professionally. Research the field before setting up an appointment, dress appropriately, and be prepared to present yourself confidently and respectfully.

❖ College at Home

While many students would like to earn a college degree, Christian homeschoolers are becoming less and less inclined to send their children off to a university only to have the values that have been taught through years of training and discipling at home challenged. They are even less inclined to pay thousands of dollars each year for the "privilege" of having their values and beliefs openly mocked. Since many fields of employment require a college degree, homeschool families are turning to college at home.

There are several ways to earn college credit and college degrees (real degrees, not hand printed ones from a diploma mill) without attending a college campus. Credits can be earned through correspondence courses, courses taken by computer via modem, public television or cable network broadcasts of college courses (though these often require attendance at a local campus for orientation and final exam), college level examinations, and life experience as demonstrated through portfolios.

Dr. John Bear and Mariah Bear have written several useful books on earning college credits and even entire accredited degrees from home. College Degrees by Mail and Internet and Bears' Guide to Earning Degrees by Distance Learning are both published by Ten Speed Press.

Most colleges today will accept transfer credits taken outside the college, however each college sets its own rules regarding how many outside credits may be applied toward a degree as well as what credits are transferable. Dr. Bear's books give information on how to obtain credits as well as contact information for many colleges and universities which offer courses or degrees off-campus. Dr. Bear also lists over 100 schools that offer degrees almost entirely by home study. Three of these will award a degree earned wholly off-campus:

- Excelsior College, Columbia Circle, Albany, NY 12203-5159
  (888) 647-2388, online: www.excelsior.edu.

- Thomas A. Edison State College, 101 West State Street, Trenton, NJ 08608.
  (609) 292-9992, online: www.tesc.edu.

- Charter Oak State College, 270 Farmington Avenue, Farmington CT 06032.
  (203) 677-5147, online: www.charteroak.edu.

The Independent Study Catalog available from Peterson's Publications (800-338-3282) is a directory which lists every course offered at each of the 71 schools listed in College Degrees by Mail and Internet.

Even taking just a year or two by correspondence or distance learning can cut the cost of a university degree nearly in half. Typical correspondence courses include a required text and assignments which are mailed to the teacher. If final exams are required, they are taken under the supervision of a proctor, usually at a local college. Distance learning courses, on the other hand, vary widely, especially since technology had been changing and developing so rapidly during the past few years. A distance learning course may include books or videos, sent to the student for independent study, followed by a proctored exam, or distance learning may mean scheduled "classes" on the Internet.

National Home Study Council

The National Home Study Council (NHSC) is an accreditation agency for home study schools. While there are many legitimate home study programs which are not a part of NHSC, it does offer a list of schools and courses which have passed its standards.

Some of NHSC's listings are Christian (like the Berean College) and others are secular (Columbia School of Broadcasting). For a free brochure listing over 100 different schools and programs, write to the National Home Study Council, 1601 Eighteenth Street N.W., Washington, DC, 20009.

Mary Pride's Big Book of Home Learning has a lot of information on these schools and the courses they offer.

Inexpensive College Courses at Home

You can also design your own college courses in the same way you designed courses for high school, only more advanced. This offers an alternative for students who may finish their high school course work before they are mature enough for college. In order to receive college credits, you can arrange to take an examination at most colleges in almost any subject.

A visit to your local college bookstore will provide access to advanced textbooks on almost any subject. Be sure to check the books thoroughly for philosophical content. Also ask about the availability of used texts.

College libraries are often overlooked as resources. Ask if non-students may get a card at the college library. If you can get a card, you have access to most college-level textbooks virtually free of charge. If library cards are only available to enrolled students, ask your local public library to request an inter-library loan of any materials you would like to borrow.

College Credit by Examination

Most colleges set a limit on how many credits may be earned by exam. For example, a college may allow no more than 30 credits to be earned by examination. If you intend to transfer to a campus-based program to finish your degree, be sure to check to see how many credits by exam can be earned, as well as which exams and which exam programs are honored.

One of the most common tests used to earn college credits is the **CLEP** (College-Level Examination Program), offered by the College Entrance Examination Board (CN 6600, Princeton, NJ 08541-6600.) The CLEP does not award college credits; each college sets its own required passing score, and each college determines how many credits it will award for passing each test.

CLEP has five general exams: English, Humanities, Mathematics, Natural Sciences, and Social Sciences-History. CLEP also offers 30 different subject exams. The cost to take the tests is about $30 each.

Your local community college may have a "CLEP Colleges" booklet available, or you may find CLEP preparation books at major book stores. There is also an official handbook, The Official Handbook for the CLEP Examinations, which may be ordered from College Board Publications, Department S95, Box 886, New York, NY 10101-0886. You may also order the handbook by phone, using a credit card, at (800) 323-7155.

Students can take CLEP exams at any age, which allows high school students working at an advanced level to earn college credit. Most CLEP exams are offered throughout the year so that students can plan to take an exam when they finish a high school course For example, a student who is working on a second-year high school Algebra course may be able to pass the CLEP for College Algebra. It makes sense to take the exam immediately after finishing the high school course, while the subject matter is still fresh. I know of several students, for example, who passed the College Algebra CLEP exam after finishing the Saxon Algebra 2 book.

Other commonly used exams for earning college credits are:

PEP (Proficiency Examination Program), offered by the American College Testing Program (P.O. Box 168 Iowa City, IA 52243.) PEP offers 43 subject exams. Prices range from $40 to $120 per exam.

AP (Advanced Placement) exams, offered by The College Board (AP Exams, P.O. Box 6671, Princeton, JN 08541-6671 or toll-free at 888/CALL-4-AP.) The AP exams were developed specifically for high school students, usually juniors and seniors, who are taking AP or honors courses during high school. However, anyone of any age may take the AP exams. Usual test centers, however, are public high schools, and often, the high schools limit who may take tests at their location. Persevere and work through the staff at The College Board—it's worth the trouble. The AP exams are one of the most widely recognized programs by universities, and each exam usually nets six credits (equivalent to a whole year course.) There are AP exams currently available in 27 subjects.

DANTES (Defense Activity for Non-Traditional Educational Support), originally designed for active military personnel, but now available to anyone. For information, write to Educational Testing Service, Mail Stop 3/X, Princeton, NJ 08541.

GRE (Graduate Record Examinations), offered by Educational Testing Service, offers a general exam and 20 different subject exams designed to test knowledge which would normally be gained by a Bachelor's degree holder in the field. According to Dr. Bear, the Regents College of the University of the State of New York will award 30 semester credits for passing the GRE (this is equivalent to a full year of college.)

Test Preparation

The most important preparation will be to write to the addresses given above and request information well in advance. If the company which offers the test has a book available to help you prepare for it, it will likely be worthwhile to purchase it. It is in the company's best interest to have their exam program be a success, and they are the best equipped to tell you what is covered in the tests they publish.

Additional books to help you prepare for the above exams are available at most libraries and bookstores. One of the more popular series is published by Barron's. The Barron's preparation books include general information on the tests, sample tests, and guidelines for study.

Credit by Life Experience/Portfolio:

Some colleges recognize that an education equivalent to that received while sitting in a class may be acquired through real life experience. It is possible, for example, to earn college credit based on spending time abroad studying another country, or based on learning that took place on the job, or even based on special seminars and training courses taken in connection with a job, hobby, or avocation.

In order to be awarded college credits for life experience, a student must be able to demonstrate that college-level learning did take place. This is usually accomplished through a portfolio—a detailed description of what was learned, including notes taken at seminars, letters of recommendation or verification, newspaper or magazine clippings, photos, or even cassettes or videos. When the student applies to receive credit based on life experience, the college assigns his portfolio to an instructor who is qualified in the particular subject area. The instructor evaluates the portfolio and makes a recommendation for the number of credits to be awarded.

Charter Oaks State College and Thomas A. Edison State College both award credits based on portfolio review. Addresses for these colleges are on page 193. When you write, request information about portfolio preparation.

❖ College on Campus

If attending a campus college or university is your goal, you will need to prepare for the admission process while you are still in high school. Competition for admission is demanding. One admissions officer at UC Berkeley told me they have so many students trying to get in, that they could literally fill their classes with "straight A" students. Most of the "top" universities could make this claim, as well. Still, as well-known homeschoolers like the Colfax family in northern California have proven, admission to even Harvard is possible.

A common complaint of college admissions officers is that all their applicants seem the same. They all study the same classes, get the same grades, and participate in the same extracurricular activities. Bright students whose individuality stands out have a good chance of getting in to colleges that are weary of the stereotypical applicant. There are several important steps that you should take while still in high school:

1. **GET A COPY OF THE COLLEGE CATALOG!** Get the admissions requirements directly from the college. Planning your high school course of study based on the recommendations of a counselor or even this book can be a waste of your time. Check the college catalog to make sure of the requirements.

2. **If at all possible, visit the college**. Often a university will sound great in the brochure or catalog (both are sales tools), but when you get there, you find it is not at all what you expected. With the high cost of college, you can't afford to be unsure of your choice.

3. **Find out the name of the admissions officer who handles non-traditional students**. Many colleges have a staff member who specializes in students who come from "unknown" high schools. Ask this officer for suggestions about what you can do to increase your chances for admission. Will the college require a transcript? Or can your eligibility be determined strictly on test scores?

   If a transcript is required, you may need to follow a specific college-preparatory course of study. On the other hand, if you will be considered on the basis of test scores alone, you may not need to bother with all the traditional courses. The sooner you can know what is required, the more time you will have to prepare.

4. **Make sure you can write!** Sounds simple, but it is amazing how many high school students are poor writers. College applications include an essay question. An excellent essay can make the difference between two otherwise equally talented candidates.

5. **Take the correct courses needed by incoming freshmen**. Each college sets its own course requirements. While two-year community colleges usually do not require specific courses, most four-year colleges do. Review the chart of typical college-bound students' graduation requirements on page 56. Ask each prospective college for a list of high school course requirements and follow the strictest list.

When to Apply

The proper time to apply for admission to most universities is in October, and no later than November, of the senior year of high school. Always check the catalog of the school you plan to attend, and make sure your application is sent on time.

Books to Help Prepare for College

There is a glut of books on the market about colleges and college admissions. Visit your local library, and check in both the reference and the loan sections. A lot of books about preparing for college are updated yearly, so the library will keep the most current edition in the reference section. Because of this, plan to spend a lot of time at the library during your college search.

Two books about college preparation that are worth owning are:

Academic Preparation for College (What Students Need to Know and Be Able to Do), available for free (single copies only) from The Office of Academic Affairs, The College Board, 45 Columbus Avenue, New York, NY 10023, (212) 713-8000. This short book contains a list of basic skills which should be learned during high school as a preparation for college. The skills listed would be an excellent guide for planning course content for high school students.

Handbook for College Admissions (A Family Guide) by Thomas C. Hayden, Peterson's Guides: Princeton, New Jersey. This is a good beginning guide for college admissions, including topics like choosing and visiting colleges, testing, what to do during high school, filling out applications, financial aid, etc.

College Entrance Examinations

Although many colleges don't place as much weight on college entrance exam scores as in the past, the test scores are one of the only ways that a college can get an objective view of what a homeschooled student can achieve.

Students must register for the exams about a month ahead. Since different colleges prefer one test over the other, check with the colleges to which you plan to apply, to make sure you are taking the test required.

Most students will be expected to take the tests during their senior year of high school, but there is no age requirement. While guidelines and suggestions vary among colleges (and even among admissions officers at the same college) a helpful suggestion from one university admissions officer is that homeschoolers take the SAT or ACT near the end of their junior year. Then, since the admissions officer may not trust the objectivity of transcripts prepared by a student's own parents, the scores will be available when the student sends his admissions application in October.

Waiting until the senior year may mean that test scores are not available until too late to help the student convince the college that his homeschool experience has provided a good preparation for college level studies. Students who take the test as juniors should include current test scores with the application, and retake the test as seniors if the college would prefer more recent scores.

There are three important exam programs for students heading to college:

PSAT (Preliminary Scholastic Aptitude Test)

Many students take the PSAT during 11th grade, as practice for the SAT. But the PSAT serves another important purpose—its scores are used to determine scholarships for the National Merit Scholarship program. Information on the PSAT can be obtained by writing to The College Board, P.O. Box 6200, Princeton, NJ 08541-6200, or by calling (609) 771-7070.

<u>SAT</u> (Scholastic Aptitude Test)

The SAT is a program of The College Board, a national nonprofit association. The SAT is developed and administered by Educational Testing Service (ETS.) There are two SATs. The SAT I takes three hours and measures verbal and mathematical reasoning abilities. The SAT II is a series of 22 Subject Tests in five general categories: English, History and Social Studies, Mathematics, Sciences, and Languages. SAT II tests take one hour each. Colleges which require SAT II tests often expect students to take three, with the choice of which three being left to the student.

The *Registration Bulletin* and information booklets, "Taking the SAT" and "Taking the Achievement Tests [the SAT IIs]," are available free from Educational Testing Service, (510) 653-5400. The *Registration Bulletin* has test dates, test center locations, registration form, test taking tips and general information about the tests. "Taking the SAT" and "Taking the Achievement Tests" describe the tests in detail, including sample questions from each section.

For more practice, there are several books available with actual tests that you can do at home. <u>The College Board Achievement Tests</u> includes 14 tests in 13 subjects. <u>10 SATs</u> has 10 actual SATs and preparation suggestions. <u>5 SATs</u> has 5 actual SATs. Although the test changes every year, the format remains the same, and these practice tests can really help. Order any of the three test books from College Board ATP, Dept. E19, P.O. Box 6212, Princeton, New Jersey, 08541- 6212. I have also seen <u>10 SATs</u> at Crown Books so you may try calling your local bookstore to get a copy faster.

Additional information about the SAT is available at The College Board's web site: http://www.collegeboard.org.

<u>ACT</u> (American College Testing Program)

The ACT is four tests in one, with sections in math, science reasoning, English, and reading. The entire ACT takes 175 minutes and is multiple choice, with only right answers counted (so making a guess and guessing wrong won't hurt your score.) The "Preparing for the ACT Assessment" booklet describes each section of the test and includes sample test questions taken from "retired" ACT tests. The "Registering for the ACT Assessment" includes a list of test sites and codes for places to send your scores. Both booklets are available from ACT at P.O. Box 414, Iowa City, IA 52243-0414, or call (319) 337-1270.

❖ High School Course Requirements for College Admissions

While colleges vary in their requirements for courses that incoming freshmen must have completed while in high school, the chart on page 56 shows a typical requirement list. The following chart will also provide a good starting place to plan, if you are doing the very preliminary planning work for a student in 9th or 10th grade. By the summer before 11th grade, you should be checking with prospective colleges or universities to make sure you will not miss any specific courses they require.

Common College Freshmen Admission Prerequisite Courses		
Subject Area	**Number of Full-Year Courses Required**	**Notes**
English	4	Some colleges require only 3 years for non-English majors.

Common College Freshmen Admission Prerequisite Courses		
Mathematics	3	Many colleges require only 2 years for non-math or science majors. However, math or science majors often need 4 years.
Social Studies	3	Many colleges require only 2 years. Most colleges have specific course requirements in the social studies field, for example, U.S. History and American Gov't..
Sciences	2	Most colleges require biology; many also require chemistry. Some colleges now require 3 years of science. Science majors may need 4 years.
Foreign Language	2	Most colleges require 2 years of the same foreign language.
Electives	4-6	Some colleges have specific additional course requirements, like fine arts, but most simply require 4-6 to additional academic courses.

❖ Sample College Admissions Information

Again, each college and university sets its own admission requirements so it will be vital to check with each campus before you apply. The following chart is presented to give an idea of the range of college information. The list is *not* a "best colleges" or a recommended list. I have simply tried to list a cross-section of public and private universities from around the country, including many well-known colleges and some not-so-well-known.

This information was taken from the *Time Magazine/The Princeton Review's* "The Best College for You," 1998 edition[15], which lists more details for over 1,000 colleges and includes a self-assessment designed to help you figure out your chances of getting into the university of your choice.

Notes: 1. The "average high school GPA" and "average SAT/ACT scores" do not represent the minimum required for admissions; they are the *average* for incoming freshmen for the 1996-97 school year.
2. The tuition rates shown do not include room and board or books.

College	Type & Affiliation, If Any	Avg. High School GPA	Avg. SAT/ACT Scores	Apply By	Average Yearly Tuition
Bethel College, St. Paul, MN	private Baptist Church		573 math/571 verbal 24 ACT		$ 13.840
Bethel College, North Newton, KS	private Mennonite	3.31	22 ACT	August 15	$ 10.290

---

[15]   Note for 2004 edition: This information is old, but can still serve as an introduction to common college entrance requirements. While the tuition has most certainly gone up, the chart will still serve to show which colleges are at the upper end of the price range. Up to date information on individual colleges can be found at the Princeton Review website: www.princetonreview.com, or at the College Board website: www.collegeboard.com.

College	Type & Affiliation, If Any	Avg. High School GPA	Avg. SAT/ACT Scores	Apply By	Average Yearly Tuition
California Institute of Technology, Pasadena, CA	private		767 math/725 verbal	January 1	$ 18,000
College of William & Mary, Williamsburg, VA	public		590-690 math 600-710 verbal 29 ACT	January 15	$ 5,032 in state $ 15,404 out of state
Colorado State University, Ft. Collins, CO	public	3.5	561 math/553 verbal 24 ACT	July 1	$ 2,258 in state $ 9,480 out of state
Duke University, Durham, NC	private United Methodist Church		650-750 math 640-730 verbal 30 ACT	January 2	$ 21,550
Emory University, Atlanta, GA	private United Methodist Church	3.7	650 math/570 verbal 28 ACT	January 15	$ 20,870
Grove City College, Grove City, PA	private Presbyterian Church USA	3.7	624 math/615 verbal 27 ACT	February 15	$ 6,576
Harvard & Radcliffe Colleges, Cambridge, MA	private		690-790 math 700-790 verbal 30-34 ACT	January 1	$ 19,770
King College, Bristol, TN	private Presbyterian Church	3.29	542 math/594 verbal 24 ACT		$ 9,560
Massachusetts Institute of Technology Cambridge, MA	private		720-790 math 650-750 verbal 30-33 ACT	January 1	$ 23,100
Midland Lutheran College, Fremont, NE	private Evangelical Lutheran Church in America	3.1	22 ACT	September 1	$ 12,300
Ohio University, Athens, OH	public	3.2	551 math/555 verbal 24 ACT	February 1	$ 4,275 in state $ 8,994 out of state
Oral Roberts University, Tulsa, OK	private		523 math/538 verbal 23 ACT	July 15	$ 9,392
Pepperdine University, Malibu, CA	private Church of Christ	3.7	600-699 math 600-699 verbal 25 ACT	January 15	$ 21,100
Princeton University, Princeton, NJ	private		675-775 math 675-775 verbal	January 2	$ 22,000
Stanford University, Stanford, CA	private		709 math/703 verbal 32 ACT	December 15	$ 20,490

College	Type & Affiliation, If Any	Avg. High School GPA	Avg. SAT/ACT Scores	Apply By	Average Yearly Tuition
Texas A&M University, College Station, TX	public		606 math/578 verbal 25 ACT	March 1	$ 1,020 in state $ 7,440 out of state
The Evergreen State College, Olympia, WA	public	3.1	550 math/595 verbal	March 1	$ 2,346 in state $ 8,295 out of state
Tulane University, New Orleans, LA	private		622 math/623 verbal	January 15	$ 19,700
U.S. Air Force Academy, Colorado Springs, CO	public	3.8	649 math/626 verbal	January 31	$ 0
University of Michigan Ann Arbor, MI	public	3.65	590-700 math 560-660 verbal 25-30 ACT	February 1	$ 5,820 in state $ 18,450 out of state
University of Central Florida, Orlando, FL	public	3.4	563 math/557 verbal 24 ACT	July 15	$ 1,829 in state $ 7,074 out of state
University of Wisconsin Madison, WI	public	3.7	620 math/610 verbal 26 ACT	February 1	$ 2,881 in state $ 9,636 out of state
Western Baptist College, Salem, OR	private	3.4	510 math/520 verbal 22 ACT	August 1	$10,490
Yale University, New Haven, CT	private		720 math/730 verbal	December 31	$ 23,100

❖ Scholarships and Financial Aid

There are many scholarships available for colleges, universities, and trade schools. Some are awarded for academic work, athletics, talents, skills, and/or school and community involvement. Some are based on merit only; some specify merit and need. Community groups, businesses, professional associations, church groups, minority groups, foundations, and labor organizations all are sources of private scholarships. Ask your local public school counseling office if there is a list of private scholarships available in your community.

There are scholarship, grant, and loan programs through both the federal and the state government. Information about government programs is available at any government college office (i.e. public community colleges, state colleges or state universities.) Information should also be available at your local public high school counseling or career office. For federal scholarships, you may write to Federal Student Aid Programs, P.O. Box 4016, Iowa City, IA 52243-4016. For state scholarships, the best source of information is likely your nearest state college.

Each college will have a financial aid office where you can get information about scholarships offered. Check the college catalog and call the college directly to ask about their financial aid and scholarship programs. There are also numerous books available at the public library about financial aid for college. Plan to spend a whole afternoon at the library just getting started with a list of possible scholarships.

CALIFORNIA SUPPLEMENT

❖ California Supplement Contents

❖ **Preface to Supplement** 205

❖ **A: Required Areas of Study** 211

❖ **B: Graduation Requirements** 215

❖ **C: Tests** 219

❖ **D: Work Permits** 223

❖ E: Driver Education & Driver Training 237

❖ Preface to Supplement

This Supplement was formerly published as a separate booklet which was included with purchases of the <u>High School Handbook</u> within California. It has always been an important part of the book for California homeschoolers, but if you live in a different state or country and have seen an older edition, this section will be new to you. You're free, of course to browse through it, but please remember that the information applies only to California. I'm sometimes asked if I'll be preparing a supplement for other states, and I anticipate being asked if Californians are getting something "extra" now that the supplement is bound together with the rest of the book. The answer to both questions is No. Other states have homeschool organizations and leaders in place who are familiar with their laws; if you need help in one of these areas, call your statewide organization or call HSLDA. I grew up in California, homeschooled my own children here, and have served in leadership with my state's homeschool organization, CHEA of California, for many years. My bizarre love of research, coupled with a need to find information that wasn't available back when I needed it, led to the gathering of this information. It would be a shame to keep it from California homeschoolers just so everyone else didn't feel left out. And as I said at the beginning, it's always been part of the book—you just may not have realized it until now.

As you are reading the legal codes quoted in this Supplement, keep in mind that interpretation and application of the codes may vary, even among attorneys. I am not an attorney. The material and opinions in this supplement are not, nor are they intended to be, legal advice. If you have legal questions, I recommend that you contact the Home School Legal Defense Association.

Home School Legal Defense Association, PO Box 3000, Purcellville, VA 20134.

The Education Codes cited are public information and should be available at your local public library. They are included in this Supplement as a handy, practical aid for parents planning to teach their children at home during junior and senior high school.

As in *The High School Handbook*, I assume that you are familiar with the law in California regarding private school affidavits, school records, etc. If you are new to homeschooling in California, purchase CHEA's *An Introduction to Home Education*, which will help you to set up your homeschool program legally.

Since there is no specific "homeschool law" in California, most homeschool families operate as private schools, either by setting up their own small school in their homes, or by enrolling in another private school which offers independent study. *An Introduction to Home Education* explains how to set up your program in either of these two ways. For this book, it is important that you understand that whether you set up your own school or join another, the appropriate legal term which applies to your school is "private school." Similarly, your students are technically private school students. This may seem to the novice to be an insignificant semantic issue; however, learning to use the appropriate term will save a lot of headaches, especially when dealing with government bureaucracies which do not understand "homeschooling."

Increasingly, public schools in California are offering independent study options or charter schools to their students. It is important to realize that independent study within the public school system is not the same as homeschooling, as the term is used in this book. Public school students, whether in a typical classroom, a public independent study program, or a charter school, are still *public school* students. As such, they are subject to different California Education Code requirements than are private school students. Their parents do not enjoy the same amount of freedom and authority over their programs, curriculum, and students as do those parents who homeschool their children privately.

If your students are enrolled in a public school program, or if you are considering enrolling them in one, I recommend purchasing the "Public School ISP & Charter School" information packet from CHEA of California. This packet will explain the important differences between homeschooling privately and being a part of a public school program.

This *California Supplement*, as well as *The High School Handbook*, is intended to help parents who are homeschooling privately, apart from any public school program. If your students are in a public school program, you should seek help from the public school teacher or administrator who oversees the program, so that you will not be confused by the private school information included in this manual.

❖ A: Required Areas of Study

The law in California does not state that private schools must require exactly the same courses that the public schools require, only that private schools *"...shall offer instruction in the several branches of study required to be taught in the public schools of the state...."* (EC § 48222)

Without comment as to whether it is unconstitutional for the state to make such requirements of private schools, but primarily for the resource value in deciding what to study in junior and senior high school, the areas of study listed in the Education Code are listed below.

Remember, the "branches of study" are required, but not the same course content. This means that while private schools in California are required to teach English, they are not required to teach it in the same way or with the same content as a public school English course. The description of what *public* schools include in the study of English is listed in the Education Code sections shown beginning on the next page, but you may choose to set up your own courses with different content than what is included by the public schools.

Here are the required branches of study to be offered by private schools in grades 7-12:

English,	**Fine arts,**
Social sciences,	**Applied arts,**
Foreign language,	**Career technical education,**
Physical education,	**Automobile driver education,**
Science,	**Parenting skills.** [15]
Mathematics,	

Public schools are required to include specific topics within their courses, but these descriptions of content are not required of private schools. Nevertheless, some parents like to see what the public school requirements are, so they are included on the following page, as written in the Education Code.

Areas of study; grades 7 to 12

---

[16]   Parenting skills is a requirement which is to be offered in grade 7 or 8. However, schools which cover parenting skills in grade 6, 7, 8, or 9 are considered to be in compliance with the requirement, even if the subject is taught in grades 6 or 9, rather than 7 or 8. This requirement does not mean a separate course is required; parenting skills are commonly taught within other courses.

The adopted course of study for grades 7 to 12, inclusive, shall offer courses in the following areas of study:

*(a) **English**, including knowledge of and appreciation for literature, language, and composition and the skills of reading, listening, and speaking.*

*(b) **Social sciences**, drawing upon the disciplines of anthropology, economics, geography, history, political science, psychology, and sociology, designed to fit the maturity of the pupils. Instruction shall provide a foundation for understanding the history, resources, development, and government of California and the United States of America; instruction in our American legal system, the operation of the juvenile and adult criminal justice systems, and the rights and duties of citizens under the criminal and civil law and the State and Federal Constitutions; the development of the American economic system, including the role of the entrepreneur and labor; the relations of persons to their human and natural environment; eastern and western cultures and civilizations; human rights issues, with particular attention to the study of the inhumanity of genocide, slavery, and the Holocaust, and contemporary issues.*

*(c) **Foreign language** or languages, beginning not later than grade 7, designed to develop a facility for understanding, speaking, reading, and writing the particular language.*

*(d) **Physical education**, with emphasis given to physical activities that are conducive to health and to vigor of body and mind.*

*(e) **Science**, including the physical and biological aspects, with emphasis on basic concepts, theories, and processes of scientific investigation and on the place of humans in ecological systems, and with appropriate applications of the interrelation and interdependence of the sciences.*

*(f) **Mathematics**, including instruction designed to develop mathematical understandings, operational skills, and insight into problem-solving procedures.*

*(g) **Visual and Performing Arts**, including dance, music, theater, and visual arts, with emphasis upon development of aesthetic appreciation and the skills of creative expression.*

*(h) **Applied arts**, including instruction in the areas of consumer and homemaking education, industrial arts, general business education, or general agriculture.*

*(i) **Career technical education** designed and conducted for the purpose of preparing youth for gainful employment in the occupations and in the numbers that are appropriate to the personnel needs of the state and the community served and relevant to the career desires and needs of the pupils.*

*(j) **Automobile driver education**, designed to develop a knowledge of the provisions of the Vehicle Code and other laws of this state relating to the operation of motor vehicles, a proper acceptance of personal responsibility in traffic, a true appreciation of the causes, seriousness and consequences of traffic accidents, and to develop the knowledge and attitudes necessary for the safe operation of motor vehicles. A course in automobile driver education shall include education in the safe operation of motorcycles.*

(k) Other studies as may be prescribed by the governing board. (EC § 51220)

*Commencing with the 1995-96 fiscal year, the adopted course of study for grade 7 or 8 shall include the equivalent content of a one-semester course in **parenting skills** and education... with content designed to develop a knowledge of topics including, but not limited to, all of the following:*

(1) Child growth and development	*(5) Personal hygiene*
(2) Parental responsibilities	*(6) Maintaining healthy relationships*
(3) Household budgeting	*(7) Teen parenting issues*
(4) Child abuse and neglect issues	*(8) Self esteem.*

This section is not intended to replace existing courses that accomplish the intent of this section. School districts may meet the requirements of this section with existing courses of study offered in any of grades 6 to 9, inclusive, that includes the course contents identified... (EC §§ 51220.5 (c) & (e))

(Bold-face type on the "branches" of study added for emphasis. The bold-face shows the required branches; the rest is description of what the public schools must include within their courses.)

The following codes do not include additional "branches of study," but add definition to the content of the courses to be offered by public schools. Again, your own school may include different content.

Driver Education:

In addition to the requirements specified in subdivision (j) of Section 51220, automobile driver education shall be designed to develop a knowledge of the dangers involved in consuming alcohol or drugs in connection with the operation of a motor vehicle. (EC § 51220.1)

For the purposes of subdivision (j) of Section 51220, a course in automobile driver education shall include, but is not limited to, education regarding the rights and duties of a motorist as those rights and duties pertain to pedestrians and the rights and duties of pedestrians as those rights and duties pertain to traffic laws and traffic safety. (EC § 51220.4)

Social Sciences:

Instruction required by subdivision (b) of Section 51220 in the area of study of social sciences shall also provide a foundation for understanding the wise use of natural resources. (EC § 51221)

Mathematics:

(a) The adopted course of study for grades 7 to 12, inclusive, shall include algebra as part of the mathematics area of study pursuant to subdivision (f) of Section 51220. (EC § 51224.5)

❖ B: Graduation Requirements

California law does not set graduation requirements for private schools; each private school sets its own requirements. Although the law does not require private schools (including private homeschools) to teach the same number of courses as public schools, it does say this:

> *Children who are being instructed in a private full-time day school by persons capable of teaching shall be exempted* [from compulsory public school attendance]. *Such school shall, except under the circumstances described in Section 30* [which covers bilingual instruction], *be taught in the English language and shall offer instruction in the several branches of study required to be taught in the public schools of the state.*
> (EC § 48222)

The branches of study which private schools teaching grades 7-12 are required to offer are listed on page 211. Obviously some of the subjects, like driver education, do not need to be taught every year. But during the six years from grades 7-12, these subjects are required by California law to be offered in your school.

❖ Public School Junior High Requirements

The state does not set a specific numbers of courses required for graduation from public junior high or middle schools. Public school junior high requirements are set at the district level. Private junior high schools set their own requirements.

❖ Public School Senior High Requirements

California's graduation requirements for all *public* high schools are listed on page 216. In addition to these state-wide public school requirements, local districts may set additional requirements for students in the public high schools within their districts. For example, although not required by state law, many districts require a course in health. Since even your public school district will vary somewhat from others within the state, you should not worry about having your own graduation requirements vary from those of other schools, whether public or private.

Also, graduation requirements vary greatly among the states, so what is required as minimal in California may not meet the requirements of another state. Many states require high school students to take a semester or year course on their state's history while in high school. California does not have such a requirement, but parents who are setting up their own graduation requirements may want to add state history. Thankfully, private schools (including those in homes) have a great deal of freedom in setting up their programs.

Again, as stated above, what the law in California does require is that private schools *"...shall offer instruction in the several branches of study required to be taught in the public schools of the state..."* (EC § 48222) The branches are the same for high school as they are for junior high, and are listed on page 211.

The graduation requirements listed here are for public schools. All that is legally required of private schools in California is to offer courses is the same "branches of study." If you do intend to pattern your school's graduation requirements after those of the public schools', take special note of items (2) and (2)(b) which will help you feel more comfortable with deviating somewhat to adapt these requirements to your family's and student's needs.

The number of credits in parenthesis was added following the "5 credits per semester" system explained on pages 36-37 of this book. The California Education Code lists the public school graduation requirements only in terms of the number of years each must be studied:

> (1) *At least the following numbers of courses in the subjects specified, each course having a duration of one year, unless otherwise specified.*
> (A) *Three courses in English.* (30 credits)
> (B) *Two courses in Mathematics.* (20 credits)
> (C) *Two courses in science including biological and physical sciences.* (20 credits)
> (D) *Three courses in social studies, including United States history and geography; world history, culture, and geography; a one-semester course in American government and civics, and a one-semester course in economics.* (10 credits US History & Geography; 10 credits World History, Culture & Geography; 5 credits American Government; 5 credits Economics)
> (E) *One course in visual or performing arts or foreign language. For the purposes of satisfying the requirement specified in this subparagraph, a course in American Sign Language shall be deemed a course in foreign language.* (10 credits)
> (F) *Two courses in physical education, unless the pupil has been exempted pursuant to the provisions of this code.* (20 credits)
>
> (2) *Other course work as the governing board of the school district may by rule specify.*
> (b) *The governing board, with the active involvement of parents, administrators, teachers, and pupils, shall adopt alternative means for pupils to complete the prescribed course of study which may include practical demonstration of skills and competencies, supervised work experience or other outside school experience, career technical education classes offered in high schools, courses offered by regional occupational centers or programs, interdisciplinary study, independent study, and credit earned at a post-secondary institution. Requirements for graduation and specified alternative modes for completing the prescribed course of study shall be made available to pupils, parents, and the public.* (EC § 51225.3)

While health is not included in the graduation requirements for public schools listed in the Education Code in § 51225.3, nor in the "areas of study" quoted earlier, it is required to be taught in **public schools** as follows:

> *... at the appropriate elementary and secondary grade levels and subject areas in personal and public safety and accident prevention, including emergency first aid instruction, instruction in hemorrhage control, treatment for poisoning, resuscitation techniques, and cardiopulmonary*

resuscitation when appropriate equipment is available; fire prevention; the protection and conservation of resources, including the necessity for the protection of our environment; and health, including venereal disease and the effects of alcohol, narcotics, drugs, and tobacco upon the human body. (EC § 51202)

Also, (again, in public schools) at the "*appropriate grade levels*," local districts are to "*adopt regulations specifying the grade or grades and the course or courses in which the instruction with respect to alcohol, narcotics, restricted dangerous drugs... and other dangerous substances shall be included.*" (EC § 51203)

New for the 2003-2004 school year is a requirement that students in public schools "*shall meet or exceed the rigor of the content standards for Algebra I.*" (EC § 51224.5) This new clause has caused some confusion among homeschoolers and other private schools. First, remember that the Algebra requirement applies only to graduation from public school. Second, if you are in a program which attempts to meet or exceed the public school graduation standards, you will want to take algebra; however a clause in the code which relates to 7th and 8th grade students has also caused confusion: "*a pupil who completes coursework in grade 7 or 8 for algebra is not exempt from the mathematics requirements for grades 9 to 12.*" (EC § 51224.5) Some have erroneously interpreted this clause to means that a student who takes Algebra I in junior high cannot receive high school credit for the course. What the clause actually means is the students graduating from public high school must complete two years of math during grades 9 to 12, and if they have not already taken Algebra 1 in junior high, then one of the two high school years must be algebra. A student who took Algebra 1 in 8th grade has satisfied the algebra requirement for high school graduation and should receive high school credit for Algebra 1 based on his 8th grade studies. It is, after all, a high school level course. However, even though the algebra requirement has been met, the student would still need to take two additional years of math in grades 9 to 12, for example, Algebra 2 and Geometry.

The chart on the following page shows graduation requirements based on the public school requirements. Before using it as a basis for your own graduation requirements, you should be aware that these requirements are subject to change. In the past, for example, there have been bills before the State Legislature which proposed the following changes:

1. Change the English requirement to four years rather than three.
2. Change the math requirement to three years rather than two.
3. Change the science requirement to specify laboratory courses.
4. Award credits toward graduation for community service.

These proposals did not become law; however, since there are similar bills nearly every year, they should serve as reminders that basing your requirements on the secular school system's goals will not give you a consistent standard.

California Public High School
Minimum Graduation Requirements

Sample

This chart covers the minimal public school graduation requirements listed on page 216.
Note that these requirements may not meet college entrance requirements.

SUBJECT	9th	10th	11th	12th	REQUIREMENTS
English					30 credits 6 semesters
Mathematics (include algebra)					20 credits 4 semesters
Science					20 credits 4 semesters
World History					10 credits 2 semesters
U.S. History					10 credits 2 semesters
American Government					5 credits 1 semester
Economics					5 credits 1 semester
Fine Art or Foreign Language					10 credits 2 semesters
Physical Ed.					20 credits 4 semesters
Applied Arts					(no set # of credits required - see page 211)
Career / Technical					(no set # of credits required - see page 211)
Driver Education					2½ - 5 credits if offered
Health					2½ - 5 credits if offered
Electives					(no set amount of credits required)

Total Credits: _____ _____ _____ _____

Cumulative Total Credits: _____ _____ _____ _____

Total Credits Required:

_____

❖ C: Tests

❖ Standardized Testing

There is no legal requirement for private school students to take standardized tests in any grade in California.

❖ California High School Proficiency Exam

Any student who passes the CHSPE will be awarded a Certificate of Proficiency by the State Board of Education. California law provides that the Certificate of Proficiency *"shall be equivalent to a high school diploma."* (EC § 48412) This means that employers or institutions in California which require high school diplomas must accept the Certificate as satisfying that requirement. Federal government agencies, out-of-state universities, etc., are not bound by California law, so you should check before relying on the CHSPE Certificate to get you a federal job or college admission.

Since the State Department of Education recognizes the Certificate of Proficiency as equivalent to a diploma, some private high schools award an honorary diploma to students who have passed.

The CHSPE may be taken by persons who, on the day of the test, are 16 years of age or older, or who have completed tenth grade, or who are currently enrolled in second semester of tenth grade. This enables some 15 year olds to take the test. But passing the test does not exempt your child from the compulsory attendance law until he is 18, unless he is

---

❖ **Some Benefits of Passing the CHSPE**

1. A student who has passed the CHSPE does not need a work permit.

2. A student who has passed the CHSPE is automatically eligible for admission to California's community colleges.

3. A student who has passed the CHSPE may enroll in correspondence courses from most universities that require a high school diploma.

4. Any California employer who requires job applicants to have a high school diploma must, by law, accept the proficiency certificate as equal to a diploma. This can alleviate problems over homeschool-awarded diplomas.

---

at least 16 <u>and</u> has his parents' permission to leave school.

There is no limit to the number of times a person may take the CHSPE, so it will do no harm to take it even before a student thinks he is ready to pass it, just for experience.

The CHSPE is required by law to be offered twice a year, once in the fall and once in the spring. Additionally, the State Department of Education may choose to offer the exam during the summer. Although the CHSPE is required to be offered twice a year, in practice this has not always happened. The CHSPE is usually administered by a separate entity, based upon a contract with the State Department of Education. In the past, contracts have had a two-year duration. At the end of the contract period, a new contract must be negotiated. It is typical for the contract negotiations to overlap one of the test dates, resulting in cancellation of one of the test dates every couple of years. More frustrating is that during this contract renewal period, parents typically hear rumors that the CHSPE will never be offered again. If you are trying to arrange to take the CHSPE during one of these contract negotiation periods, be aware that "never offered again" probably means "never offered again by this particular test administrator." In all likelihood, the contract will be awarded to a different entity and will be rescheduled. If the fall test is canceled, you may have to wait until spring, or vice versa. But since the test is mandated by law, and since the test fees collected pay for its administration, it will not be permanently discontinued without an action by the California Legislature.

CHSPE Registration forms, which include test information and some sample questions, are available at your local library. You may also visit the CHSPE web site at www.chspe.com to download an application, the latest calendar of test dates, sample test questions, and general information.

The test dates are typically set for two to three years at a time, depending on the contract in effect. Note that the registration deadline may refer to the date the application must be *received*, not the postmark. Also, there are usually a few walk-in sites available throughout the state, so if you don't get your application in on time, you can call to see if there is a testing site nearby at which you can register on the day of the test.

Many home-educated students plan to take the proficiency test at age 16, then continue to junior college or take college courses at home. Following this plan, by 18, these students will have already earned an AA degree, or be ready to transfer to a university as a junior, or have completed a certificate course such as nursing or real estate. Students who take college courses at home are often even farther along in their college studies by age eighteen, some even ready to graduate with a Bachelor's degree.

CDS Code Numbers

The Registration form for the CHSPE has a space for a seven-digit "CDS Code Number." If you have an assigned number on your affidavit, your CDS code number will be in this format:

12   12345   1234567   12 12

The first three groups of digits are your school's identification number. The last two sets of digits (two each) are not part of your school's number. The number that should be included on the CHSPE registration is the third group of digits (the seven-digit number.) These seven digits are unique to your school, the first two sets of digits relating to county and district.

- **If you are enrolled in a private ISP** (Independent Study Program), ask the administrator for the CDS code number for your school.

- **If you filed a private school affidavit, *and* there are more than five students enrolled** in your private school, this number should appear on the upper right corner of an old copy of your school's affidavit when it is sent by your county each fall. Or, if you are a new school, having just filed your affidavit for the first time, (but with more than five students), your county will probably send you either a copy of your affidavit with the number filled in, or a postcard with your school's assigned number. If you do not yet have your assigned number at the time the registration for the CHSPE is due, simply write "applied for" next to the appropriate space on the form.

- **If your school has five or fewer students but you filed an affidavit for your school in October 1990 or before,** your number no longer appears on your blank affidavit each year, but it is still the correct number for your school. Look on an old affidavit (1990 or previous) and use the number shown.

- **If your affidavit was first filed in October 1991 <u>or later</u>, and your school includes five or fewer students,** you do not have a CDS code number. Don't panic—you don't need one. Simply write "N/A - homeschool" or, if you prefer, "N/A - Small Private School with no CDS code number" next to the space for the number.

❖ D: Work Permits

Work permits can be a hot issue in some counties. If you are informed regarding the law, you may have better success in trying to get a permit from a hostile county. In addition to having to follow stringent state and federal laws, each school district implements its own policies regarding the issuing of work permits. This means that there is a variety of procedures across the state, so worked for your friend may not work for you.

In addition to inconsistencies of policy, a potential problem for homeschoolers is that the person who issues the work permit also has the power to revoke it. *"If evidence is shown, **to the satisfaction of the authority issuing the permit to work**, that the school work or the health of the minor is being impaired by the employment, that authority may revoke the permit."* (EC § 49116) (Emphasis added.) The permit may also be revoked if the *"issuing authority"* believes that any provision or condition of the permit is being violated. (EC § 49164)

One official at the State Department of Education said that since he believes non-credentialed parents cannot teach their own children, he considers most homeschooled students to be truant. He further stated that truants cannot get work permits. The fact that this was his personal opinion (rather than a definition supported by law) makes this type of situation especially difficult to deal with. However, since work permits are issued at the local level, not at the state level, parents may not encounter such a prejudiced attitude at all.

Most of the high school students in California who want a work permit are able to get one. We tend to hear about the few who have a problem, not the majority who don't. But knowing that there have been some problems over work permits should serve as a caution to all that there is a need for a careful, professional attitude. Know the law and find out the standard procedure in your locale before you charge in. When you need to ask questions, do so in a confident, business-like manner.

Minors working in the entertainment industry are subject to different work permit laws and there are different procedures for obtaining work permits for the entertainment industry. These laws and procedures are discussed beginning on page 233.

The Department of Labor publishes an informative pamphlet on work permits and child labor in general. The pamphlet is called "Child Labor Law Pamphlet" and is available online at www.dir.ca.gov/dlse/. Much of the information in this chapter is derived from the pamphlet.

❖ Child Labor Law Restrictions

Federal labor laws and state laws both govern the employment of minors. When federal and state laws both apply, the more restrictive law prevails. The purpose of the work permit is to protect minors in several ways: they must not work full time (a few exceptions) so that they can attend school (EC § 49100); there are certain fields in which minors may not work (for their safety) (EC § 49164); their parents or guardians must approve of the job (EC § 49110); and the job must not endanger the health or education of the minor (EC § 49164).

Child labor laws are taken seriously in California. Violations can result in stiff penalties for employers and for parents:

> *Any person, or agent or officer thereof, employing either directly or indirectly through third persons, or any parent or guardian of a minor affected by this article who violates any provision hereof, or who employs, or permits any minor to be employed in violation hereof, is guilty of a misdemeanor, punishable by a fine of not less than one thousand dollars ($1,000) nor more than five thousand dollars ($5,000) or imprisonment in the county jail for not more than six months, or both. Any person who willfully violates this article shall, upon conviction, be subject to a fine of not more than ten thousand dollars ($10,000) or to imprisonment in the county jail for not more than six months, or both. No person shall be imprisoned under this section, except for an offense committed after the conviction of that person for a prior offense under this article.* (Labor Code § 1303)

There are additional penalties for various violations. For example, if a minor is found working in a prohibited industry, such as working with power tools on a construction site, the penalty assessed to the employer or other person who allowed the minor to work there is a minimum fine of $5,000 for each violation.

❖ When to Get a Work Permit

Work permits are needed by minors (ages 12-18) who have jobs. *You do not get a work permit until you have been offered a job.* Each permit is issued for a particular job. If you change jobs, you will need a new permit. Also, work permits issued during the school year expire five days after the opening of the next school year. So you will need a new permit at the beginning of each new school year. (EC § 49118)

Students Who DON'T Need A Work Permit

The law says that minors under the age of eighteen must have a permit to work. (EC § 49160) However, there are a number of exceptions:

1.   *"Any minor who has been graduated from a high school maintaining a four-year course above the eighth grade of elementary schools, or who has had an equal amount of education in a private school or by private tuition, or who has been awarded a certificate of proficiency"* does not need a work permit. (EC § 49101)

   If your student is 16 or 17 years old and has passed the CHSPE (see page 219) or has graduated from high school, he does not need a work permit. If there are any problems, the student may ask for a "certificate of age" from the County Superintendent. When getting this certificate, the student should be accompanied by a parent or guardian and should bring his birth certificate and "Certificate of Proficiency," (received when he passed the CHSPE) or his high school diploma. *"The certificate of age shall serve as a permit to employ a minor who is not by law required to attend school, and who is otherwise required to hold a permit to work." (EC § 49114)*

2. *"In order that children may be disciplined and trained in habits of work and industry by their parents, guardians, or other persons standing in the place of parents, nothing in this chapter shall require a permit to work to be issued to any minor or require a permit to employ to be issued to the parent or guardian when the work or intended work to be performed by the minor is performed upon or in connection with the premises owned, operated, or controlled by the parent or guardian. Nothing in this section shall be held to affect existing provisions of law which require permits to work to be issued to minors employed in manufacturing, mercantile, or similar commercial enterprises by their parents or guardians, or to do work which is otherwise forbidden..." (EC § 49141)*

    Nothing in this article ... shall prohibit or prevent either of the following: (a) The employment of any minor at agricultural, horticultural, viticultural, or domestic labor during the time the public schools are not in session, or during other than school hours, when the work performed is for or under the control of his parent or guardian and is performed upon or in connection with premises owned, operated or controlled by the parent or guardian. (LC § 1394)

    Because work for parents is covered in both the Education and Labor Codes, and because each code addresses the topic differently, there is some disagreement about when children are exempt from work permit requirements when working for their parents. It appears that as long as the work being performed is not of a type prohibited, such as working of certain power tools, your child may work for or with you, his parents, or for adults who are standing in your place (in other words, relatives, close friends, church elders, etc. who are known to the family) without a permit, except in manufacturing, mercantile, or similar commercial enterprises, or work which is otherwise forbidden for minors.

3. Minors who are self-employed do not require permits.

4. Minors *irregularly* employed in odd jobs in private homes, such as baby-sitting, lawn mowing, and leaf raking, do not need to obtain a work permit.

5. Minors engaged in the sale and distribution of newspapers or magazines are often self-employed, and thus do not require permits. Minors who are at least 14 years of age and employed to deliver newspapers to consumers do not require permits, whether or not they are self-employed. (EC § 49112(d))

6. Minors of any age who participate in any horseback riding exhibition, contest, or event, whether or not they receive payment for services or prize money do not need to obtain a work permit. (EC §§ 49119, 49165; LC § 1308(b)(3)) **Note:** Minors under 16 years of age are prohibited from participating in any rough stock rodeo event, circus or race. "Rough stock rodeo event" means any rodeo event operated for profit or operated by other than a nonprofit organization in which unbroken, little-trained, or imperfectly trained animals are ridden or handled by the participant, and shall include, but not be limited to, saddle bronc riding, bareback riding, and bull riding. "Race" means any speed contest between two or more animals that are on a course at the same time and that is operated for profit or operated other than by a nonprofit organization. (LC 1308(b)(3))

❖ Where to Get a Work Permit

First, according to the California Education Code, it is the Superintendent of the school district in which a student lives who has the ultimate authority to issue work permits to minors in his district, regardless of where the minor attends (or doesn't attend) school. The reason for this is that the Legislature, in passing laws related to child labor, desired to make sure that children would not be working when they ought to be in school. (Think of the "olden" days when children were sent out as chimney sweeps rather than being taught to read.) So the Superintendent has the job of making sure that children aren't being exploited by going to work instead of school.

Second, the Superintendent of the local school district has the authority to delegate others to issue permits in his place. This is the rule across the state, for every school district, by state law:

> It is the intent of the Legislature that school district personnel responsible for issuing work permits to minors have a working knowledge of California labor laws as they relate to minors; and further, that personnel be trained to provide the pupils practical personal guidance in career education. **The superintendent of any school district in which any minor resides**, a person holding a services credential with a specialization in pupil personnel services authorized by the superintendent in writing, or a certificated work experience education teacher or coordinator authorized by the superintendent in writing, **may issue to certain minors permits to work**. If the minor resides in a portion of a county not under the jurisdiction of the superintendent of any school district, the permit to work shall be issued by the superintendent of schools of the county, by a person holding a services credential with a specialization in pupil personnel services authorized by the superintendent in writing, or a certificated work experience education teacher or coordinator authorized by the superintendent in writing. No permit to work shall be issued until the written request therefor from the parent, guardian, foster parent, or residential shelter services provider, has been filed with the issuing authority.

> In the event that the certificated person designated by the superintendent to issue work permits is not available, and delay in issuing a permit would jeopardize the ability of a pupil to secure work, a person authorized by the superintendent may issue the work permit.

> In the event that a district does not employ or contract with a person holding a services credential with a specialization in pupil personnel services or with a certificated work experience education teacher or coordinator, the superintendent may authorize, in writing, a person who does not hold that credential to issue permits to work during periods of time in which the superintendent is absent from the district. (EC § 49110) (Emphasis added.)

> **The superintendent of any school district may designate the principal or other person having charge of a private school** within the district, in which pupils are enrolled pursuant to Section 48222, as a person authorized **to issue work permits to pupils of the school**, in accordance with this chapter. Where the pupil resides in a portion of the county not under the jurisdiction of the superintendent of any school district, the county superintendent of schools may designate the principal or other person having charge of a private school as the person authorized to issue such work permits. The superintendent of the school district, or the county superintendent of schools as the case may be, shall periodically ascertain that the designated person has complied with the requirements of this chapter pertaining to issuing authorities. (EC § 49110.1) (Emphasis added.)

Remember that it is the Superintendent of each school district who has authority both to issue permits and to authorize someone else to issue them. The policies of each district therefore vary. Most commonly, the Superintendent authorizes one or more persons in the district to issue permits. Much depends on the size of the district and on the number of high schools, both public and private, within it. Usually the Superintendent authorizes a person at the local public high school to issue permits to the public school students enrolled in it. Often this is a career or guidance counselor. For students who do not attend the local public high school, there is a variety of scenarios:

1) The public school person who is authorized to issue permits to students enrolled in his school may also be authorized to issue permits to private school students in the district, OR

2) The private school students may need to go directly to the office of education and obtain work permits there (not usually directly from the Superintendent, but more likely from his authorized staff person), OR

3) The Superintendent may authorize a private school principal to issue permits to students in their school, OR

4) The Superintendent may authorize a private school official (or other person) to issue permits for all private school students from all private schools.

These are the most common scenarios, but there could be another system in your district. Therefore, the bottom line is that you will need to find out which system is in place in your district. In order to find out the system in place in your district, follow these steps:

If you are enrolled in a private independent study program (ISP), your principal may have (or be able to get) permission from the district superintendent to issue work permits, or the principal will find out where the students in your ISP should go to get one.

If you have filed your own private school affidavit, call your local school district, and ask where students *from private schools* should get work permits. If asked, tell them you are enrolled in a small private school that does not have authority to issue work permits.

If you have not filed an affidavit and are not enrolled in a private ISP, you may be able to get a work permit through the same means as someone who has filed an affidavit. Your student may be considered truant because he is not enrolled in a school, or he is enrolled in a school which is not in compliance with the state law (since your school has not filed an affidavit), so avoid discussions about this when applying for a work permit.

If your student is offered a job in the entertainment industry, see the section beginning on page 233.

❖ Authority to Issue a Work Permit

A key is that when the Superintendent grants authority for someone to issue permits, he also grants that authority **only as to certain students**. Most commonly, this means that the public school person who issues permits can *only* legally issue them to students enrolled in his own school. However, as noted above, it is also common to find a district in which a public school person has authority to issue permits to all students who reside in a district, regardless of which school they attend.

One common error is that some homeschool parents have thought that as long as they could get a blank form, they could fill it out and their child would then have a valid work permit. This is not so. Only a person authorized by the Superintendent of the school district may issue permits, and then only to the students to whom he is authorized to issue them. Stiff fines can be imposed on employers who employ students who do not have valid permits, so it's an important issue. You can't just get a form from a nice school official who has extras and then issue it yourself.

❖ Going to get the Work Permit

If your district's policy is to have all work permits issued by the public school, go to the local high school to get a work permit. A parent should accompany the student. Be prepared to give the name and phone number of your private school, and the name of the business, name of employer, and phone number where the minor has been offered a job. If the public high school issues permits to all private school students in the district, you should have no problems in getting one issued to you.

There have been some cases in which homeschooled students were denied a work permit simply because they were being home educated. Because of these cases, it is best to be prepared ahead of time. The most important tip is that you should not mention the words "homeschool." The reason is that "homeschooling" is a term coined by home educators. It is not a "legal-ese" definition.

Consider this—when dealing with public school officials, must other private schools explain that theirs is a "Montessori school" or a "Waldorf School" or a "Catholic Boarding School?" Of course not. They are simply private schools. Do not confuse the issue by using home educators' jargon. The correct legal term which the public school officials will understand is "private school," whether that school is based at a large campus, renovated storefront, or a residence. Use the correct terminology, and you will avoid many questions and problems.

Whatever your district's policy on work permits for private school students, it should apply to you. You may talk to someone who believes your school is not legal. This has not been shown in a court of law. But if you want to get a work permit, not argue legalities, be polite and friendly. Try to keep the conversation to the issue at hand—getting your private school student a work permit. If necessary, end the conversation with a "Thank-you for your time" and call another person in the district. It is possible that there is another person in your area who can give work permits.

❖ If You Are Denied a Work Permit

1. Find out why you were denied. It may be a reason that is easy to remedy. Perhaps they simply need a proof of age or a signature by your school principal.

2. Help your student to get a job in a situation where a work permit is not needed, i.e. for you or for a close family friend who does not work in a manufacturing or merchant business.

3. If you feel your student simply must have a job which requires a work permit, and if it was denied because you operate as a private school in your own home (you file an affidavit), consider joining a private independent study program (ISP) that issues work permits.

4. Contact Home School Legal Defense Association if you are a member. They may be able to tell you of any new changes affecting the laws related to work permits.

❖ Work Permit Forms

Two separate forms are needed in obtaining a work permit. Usually, both forms can be filled out at once, after a job offer has been made to the student.

Form B1-1 is a "Statement of Intent to Employ Minor and Request for Work Permit." This form has a section for the minor, a section for the school, and a section for the employer to complete before a work permit is issued. A copy of the Form B1-1 is shown on page 230.

Form B-1, the "Request for Work Permit and Statement of Intent to Employ Minor," has two copies: the first copy is to be kept by the issuing authority (this will be the place you received the form—probably either a local public school, private school, or County Office of Education.) The second copy is to be kept by the employer.

Form B1-4 is the work permit (called a "Permit to Employ and Work.") A copy of the B1-4 is shown on page 231.

The "Permit to Employ and Work" also has two copies: the top one is to be kept by the employer, and the second copy is to be returned to the issuing authority. If you want to have a copy for your own records, you will need to make a photo copy before returning the forms to the issuing authority. (This is not necessary, legally, but some families like to keep a copy with their school file.) If you do keep a copy of the permit, it is *not* part of your student's cum file and is *not* transferred to another school.

Form B-4, the "Permit to Employ and Work," is technically issued after the "Request for Work Permit and Statement of Intent to Employ Minor," but often both forms will be given to you at the same time. The usual procedure is for you to take both forms to the employer to fill out; then return with them to the person who is issuing the permit. The issuing authority will check the forms, sign the permit, and either give you the two copies to be returned to the employer or will mail the employer's copy. Of course, each official may vary this slightly. Just be sure you listen carefully and understand the instructions given to you when you get the forms. There are stiff penalties for employers who hire minors without having these forms properly issued.

The following two samples include the information as it is on the actual forms, but are samples only. They may not be used in place of the actual forms.

Statement of Intent to Employ Minor and Request for Work Permit
Not a work permit—Print all information except signatures

For Minor to Complete

▶

Minor's name (last name first)	Social security number	Date of birth	Age	Grade

Street address	City	ZIP code	Home telephone

School name

Street address	City	ZIP code	School telephone

For Employer to Complete (Please review rules for employment of minors on reverse.)

▶

Name of business

Maximum number of hours of employment when school is in session:

Mon. _____ Tue. _____ Wed. _____ Thurs. _____ Fri. _____ Sat. _____ Sun. _____ Weekly = _____

In compliance with California labor laws, this employee is covered by workers' compensation insurance. This business does not discriminate unlawfully on the basis of race, ethnic background, religion, sex, sexual orientation, color, national origin, ancestry, age, physical handicap, or medical condition. I hereby certify that, to the best of my knowledge, the information herein is correct and true.

Supervisor's signature	Supervisor's name (print or type)

For Parent or Guardian to Complete

This minor is being employed at the place of work described with my full knowledge and consent. I hereby certify that, to the best of my knowledge, the information herein is correct and true. I request that a work permit be issued.

In addition to this employer, my child is working for:

_____
Name of business

Signature of parent or legal guardian	Date

For School to Complete

▶
_____
Evidence of minor's age

_____
Signature of verifying authority

Type:
Regular _____
Vacation _____
Year-Round _____
Work Experience Education _____
Other (specify) _____

CALIFORNIA DEPARTMENT OF EDUCATION FORM B1-1 (revised 6/03)

PERMIT TO EMPLOY AND WORK

Expires: _____
(No later than five days after beginning of next school year.)

Type: Regular _____ Work Experience Education _____
Vacation_____ Other (specify) _____
Year-Round ____ (specify schedule under "Other remarks")

Maximum Work Hours

School In Session

(Any week in which public school is scheduled for at least one day.)

Mon .- Thurs. _____ Friday* _____ Sat. __8__ Sun. __8__

*And any schoolday that immediately precedes a non-schoolday. e.g., a school holiday

Weekly Maximum _____ Spread of Hours ** _____

School Not In Session

(Any week in which public school is not scheduled for at least one day.)

Monday through Sunday __8__

Weekly Maximum _____ Spread of Hours** _____

** Ages 14 and 15: 7 a.m.-7 p.m. on any one day except June 1 through Labor Day when the hour is extended until 9 p.m. (L.C. 1391).
Ages 16 and 17: 5 a.m.-10 p.m. on until 12:30 a.m. preceding any non-schoolday (L.C. 1391).

Spread of hours that minor must be in school _____ (required for "Regular" and "Year-Round" permits only)

Remarks

- May not be employed in or around hazardous occupations and/or equipment as specified in the Fair Labor Standards Act, U.S. Department of Labor Bulletins 101 and 102, California Labor Code, and California Code of Regulations, Title 8.
- Work Permit does not verify citizenship.
- Under 18 years of age, may not drive a vehicle on public streets as a condition of employment [V.C. 12515 and L.C. 1294.1(b)]
- Other remarks/limitations: _____
_____
_____
_____

Valid only at:

_____
Name of Business

Minor's Name (last name, first)	Social Security Number	Date of Birth	Age at Issuance
			(___)_____
Street Address	City	Zip Code	Home Telephone
			(___)_____
School Name Street Address	City	Zip Code	School Telephone

_____   _____   _____
Signature of Minor   Signature of Issuing Authority   Date

Employer's Worker's Compensation Insurance Company

Maximum number of hours of employment when School is in session:

_____

California Department of Education Form No. B1-4 (revised 11/97)

❖ Hours That Minors May Work

Federal law and state law both cover hours that minors may work. Again, where the two laws have different provision, the more stringent law takes precedence. The regulations are listed on the back of the work permit and are summarized on the chart below.

	Ages 16 & 17 Must have completed 7th grade to work while school in session.	Ages 14 & 15 Must have completed 7th grade to work while school in session	Ages 12 & 13
SCHOOL IN SESSION *	4 hours per day on any schoolday. 8 hours on any non-schoolday or on any day preceding a non-schoolday. 48 hours per week. Work Experience Education students & personal attendants** may work more than 4 hours on a schoolday, but never more than 8.	3 hours per schoolday outside of school hours. 8 hours on any non-schoolday. 18 hours per week. Work Experience Education students may work during school hours & up to 23 hours per week.	May be employed only during school holidays and vacations (usually construed to include weekends). May never be employed on any schoolday, either before or after school. Daily and weekly work hour maximums while school is in session are not specified in statute, but may not exceed the maximum allowed when school is not in session or the maximum stated on permit. Not eligible for Work Experience Education programs.
SCHOOL NOT IN SESSION	8 hours per day. 48 hours per week.	8 hours per day. 40 hours per week.	8 hours per day. 40 hours per week.
SPREAD OF HOURS	5 a.m. – 10 p.m. However, until 12:30 a.m. on any evening preceding a nonschoolday. WEE students, with permission, until 12:30 a.m. on any day. Messengers: 6 a.m. – 9 p.m.	7 a.m. – 7 p.m., except that from June 1 through Labor Day, until 9 p.m.	7 a.m. – 7 p.m., except that from June 1 through Labor Day, until 9 p.m.

* Statutes governing workhours for 14- and 15-year-olds use the phrase, "while school is in session", for the three-hour day, 18-hour week. California provides no precise definition of this phrase. However, the phrase is also used in federal regulations from which California's standard is derived. (29 CFR 570.35(a)) The U.S. Department of Labor considers the term "school in session" to mean the scheduled schooldays of the public school system in the county where the minor resides. A school week under federal standards is any week during which school is in session for at least one day. Thus, school is considered in session during any week that has at least one scheduled schoolday. Since the school session is derived from the schedule for the county's public schools, school may be considered in session for a minor who attends a private school that is closed during the summer if the public schools are in session at that same time.

** "Personal attendant" includes baby-sitters and means any person employed by a private householder or by any third party employer recognized in the health care industry to work in a private household, to supervise, feed, or dress a child or person who by reason of advanced age, physical disability, or mental deficiency needs supervision. The status of 'personal attendant' shall apply when no significant amount of work other than the foregoing is required.

With few exceptions, all employees are entitled to one day of rest in seven. (LC §§ 551, 552) Days of rest may be accumulated providing that in each calendar month the employee receives the equivalent of one day of rest in seven. (LC § 554) A violation of Sections 551, 552 and 554 is a misdemeanor. (LC § 553) School attendance is not considered work time.

Under extreme conditions, it may be possible for an age 14-16 non-graduate minor student to obtain a permit for full-time work. This is only permissible if the parent or guardian is incapacitated through illness or injury, if the father has died or deserted the family, and if aid for the family cannot be secured in any other way. A full investigation would be required to verify these circumstances.

There are a number of exceptions to the rules regarding work hours. If your student desires to work different hours than what is allowed on the chart, review the Department of Labor's pamphlet online.

❖ Working in the Entertainment Industry

Different rules apply to minors who desire a permit to work in the entertainment industry. Businesses who employ minors in this industry are typically well-versed in the rules and should be able to help if you have problems obtaining a permit.

There are two basic types of entertainment industry work permits: blanket work permits and individual work permits.

Blanket Permits

Blanket permits are for "groups of minors hired for special events or particular productions lasting a limited time." Employers who hire such groups will most likely help you with the procedure. Basic requirements are that there must be at least one accompanying parent or guardian for every 20 minors. Each student will need a school verification and parental consent form, but the employer should be able to provide these for your student. One blanket permit is issued for the whole group and a list of the minors' names is attached. These permits expire at the end of the special event for which they are issued.

Individual Permits

Minors working in entertainment industry jobs for which a blanket permit does not apply, will need an individual permit. The application may be downloaded and printed from the Department of Labor Standards Enforcement website: www.dir.ca.gov/dlse/DLSEForm277.pdf, or you may get a copy from any DLSE office. A sample copy of the application appears on page 235. Once you have printed the form, the parent or guardian must complete the top part of the form, and then print and sign his or her name.

An authorized school official must complete the "School Record" section in the middle part of the form, and then sign it, print his or her title or position, and affix the school's seal or stamp. The DLSE instructions include the following description of who constitute an authorized school official: "i.e., principal, vice principal, dean, headmistress, headmaster, counselor or the minor's teacher." Also, the instructions specifically state that "Minors who attend a private full-time day school must obtain the written verification from the principal or other person having charge of the private school." To clarify, follow the directions on the next page for obtaining the school official's signature.

If you are enrolled in a private independent study program (ISP), then your school's principal or headmaster should sign the form and affix the school stamp or seal.

If you have filed your own private school affidavit, the person listed as principal on your affidavit should sign. If your school does not have a stamp or seal, you may want to purchase one from a stationery or office supply store. The seal should have the school name and the words "official seal" on it.

If you have not filed an affidavit and are not enrolled in a private ISP, you will probably not be able to get a work permit because your student is legally considered truant.

The process for getting an individual permit is different for work during school vacation or holidays. First, obtain and complete the top part of the application as discussed abo ve. Then, instead of having the school official complete the middle part and affix a seal, simply attach the student's most recent report card to the application and send or take it to any office of Department of Labor Standards Enforcement. A letter from the school principal stating that the "minor is 'satisfactory' in all academic subjects, health and attendance" may be sent instead of the report card. However, if the principal and the parent are the same person, a report card in standard school format may raise fewer questions. Entertainment permits that are issued based on report cards will be effective only when school is not in session.

Once the application form is complete, you may mail or take it personally it to the nearest DLSE office. If you mail it, include a self-addressed stamped envelope. The permit will be mailed to you.

If your student has previously had an entertainment industry work permit and is seeking to renew it, follow the same procedures described above, but also include a copy of the old permit.

At their discretion, the DLSE may also require a physical examination to ensure that the minor is physically able to perform the duties required.

Exception: Minors of any age may appear in the following venues without permits:

1. In any church, public or religious school, or community entertainment;

2. In any school entertainment or in any entertainment for charity or for children, for which no admission fee is charged;

3. In any radio or television broadcasting exhibition, where the minor receives no compensation directly or indirectly therefor, and where the engagement of the minor is limited to a single appearance lasting not more than one hour, and where no admission fee is charged for the radio broadcasting or television exhibition;

4. At any one event during a calendar year, occurring on a day on which school attendance is not required or on the day preceding such a day, lasting four hours or less, where a parent or guardian of the minor is present, for which the minor does not directly or indirectly receive any compensation.

STATE OF CALIFORNIA
Division of Labor Standards Enforcement

APPLICATION FOR PERMISSION TO WORK IN THE ENTERTAINMENT INDUSTRY

THIS IS NOT A PERMIT ☐ NEW ☐ RENEWAL

PROCEDURES FOR OBTAINING WORK PERMIT

1. Complete the information required below.
2. School authorities must complete the School Record section below.
3. For minors 15 days through kindergarten, please attach a certified copy of the minor's birth certificate. See reverse side for other documents that may be accepted.
4. Mail or present the complete application to any office of the Division of Labor Standards Enforcement for issuance of your work permit.

Name of Child	Professional Name, if applicable

Permanent Address	Home Phone No.

School Attending	Grade

Date of Birth	Age	Height	Weight	Hair Color	Eye Color	Sex

Statement of Parent or Guardian: It is my desire that an Entertainment Work Permit be issued to the above named child. I will read the rules governing such employment and will cooperate to the best of my ability in safeguarding his or her educational, moral and physical interest. I hereby certify, under penalty of perjury, that the foregoing statements are true and correct.

Name of Parent or Guardian (print or type)	Signed	Day time phone #

SCHOOL RECORD

☐ I certify that the above-named minor meets the school district's requirements with respect to age, school record, attendance and health.
☐ Does not meet the district's requirements and permit should not be issued.

Authorized School Official	Date	
School Address	School Telephone	[School Seal or Stamp]

HEALTH RECORD
COMPLETE THIS SECTION IF INSTRUCTED TO DO SO OR IF INFANT UNDER ONE MONTH OF AGE

Name of Doctor _____ Address _____ Telephone Number _____

I certify that I am Board Certified in pediatrics and have carefully examined
_____ and, in my opinion:

He/She is physically fit to be employed in the production of motion pictures and television.
If less than one month, infant is at least 15 days old, was carried to full term, and is physically able to perform.

_____ M.D.   _____
Signature   Date

❖ E: Driver Education & Driver Training

In California, minors may not obtain provisional driver's licenses unless they have taken "approved" courses in driver education and driver training. Note that there are two separate courses involved: **Driver Education** (the classroom course) and **Driver Training** (the behind-the-wheel course.)

Current law allows Driver Education and Driver Training (DE/DT) to be offered by public high schools, private high schools, and commercial driving schools. A parent may not teach the course to his own child *unless* the parent also happens to be a teacher at the student's high school or is a licensed driving instructor. If you are a private school teacher, whether in a large campus-based school, a private ISP, or your own small school based in your home, then you may teach DE/DT to students in your class, just as you may teach any another class. Remember, however, that you are teaching DE/DT in your capacity as a private school teacher—not as a parent. This is an important distinction in dealing with the Department of Motor Vehicles.

Parents whose children are enrolled in a private ISP should verify with the administrator that the parent is the actual teacher. For example, are your teacher qualifications kept on file by the private ISP? Are you included in the number of teachers tallied on the private school affidavit? In some ISPs, parents are only teachers' aides and in this case, the parents cannot teach DE/DT.

❖ Communicating with DMV

It is important that all communications with the DMV be in writing, never by telephone. There have been instances in which private schools have received letters from the DMV listing a phone number and an invitation to call with questions. However, experience has shown that telephone calls usually worsen the situation by setting up an opportunity for private school administrators to be asked questions for which they are unprepared, only to have their hesitancy or incorrect responses used as reason for further denials or delays.

Although corresponding by mail is slow and requires patience, take the time to write all questions or requests. If there is no response, if you receive a request from DMV for more information, or if you receive a denial letter, take time to write again. Allow at least 30 days for DMV to respond to each letter or request you send before writing again.

All private schools must offer driver education (the classroom course) because it is one of the "branches of study" required in the Education Code. (See page 211.) In addition, private schools *may* offer driver training (the behind-the-wheel course), but there is no requirement that they offer driver training at all. Even with the requirement that private schools offer driver education, there is nothing to require their driver education course to be an "approved" one. An approved course is necessary only if your students intend to use your school's course to fulfill the requirements for obtaining an Instruction Permit or Provisional Driver's License.

As with any other course offered in private schools, content varies from school to school. Private schools who want to fulfill their requirement to offer driver education as a "branch of study," but who do not wish to provide an "approved" course which allows students to obtain drivers' licenses, do not need to follow the course descriptions on the following pages. However, schools who want their students to be able to use their driver education courses to obtain licenses will want to follow the descriptions shown.

An "approved" course is one that is *"maintained pursuant to provisions of the Education Code."* (Vehicle Code § 12814.6) It is important to note that private schools are not required to use state-credentialed teachers for any subject, including driver education or driver training. Even "approved" courses in private schools do not require credentialed or certified teachers.

Because of DMV's policy review and subsequent clarification of their regulations, there are currently four options for private school students to take "approved" DE/DT courses:

❖ Definitions of Terms

Before working with the DMV, know the following terms:

Approved Course: a DE/DT course maintained according to the appropriate provisions of the California Education Code.

Driver Education: the classroom course.

Driver Training: the behind-the-wheel or laboratory course.

Instruction permit: the permit issued by DMV which allows a student to practice driving accompanied by a licensed driver at least 25 years old.

Provisional License: the driver's license issued to drivers of ages 16-17. This license becomes a regular driver's license when the driver turns 18 years old.

Requisition Form: the form (DL 396) used by schools to order materials from DMV.

Student License: the license issued by a school principal which allows a student to drive under the supervision of the Driver Training instructor.

1. Take the course at the private school at which the student is enrolled full-time.

2. Take the course at another private school which will allow your student to take the course. The student must either take the course *for free*, or if tuition is charged, the student must be enrolled in more than just DE/DT. For example, a student who takes at least one additional academic course may also take DE/DT, and the student may be charged tuition for all courses taken.

3. Take the class at a licensed commercial driving school. Check prices at several schools, or get several high schoolers together and ask about a group rate.

4. Wait until your student is age 17½ to get an instruction permit, and then age 18 to get a driver's license. In this case, approved driver education and driver training courses are not required.

❖ Non-approved Courses

Driver education has become a hot issue during the past few years, largely because of animosity from commercial driving schools, which are highly regulated, toward private high schools, which are not. Commercial driving schools have pressed for legislation to "level the playing field" by regulating private high schools. At the same time, new educational trends have raised the stakes: online and distance programs have started up lower-cost programs which have drawn students away from the commercial schools operating in classrooms.

With the onslaught of new course offerings, DMV has attempted to review and clarify their policies and regulations, with only limited success. In the past few years, DMV has filed several law suits to shut down distance-learning driver education programs. Although DMV lost these cases, the battle clearly has just begun. One area which has become a focus of attention is "private schools" offering only driver education. As stated previously, private schools can offer driver education as part of their course of study. However, some program operators have discovered that the private school laws are much more flexible than the commercial school laws. So some driver education programs which have formerly operated under the commercial driving school regulations have chosen to file private school affidavits and declare themselves to be private high schools even though they are open about the fact that the only course they offer is driver education. Sadly, this has brought all private schools under scrutiny and current efforts are being made to limit private school freedoms in order to halt commercial driving schools from circumventing the legal restrictions imposed upon them by the Vehicle Code.

The bottom line for families considering enrolling in a driver education program offered by someone else is that there are many schools offering programs which are not in compliance with the law even though they have not been shut down. However, considering the spotlight that has been focused on driver education programs, particularly within private schools, the situation is likely to change. This means that students who are enrolled in questionable programs could find their certificates of completion or instruction permits denied by DMV. Worse, private schools could face legislative battles over freedoms affecting all their programs because of the problems over driver education.

Parents should check out any program offering driver education before enrolling. Find out whether the certificate of completion offered is a private school form or a commercial school form. If it's a commercial school, check it out by calling the DMV. If it's a private school, make sure it's in compliance with the laws, not only by filing an affidavit, but by offering courses in all the branches of study listed on page 211, and by having students enrolled in those courses. Remember that simply filing an affidavit does not create a school.

❖ Enrolling Outside Students

The DMV has stated that their interpretation of the law is that if private schools charge tuition for DE/DT courses, they may not offer the courses to outside students. According to the DMV, if a private or public high school allows an outside student to enroll *only* for DE/DT, and if the school charges tuition for the course, then the school is acting as a commercial driving school for that student. The DMV maintains that it is possible to operate both a private secondary school (in the case of students who are enrolled full-time) and a commercial driving school (in the case of students who take only DE/DT for a fee) at the same time.

A commercial driving school is defined as a *"business which, for compensation, conducts or offers to conduct instruction in the operation of motor vehicles."* (VC § 310.6) Commercial driving schools are licensed by the DMV and have strict requirements for instructors and course content.

To avoid problems with the DMV, offer driver education and driver training only to your full-time enrolled students, that is, those students who are included in the tally of students on your private school affidavit and who are exempt from attendance at public school because they are "instructed in a full time day school" (EC §48222.) The

DMV has stated they will not send forms to any school which appears to be offering DE/DT for a fee to outside students, unless the school is licensed to operate as a commercial driving school.

❖ Teaching Driver Education & Driver Training

The rest of this section will concern teaching driver education and driver training as a part of a private school's curriculum, and assumes that you desire to teach an "approved" course so that your students will be able to use it to fulfill the requirements to get their provisional drivers' licenses. Whether you are going to teach only driver education, or both driver education and driver training, you must plan ahead.

The required paperwork is available to schools for free from the DMV in Sacramento, but may be ordered *only once per year*, so you need to know ahead of time how many students will be taking your course during the year, including all courses in fall, spring and summer terms. The paperwork from DMV includes Student Examinations on the Vehicle Code, Parent-Teen Training Aides, Student Licenses, Secondary School DE/DT Handbooks, and all the necessary forms and certificates to be used by schools. Textbooks, workbooks, and other teaching materials for use in the classroom are not available from DMV. Some sources for these items are listed on page 247-248.

Schools should always communicate with DMV in writing, not by telephone. Of course, when students apply for instruction permits or provisional drivers' licenses, they will visit a DMV field office in person, accompanied by a parent. However, in this situation, the parents are following standard procedure as parents of minor applicants; they are not representatives of a school.

❖ Ordering Materials from the DMV

Private schools must request materials from DMV *after* their annual affidavit has been filed and processed for the school year in which they intend to use the materials. This allows the DMV to verify that the affidavit is on file for the current year. Private schools may begin teaching driver education courses at the beginning of the school year; they simply won't receive the completion certificates and other forms from the DMV until later in the fall term. Private schools may still order materials from DMV *only once* per year.

In ordering materials, requests are sent to DMV by the private school administrator, not individual teachers. Materials must be ordered on the DMV Requisition Form (DL 396). So the first step in ordering materials from DMV is to obtain a copy of the DMV's Requisition Form. Then the form must be filled out and returned to DMV for processing and filling of the order.

Obtaining a DMV Requisition Form (DL 396)

Send a letter on school letterhead requesting the DMV to send you a Requisition Form. If your school has a CDS code number, include it. You may send your request in September so that you will have your Requisition Form when you file your private school affidavit in October. Mail your request for a Requisition Form to the DMV address shown in the sample letter at the right.

In the past, some schools have been denied Requisition Forms. The letters of denial indicated that the schools would need to verify that they were "bona fide" schools, by sending various documents to the DMV, such as school catalogs, courses of study, etc. There is no law requiring such items to be sent to any state agency, nor is there any requirement for private schools even to have these kinds of things.

The DMV has stated that their policy has been revised so that the Requisition Form will be sent upon request to any school. However, it is possible that your school could receive a denial letter from the DMV. If so, the letter should state the reason for denial. You may be able to solve the problem simply by sending another letter clarifying your request. See the section on "Handling DMV Denials" on pages 251-253 before responding to a denial from DMV, and remember to respond in writing, never by telephone.

Using the Requisition Form to Order Materials from DMV

Ordering materials from DMV requires planning ahead. If you sent a request to DMV for a Requisition Form in September, you should have it on hand by the time you file your annual private school affidavit in early October. If you did not request a form in September, you can do so at any time of year, as long as you only order materials from DMV once per year. Keep in mind, however, that in the past, the DMV has revised forms and materials during the early spring, with new versions not being ready until as late as summer. So if you request a Requisition Form or try to order materials during late spring or early summer, you may wind up being delayed until the end of summer, only to find that you now need to wait until you file your private school affidavit again before the DMV will fill your order.

Here is a suggested time table for preparing and ordering materials from DMV:

1. During enrollment or planning for fall term, determine how many students will take driver education, driver training, or both in the upcoming full year, including fall, spring, or summer sessions.

2. You may start your course at any time, using the teaching materials you have selected, even though you do not yet have your forms from DMV.

3. In early September, send your request for a Requisition Form (DL 396) to DMV, as discussed on page 240. Remember that DMV sometimes changes their Requisition Forms, and if they are making changes, there will likely be a delay in sending the forms to schools.. Even without changes causing delays, it commonly takes at least 30 days to receive a response from DMV when you write to request the form. Be patient. If it has been more than 30 days <u>and</u> is past September of the year in which you plan to use the DMV materials you are ordering, <u>and</u> you have received no response from the DMV, resubmit your request in writing. All communication with the DMV should be in writing, never by telephone.

4. Between October 1 and October 15, file your private school affidavit. After October 15, send in your DMV Requisition Form.

5. In the past, the DMV required schools ordering materials for the first time, or schools which had not ordered materials for the previous year, to provide the DMV with a letter of verification that the affidavit was filed. Currently, most school districts and the State Department of Education have refused to provide such letters because of concern that the letters would be used to claim that a particular private school was "approved" or "endorsed." Further, most affidavits are now filed online rather than via mail to the local district. Therefore, the DMV dropped their requirement for such a letter to be provided and instead now requires that a copy of the private school affidavit be included with the completed Requisition Form *each time* a school orders materials.

6. Be sure that when you are filing your private school affidavit, before you click "send" on the online form, print a copy of your filled-in form to save.

7. Because the DMV has changed their forms and policies every few years during the past decade or more, it is possible that procedures have changed by the time you are reading this book. A supplemental memo, "Update on Private Schools and the DMV," may be available from CHEA at nominal cost to those who have purchased this manual. Before you fill out and send in your Requisition Form, call CHEA at (562) 864-2432

to ask if you need an update. Be prepared to give the publication date from the front cover of this book so the staff person answering your call can compare the date of this edition with any updates available.

Please be aware that the information in this book and any supplemental memo is prepared to the best of our ability, but that neither CHEA nor this author can guarantee that the DMV will honor requests or orders. We only wish we had that kind of control! If you fill out the form according to the directions on the memo, but receive a denial from DMV, see the section on "Handling DMV Denials" on pages 251-253 before taking action.

To avoid having to check with DMV to find out which certificates and DE/DT forms have been revised each year, schools should order only what is needed for one year and reorder all items each year. Also be sure to order the *Secondary School DE/DT Handbook* (DL 612) each year. This manual explains in detail how to fill out each of the DE/DT forms, and how and when to issue Student Licenses. It is updated yearly. Be sure to read all directions carefully before filling out or issuing any forms or certificates.

Finally, be aware that "Certificates of Completion" are currently numbered and tracked. Schools may not obtain forms from anyone other than DMV. For example, a school may not use "extra" forms from another school in the area which ordered more than they needed. The DMV has stated that they are considering bar-coding the forms in the future. This is reportedly so that they can make sure that the forms are not misused, and also so that they can begin to study the effectiveness of the various driver education and driver training courses. For example, they may track the number of tickets received by teen drivers and where the teens took DE/DT to see whether training at commercial schools is superior to training in high schools. They also may track attendance at traffic violators' schools to monitor their effectiveness.

Filling Out the DMV's Authorization/Requisition for Driver Instruction Forms

If you have received the Requisition Form (DL 396), there should be a memo attached, entitled "Ordering Driver Instruction Supplies." Several items in the memo and on the form itself, have caused confusion among private schools. The following is intended to clarify the instructions as they apply to private schools. It is not intended as, nor should it be construed as, legal advice.

It will be most helpful to have your DMV memo and DL 396 handy as you read through this information. For your convenience, it is laid out in the same way as the DMV materials.

Understanding DMV's Memo: "ORDERING DRIVER INSTRUCTION SUPPLIES"

1. REQUISITION PROCEDURES

DMV will allow private schools to order only one time for each school year; however, there is no deadline for when that order should be submitted. Most private schools will find it easiest to order their materials at the end of October, after having filed their private school affidavits for the year.

3. ELIGIBILITY REQUIREMENTS

- THE REQUESTER SCHOOL MUST BE A SECONDARY SCHOOL AS DEFINED IN E.C. §52. THE SECONDARY SCHOOL MUST OFFER THE CURRICULUM OUTLINED IN E.C. §51220.

E.C. §52: "The secondary schools of the state are designated as high schools, technical schools and adult schools." This section of code applies to public schools. Therefore, private schools should ignore this requirement.

E.C. §51220: Not all of this code section is applicable to private schools; only the "branches of study" as referred to in E.C. §48222 are required. The "branches" listed in the E.C. are English, social sciences, foreign language, physical education, science, mathematics, fine arts, applied arts, career technical education, automobile driver education, and parenting skills.

- THE REQUESTER SCHOOL MUST BE A... PRIVATE SCHOOL AS DEFINED BY VEHICLE CODE §492 AND EXEMPT UNDER E.C. §48222.

V.C. §492: "A 'private school' is any school whether conducted for profit or not, giving a course of training similar to that given in a public school at or below the twelfth grade, including but not limited to schools owned or operated by any church." (It is important to note that this definition in the vehicle code is only for the purposes of the vehicle code and does not apply to subjects other than those in the vehicle code.)

E.C. §48222 does not exempt private schools from anything and the use of this code in this context by DMV is inaccurate. E.C. §48222 exempts *pupils* from attendance at public school, if the private school of attendance is a "full-time, private day school," if courses are taught by "persons capable of teaching," if courses are "taught in the English language," and if instruction is offered "in the several branches of study required to be taught in the public schools." These branches are listed in E.C. §51220.

- THE DE/DT COURSES OFFERED BY THE REQUESTER SCHOOL MUST BE MAINTAINED PURSUANT TO E.C. §51220(J), §51852(A), AND §51852.

E.C. §51220(j) covers required elements for an "approved" course in driver education. These elements must be included in any course for which a school intends to issue a DMV Certificate of Completion. E.C. §51852 covers several options for driver training. The DMV's inclusion of §51852(a) is confusing, since that code outlines only one of several possible options for "approved" driver training courses. Private schools are covered in E.C. §51852(h), which requires a minimum of six hours of on-street behind-the-wheel training.

- THE DRIVER EDUCATION/DRIVER TRAINING INSTRUCTORS, WHO WILL HAVE CONTACT WITH MINOR PUPILS MUST HAVE EITHER A VALID TEACHING CREDENTIAL OR A CRIMINAL RECORD SUMMARY PER E.C. §44237 AND §44830.

Private school instructors are not required to have state credentials. Criminal record summaries are used by private schools only when making hiring decisions. It is a misdemeanor for a private school to disclose to anyone, including the DMV, whether or not an instructor has a criminal record summary or not. DMV may, however, have a legitimate interest in requesting the names of DE/DT instructors, as the instructors are required to sign certificates which students hand in at DMV field offices when obtaining instruction permits or driver licenses. Having the names of the instructors listed should be used by DMV only to verify that the signer of the form is indeed authorized by the named school to teach DE/DT.

- A VIOLATION OF THESE ELIGIBILITY GUIDELINES MAY RESULT IN THE LOCAL DMV FIELD OFFICE'S REFUSAL TO ACCEPT DL 356 AND DL 391 CERTIFICATES, AND/OR THE SCHOOL BEING DENIED FURTHER DE/DT SUPPLIES FROM THE DEPARTMENT.

The DMV does not have authority to impose guidelines or requirements other than those imposed by the legislature through law. However, private schools are required to comply with current laws, and those schools which are not in compliance should be aware that their students may be denied licenses and permits by the local DMV offices.

Understanding DMV's "AUTHORIZATION/REQUISITION" FORM

SECTION 2: TO BE COMPLETED BY ALL REQUESTERS.

☐ THIS IS A SECONDARY SCHOOL TEACHING AT THE HIGH SCHOOL LEVEL.

Education Code §52 applies to public schools. Private secondary schools should leave this box unchecked.

☐ THIS IS A PUBLIC SCHOOL AUTHORIZED BY THE DEPARTMENT OF EDUCATION.

Applies to public schools only. Private schools should leave this box unchecked.

☐ THIS SCHOOL OFFERS DRIVER EDUCATION AND/OR DRIVER TRAINING AS PART OF THE FULL TIME CURRICULUM TO FULL TIME STUDENTS ENROLLED IN THIS SCHOOL.

Private schools may not offer DE/DT courses to outside students for a fee. Doing so places them in the category of commercial driving schools, which must be licensed by DMV and must order DE/DT materials on a different requisition form. Private schools offering DE or DT only to their own full-time students as part of their regular course of study should check this box.

☐ THE DRIVER EDUCATION AND DRIVER TRAINING COURSES ARE MAINTAINED PURSUANT TO THE PROVISIONS OF THE EDUCATION CODE AND PURSUANT TO VEHICLE CODE SECTION 12814.6.

The provisions of the E.C. are those listed previously. V.C. §12814.6 is the Brady-Jared Teen Driver Safety Act, which requires that the actual courses be in compliance with the E.C., and provides regulations regarding the time period for students to obtain instruction permits or licenses, etc. Private schools offering DE or DT must check this box in order to obtain DMV materials.

SECTION 3: TO BE COMPLETED BY ALL PRIVATE SCHOOLS.

☐ THIS IS A PRIVATE SCHOOL AS DEFINED IN CVC §492.

California Vehicle Code §492 is quoted on page 243. Private schools offering DE or DT must check this box in order to obtain DMV materials.

☐ THIS IS A PRIVATE SECONDARY SCHOOL THAT COMPLIES WITH EDUCATION CODE 33190 AND 33191.

E.C. §33190 is the code which gives the requirement for the annual filing of an affidavit by private schools. E.C. §33191 is the code which gives the requirement for obtaining finger prints and criminal record summaries for non-credentialed applicants for employment who are paid employees of the school and who have regular contact with children. Private schools should check this box.

☐ ENCLOSED IS A CURRENT COPY OF THE 'AFFIDAVIT OF PRIVATE SCHOOL' (R-4) FILED WITH THE SUPERINTENDENT OF PUBLIC INSTRUCTION AS REQUIRED BY EDUCATION CODE SECTION 33190.

Private schools should include a copy of their current affidavit when submitting the Requisition Form to DMV. Because the affidavit is not filed until between October 1 and October 15, private schools will need to delay the submission of their Requisition Form to DMV until *after* they have filed their affidavit.

☐ ENCLOSED IS WRITTEN VERIFICATION FROM THE SCHOOL DISTRICT ATTENDANCE SUPERVISOR OR BOARD OF EDUCATION DESIGNEE....

E.C. §48222 addresses *students*, not schools. It makes no sense to expect the School District Attendance Supervisor or Board of Education Designee to provide written verification that a *school* is exempt from compulsory attendance. Further, DMV is not authorized to require any kind of verification or approval of private schools by the Board of Education or school district employees. Private schools should leave this box unchecked.

SECTION 4: ADDITIONAL INFORMATION

This section gives the DMV's own definition of an "employee;" however, since the California Education Code provides a definition of employees for purposes of compliance with the law requiring fingerprints, this section of the Requisition Form may be disregarded.

SECTION 7:

The DMV has stated that for their purposes, they include both paid and volunteer instructors in their meaning of the word "employee." Therefore, it is unnecessary for private schools to change the words "employed by" which are printed on the Requisition Form, as had been recommended in previous years. Teaching credentials are not required of private school instructors and the DMV has no oversight of nor legitimate interest in credentials even for those who do have them. Furthermore, private schools should not give the DMV information about whether or not their instructors have criminal record summaries, as doing so is prohibited by law. Private schools should simply list all DE/DT instructors at their school. Write "n/a" under both the Teaching Credential and Criminal Record Summary headings for each instructor listed and attach a letter on school letterhead that says "our school is in compliance with all requirements relating to California teaching credentials and criminal record summaries as outlined in EC §§ 33190, 33191, and 44237. However, private schools are prohibited by law from releasing information to any person or agency relating to the criminal record of any employee."[17]

❖ Planning the Content of Your Courses

The general requirements for course content in "approved" courses are very minimal, so private schools should have no trouble surpassing them. The codes quoted in this section from the Education Code apply to your course to have it be an "approved" one. In general, it is up to the private school administrator to make sure his school's course meets the requirements of the Education Code, thus making his school's course an approved one. If there is a complaint filed against the school, or if the DMV has a reason to believe that the private school is not in compliance with the course requirements, then DMV may investigate. If DMV finds that a school is not in compliance, they may refuse to issue materials or honor course completion certificates from the school. If the school disputes DMV's decision, they would have to appeal in court.

Effective January 1, 2004, students may no longer take both driver education and driver training at the same time. (V.C. 12814.6(a)(3)(D)) Instead, students must complete the driver education portion of the course first, and then take driver training. The sequence of forms used, certificates given, and courses taken is shown below. The steps listed are intended to give you an overview of the course for planning purposes. The DMV may change requirements or forms, so it is important to follow the directions in the latest *Secondary School DE/DT Handbook* (DL 612).

---

[17]   Note that the DMV's definition of "employee" includes volunteers. However, E.C. § 44237 clearly requires criminal record summaries only for "applicants" for "paid" employment. Therefore, volunteer DE/DT instructors should be included on the list of instructors on the Requisition Form. Your school is in compliance with E.C. § 44237 if paid employees have either a teaching credential or a criminal record summary and if volunteers do not. The DMV has no authority to require criminal record summaries of volunteers, whether they call them employees or not.

Sequence for Completing the Courses and Issuing the Forms

1. Student in grade 9, 10, 11, or 12 takes classroom course of Driver Education.

2. Student completes classroom course and receives "Certificate of Completion Driver Education" (DL 387) with the box checked showing completion of classroom driver education.

3. Student who is at least 15 years and six months old enrolls in the "behind-the-wheel" course of Driver Training. Upon enrollment, the student's parents sign the "Statement of Consent to Issue and Acceptance of Liability" (DL 119). This form is kept by the school in the student's file until the student is 21 years old. Upon receipt of the signed "Statement of Consent..." (DL 119), the school issues a Student License (DL 118).

4. The student applies at the local DMV office for an Instruction Permit. He must pass a written exam at the DMV before he is issued the Instruction Permit. The Instruction Permit is not valid until the Driver Training course has begun. After the first behind-the-wheel lesson, the instructor dates and signs the Instruction Permit below the statement that explains that the permit is not valid until behind-the-wheel lessons have begun.

5. Student completes Driver Training and receives another "Certificate of Completion of Driver Training" (DL 388A), this time with the box checked showing completion of driver training.

6. Student practices driving, accompanied by a licensed driver at least 25 years old. The accompanying adult must sit in the front seat, where he can assist the student if necessary. The student must complete at least 50 hours of practice, in addition to the driver training course, before he applies for a license. Ten of the practice hours must be when it is dark.

7. Student who is at least 16 years old and who has had his Instruction Permit for at least six months applies at local DMV office for a Provisional License. He must pass a behind-the-wheel driving test before he is issued a Provisional License.

❖ Driver Education — The Classroom Course

These three code sections cover the requirements for driver education courses:

The adopted course of study for grades 7 to 12, inclusive, shall offer courses in the following areas of study:
... (j) Automobile Driver Education, designed to develop a knowledge of the provisions of the Vehicle Code and other laws of this state relating to the operation of motor vehicles, a proper acceptance of personal responsibility in traffic, a true appreciation of the causes, seriousness and consequences of traffic accidents, and to develop the knowledge and attitudes necessary for the safe operation of motor vehicles. A course in automobile driver education shall include education in the safe operation of motorcycles. (EC § 51220)

... automobile education shall be designed to develop a knowledge of the dangers involved in consuming alcohol or drugs in connection with the operation of a motor vehicle. (EC § 51220.1)

A course of instruction in automobile driver education shall:

(a) Be of at least 2½ semester periods[18] and shall be taught by a qualified instructor[19];
(b) Provide the opportunity for students to take driver education within the regular schoolday, and within the regular academic year...
(c) Be completed by the student within the academic year or summer session in which it was begun.
(EC § 51851)

There has been disagreement about whether the following California Administrative Code section applies to private schools. Since the topics are basic enough to warrant being included in any driver education course, my advice is to err on the side of safety and to keep your courses above reproach by including these aspects in your course:

(1) Driving is your responsibility.
(2) Major causes of accidents.
(3) The driver.
(4) Natural forces affecting driving.
(5) Signs, signals, and highway markings, and highway design features which require understanding for safe operation of motor vehicles.
(6) California Vehicle Code, rules of the road, and other state laws and local motor vehicle laws and ordinances.
(7) Differences in characteristics of urban and rural driving including safe use of modern expressways.
(8) Critical vehicle systems and subsystems requiring preventive maintenance.
(9) Pedestrian safety.
(10) Effects of alcohol and drugs.
(11) Motorcycle safety. (CAC Title 5, 10020)

Books and Resources for Driver Education

The DMV has developed a curriculum for Driver Education and is hoping to have all "approved courses" use their curriculum to ensure minimum standards are met. The curriculum is available online for free at the DMV's website: www.dmv.ca.gov/dmv.htm.[20] At this writing, the curriculum is not required. However, it covers the Driver Education course thoroughly and is therefore recommended.

The California Driver Handbook, a booklet published by the DMV, is available in bulk from the DMV in Sacramento when you order materials, or you can pick up individual copies at your local DMV office or download it from the DMV website. The handbook covers all the basic required material listed in the codes above.

---

[18]   2½ semester periods is equal to 30 hours during the regular school year, and slightly less during the summer term.

[19]   A "qualified instructor" is one who meets the requirements for all instructors in private schools: he must be "capable of teaching," as listed in EC § 48222. This determination is made by the private school administrator.

[20]   While the website is subject to change, at this writing, to reach the driver education course curriculum, first go to the DMV website: www.dmv.ca.gov/dmv.htm. From the menu on the left side of the screen, choose "Vehicle Industry & Commercial Permits." At the next screen, choose "Occupational Licensing." The next screen has a menu on the right side of the screen: choose "Driver Education Curriculum" from the bottom right side.

Each student in your course should be given a copy of the <u>California Driver Handbook</u>. Some instructors use this guide as a teaching tool for the course, going through it together in class. Others will require students to read it on their own, testing them on the material or requiring a written report as evidence of the student's having studied it.

Your students will have to pass a written test at the DMV before they can receive Instruction Permits. The test questions are based on the <u>California Driver Handbook</u>. To prepare for this test, most schools order the "Student Examination on Vehicle Code" (DL 5B.) This test could be given at the end of your course, with students being required to pass it before they can receive their certificate of completion, or you could use it as a pre-test at the beginning of the course, and then give it again at the end to measure progress. The DMV website listed above has practice written exam questions which students can use online.

The local DMV office may also have several brochures available which you could use to supplement your course. For example, one brochure explains the requirements of the Brady-Jared Teen Driver Safety Act. One pamphlet with particularly useful exercises for classroom discussion is called "But It Wasn't Really My Fault." It contains "collision reports" with diagrams and requires the student to figure out which driver was at fault in each accident described.

In addition to the materials from DMV, a number of textbooks are available from various publishers. <u>Responsible Driving</u> is available from Glencoe/McGraw Hill: www.glencoe.com or (800) 334-7344 <u>Drive Right</u> is available from Prentice Hall: www.phschool.com or (800) 326-4259. Both books are available in student and teacher editions, and both publishers offer videos and other supplementary programs to go with them. Additionally, both programs have online resources available to students and teachers.

One source of supplementary materials for your course is the California Highway Patrol. Call your local CHP office (listed in the state government section of your phone book) and ask for the Public Affairs Officer. The CHP has handouts available and films for loan. Usually, an officer is available to come to a group class and give a talk to the students, show films, and answer questions. Many schools make use of this service for one of their class periods. Several driver safety brochures are available online at www.chp.ca.gov.

The American Automobile Association is also a good source of supplementary materials. The AAA has brochures and videos available: www.aaafoundation.org.

Completing Driver Education and Obtaining an Instruction Permit

Upon completion of the classroom Driver Education course the instructor or school official issues the student a Certificate of Completion (DL 387) showing completion of classroom driver education.

The student will take the Certificate of Completion for driver education, the application form (which must be signed by *both* parents), an original or certified copy of his birth certificate, his social security card, and $12.00 to the DMV. The application is the "Application for Noncommercial Driver License, Identification Card or Name Change" (DL 44), and is available at any local DMV office, or schools may order enough to give out to their students with the certificates of completion.

If the student passes the DMV's written test, he should receive his Instruction Permit. However, the Instruction Permit is not valid until the student has begun his driver training class.

❖ Dealing with the DMV in Person

Going to the DMV to obtain an Instruction Permit may be the first experience your students will have in dealing directly with a government agency. It is a good idea to brief them so they are less likely to encounter problems. Instruct your students to dress nicely (a business-like demeanor always helps) and to simply submit their correctly completed forms as any other student would do.

Remind your students that the legal term for their educational status is "private school student." While "home schooling" has become a popular colloquial term, there is no distinction in the California Education Code or Vehicle Code between private schools whether the students meet at a large campus or a home, whether there is an enrollment of 200 or only one, etc.

If the DMV clerk asks where the student received his training, he should say, "At my high school." If pressed, he should give the name of his private school. If the accompanying parent is also the DE/DT teacher for the student and is asked about this, he should simply state, "I am a teacher at ___ School." Sometimes it helps to have the parent who did not sign the Certificate of Completion be the one who takes the student to the DMV. Then the parent can say, if asked, "My spouse is a teacher at ___ School."

Do not be drawn into an argument; if necessary, ask what other information the DMV would like and arrange to return at another time. DMV denials are best handled from home by mail.

❖ Driver Training — The Behind-the-Wheel Course

Private schools and public schools are exempt from (Vehicle Code § 11100) requirements to have a "driving school license" or "driving instructor license" if driving instruction is included as part of the schools' curriculum. Private schools are also exempt from the requirements in California Education Codes §§ 41906-7 that qualified driving instructors have a "designated subjects credential" or that they pass particular courses or exams, as long as the private school is not seeking reimbursement from the Department of Education for excess costs of driver training.

However, as with driver education, the driver training course must comply with the requirements of the Education Code in order to be "approved," and thus meet the requirements for obtaining a provisional driver's license. The Education Code sections related to driver training in private schools are straightforward:

A course of instruction in the laboratory phase of driver education shall include, for each student enrolled in the class, instruction under one of the following plans:

... (five plans listed for public school programs)...

(f) For purposes of this section, one hour means 60 minutes including passing time....
(h) Nothing in this section shall be construed to direct or restrict courses of instruction in the classroom phase or the laboratory phase of driver education offered by private elementary and secondary schools or to require the use of credentialed or certified instructors in the laboratory phase of driver education offered by private elementary and secondary schools, except that each student enrolled in a course shall satisfactorily complete a minimum of six hours of on-street behind-the-wheel driving instruction. This section shall not be construed to limit eligibility for a provisional driver's license for pupils who have completed driver education or driver training courses offered in private elementary or secondary schools.

(i) For the purposes of this section, private elementary or secondary schools are those subject to the provisions of Sections 33190 and 48222.[21] *(EC § 51852)*

The behind-the-wheel portion of a driver instruction course is begun after a student has completed Driver Education and when he is at least 15 ½ years old.

Before beginning any actual driving, the student must have the proper forms filled out. Again, all the necessary forms are ordered from DMV on the Requisition Form (DL 396) and the information for completing each form properly is in the *Secondary School DE/DT Handbook,* which is ordered at the same time.

After the first driving lesson, the teacher of the driver training course should sign and date the Instruction Permit below the statement that explains that the permit is not valid until behind-the-wheel lessons have begun.

The driver training instructor keeps the Student License (issued by the school principal) in the car during training sessions. After the course is completed, the private school may keep the Student License (DL 118) in the school files or may destroy it. The signed "Statement of Consent to Issue and Acceptance of Liability" (DL 119) should be retained in the school file until the student is 21 years old.

As stated in EC § 51852, students who take driver training at their private school must complete a minimum of six hours of driving lessons. If the parent is also the driver training teacher, it is important to note that these six hours of *lessons* are separate from the 50 hours of *practice* that the student does while he has his Instruction Permit.

A good guide for private secondary schools would be to include all the skills listed in the box on the next page and especially those listed in the *California Driver Handbook* that the student will be expected to demonstrate at his DMV driving test.

The *Parent-Teen Training Aide* (DL 603) which is given to the student when he receives his Instruction Permit has a list of skills to be practiced with the parent. This guide is available to the instructor (one per instructor) through the Requisition Form (DL 396). The *Parent-Teen Training Aide* is also available online at www.dmv.ca.gov/pubs. The skills listed in the *Parent-Teen Training Aide* should also be covered in the Driver Training course.

Completing Driver Training and Obtaining a Provisional License

Upon completion of the driver training course, the instructor signs a "Certificate of Completion of Driver Training" (DL 388A) to indicate that the student has completed Driver Training. The student takes the certificate to the DMV when he applies for a Provisional Driver's License.

There could be some confusion at local DMV offices when a student brings in forms that have the same signature for both parent and for instructor or school official. While it is legal for an instructor and a parent to be the same person, there are some DMV officials who question the objectivity of parents who teach their own children. (I have never heard of the DMV questioning the objectivity of a licensed private driving school instructor or public school Driver Training teacher who taught his own child, however.) The DMV may restrict instruction permits if it is determined "to be appropriate to assure the safe operation of a motor vehicle by the permittee." (Vehicle Code § 12509) Reread the section, "Dealing with the DMV in Person," on page 249 *before* going for the license.

---

[21] EC § 33190 deals with the annual filing of the private school affidavit. EC § 48222 addresses the private school exemption to compulsory public school attendance. See CHEA's manual, *An Introduction to Home Education*, for more information on private school affidavits, compulsory attendance, and other requirements of private schools.

Most problems have been avoided by knowing the correct "legalese" terminology when talking to the DMV. Remember that if a parent happens to be the student's teacher, it is in the capacity as "private school teacher" that he taught his child driver training. There is nothing in the law to prohibit this.

❖ Brady-Jared Teen Driver Safety Act

On July 1, 1998, the Brady-Jared Teen Driver Safety Act (V.C. § 12814.6) took effect, imposing a "graduated" licensing program for minors. During the first six months that a minor has his provisional driver's license, he cannot drive between midnight and 5:00 a.m., nor can he carry passengers under age 20, unless he is accompanied by a parent, guardian, or licensed driver over age 25. During the second six months, he can carry passengers of any age, but still cannot drive between midnight and 5:00 a.m. There are exceptions for driving to and from work, school, medical appointments, etc. Details about the new rules enacted by the Brady-Jared Teen Driver Safety Act should be covered in the DMV materials, such as the *California Driver Handbook* and the *Parent-Teen Training Aide*.

❖ Handling DMV Denials

Driver Training Skills
(from the California Administrative Code, Title 5, § 10043)

(A) Pre-driving activities
 1. Safety check outside car
   a. Tire condition
   b. Trunk (spare tire, jack, etc.)
   c. Hood properly closed
 2. Safety check inside car
   a. Seat adjustment
   b. Mirror adjustment
   c. Doors locked
   d. Seat belts fastened
 3. Auxiliary equipment
   a. Headlights & dimmer switch
   b. Instrument panel lights
   c. Windshield wipers
   d. Defroster

(B) Starting
 1. Foot on brake
 2. Parking brake
 3. Blind spot check

(C) Moving car
 1. Blind spot check
 2. Driving straight
 3. Steering
 4. Speed control
 5. Stopping car
 6. Clutch and gear use
 7. Right of way

(D) Turning skills
 1. Curb pullout
 2. Left and right turns
 3. Mirror use
 4. Position in lane
 5. Over/understeering
 6. Speed control

(E) Lane changing
 1. Blind spots
 2. Signaling
 3. Changing one lane at a time
 4. Speed control
 5. Traffic

(F) Intersections
 1. Blind
 2. 4-way
 3. Railroad crossings

(G) Skilled turning maneuvers
 1. U-turns
 2. Backing
 3. Three-point turn/ Y turns

(H) Defensive driving
 1. Space cushion
 2. Hazard recognition
 3. Visual search
 4. Speed selection for conditions

(I) Heavy traffic
 1. Exposure to heavy area traffic (freeway, highway, boulevard)

(J) Secure car
 1. Parking brake
 2. Shift to park
 3. Lock doors
 4. Setting wheels and controls

Before addressing specific problems, it's important to cover two general issues that apply to any problem with DMV. First, please be patient. That is hard to ask of 16 year olds who feel they simply must drive right away. But DMV, typical of bureaucratic agencies, moves very slowly, especially in dealing with problems or unusual circumstances.

Second, this manual makes *no guarantee* that if you follow every direction listed, you will necessarily work out your problem with DMV. The best solution is to be careful to avoid problems in the first place. Make sure you have the most up-to-date information before filling out any DMV forms. Fill in all forms in a neat and business-like manner, with no cross-outs, white-out, etc. If a problem cannot be avoided, please do not make DMV think your problem is so large that "something must be done immediately"—the usual "fix" is another detailed policy or a legislative proposal, which inevitably makes the situation worse, not better.

If DMV Won't Send a Requisition Form

If you are denied a Requisition Form, you should receive a letter from the DMV explaining why you were denied. Some of the letters include a phone number and invite you to call to discuss the problem. Don't do it. Handle all communications with DMV in writing, using a business letterhead and professional format. If you call, they will ask questions which will stump you, and then they'll likely deny your request again.

Most of the Requisition Form denial letters sent out in the past few years have to do with the criminal record summary requirement for paid employees. If you get such a letter, send your form in again, this time adding a letter on school letterhead stating that you are in compliance with the law regarding criminal record summary checks.

It has been a number of years since the DMV has requested additional documentation from schools to ostensibly show that the school is "bona fide." Nevertheless, it is conceivable that such a request could be made. As a matter of principle relating to the freedom from government evaluation of private school programs, I have recommended that private schools do *not* send additional "proof" documents to the DMV or any other government agency without a court order to do so. Complying with requests to evaluate private school programs to determine whether they are "bona fide" could set a precedent for similar future actions by other agencies.

This presents the recipients of DMV's Requisition Form denial letter with two options: 1) you could arrange for your students to take the course at a commercial driving school, or 2) you could respond to DMV's concerns without including the requested proof documents. If you desire to respond to DMV, a sample letter is shown below. Remember that such a letter should only be sent by *full-time, private day schools* in compliance with E.C. §§ 33190 & 48222, and only regarding those students who attend your school on a full-time basis. Your letter will need to be

---

Sample Letter in Response to DMV letter denying request for a Requisition Form

This letter is in response to your request for clarification of our school's procedures related to obtaining criminal record summaries as required by the California Education Code. We are in full compliance with the requirements of this code and obtain the required criminal record summaries for all applicants for employment in our school. Criminal record summaries are not required for non-paid instructors, nor for parents working exclusively with their own children in a private school.

Our school, [name of school], is a full-time, private day school in compliance with California Education Code, requiring the annual filing of an affidavit. A copy of our affidavit for the current school year is attached. All information on the affidavit is true, as certified on it by my signature.

Students enrolled in our school are exempt from attendance at public school under E.C. 48222. Our school offers the following course of study for students in grades 7-12: English, Social sciences, Foreign language, Physical education, Science, Mathematics, Visual and performing arts, Applied arts, Career Technical education, and Automobile driver education. As indicated on our affidavit, students who complete our course of study are eligible to receive a diploma from our school upon graduation.

Our school currently includes [total number of all enrolled students] students, with [number taking DE/DT] planning to take DE/DT during the next school year. The student(s) taking DE/DT at our school are full-time students at [name of your school] -- they are not enrolled in any other public or private high school.

The information provided on our affidavit and in this letter should serve your need to verify that we are a bona fide private school in compliance with current law.

---

customized depending on the information DMV has requested. If you haven't received a response after 30 days, send another letter, briefly stating that you have had no response to your letter and include a copy of your original letter.

If DMV Won't Send Your Materials

The second point at which the DMV might send you a denial letter is when you send in your filled-out Requisition Form to get your certificates and other materials. The standard materials denial from DMV states that "you do not qualify for driving instruction forms... because you have either failed to provide sufficient information or documentation, and/or you do not illustrate that your school is complying with the appropriate education and/or vehicle code sections." You have two options for responding to this kind of a denial.

First, you can write a letter to DMV explaining the reason for the response you gave on your Requisition Form, i.e., "Criminal Record Summaries are requested for all applicants for employment at our school as required by E.C. 33190; however, such records are destroyed after hiring decisions are made and disclosure of information regarding criminal records is prohibited by law." Allow another 30 days for DMV to respond to your letter.

If the school year has already begun and you seem to be facing delays from DMV which could extend past the end of the first semester, you may wish to recommend that your students take driver education or driver training from a local commercial driving school.

If Your Student is Denied a Provisional License or Instruction Permit

If your student is denied an Instruction Permit or Provisional Driver's License, the denial was most likely given in person at the local DMV office. The most common reason (aside from failing the exam) is that the student or parent was unable to give adequate answers to questions about the DE/DT courses the student took. Be sure your students are well prepared before they go. Remember that the personnel at local offices, even the managers, are not responsible for setting policy, nor do they have the authority to waive policies. Both students and parents should be prepared to calmly explain that the course was at a private high school, using correct legal terminology. They should also be prepared to state that they would be happy to return at another time after checking for the correct answers to any questions or problems. Do not feel pressured to solve the situation on the spot.

While focusing on problems you might encounter is important to help you avoid them, that does not mean you *will* have problems. For most schools and for most families, the process goes quite smoothly, once the basic procedures are understood.

❖ F: Admission to California's Public Colleges

The Donahoe Higher Education Act states:

(a) It is hereby declared to be the policy of the Legislature that all resident applicants to California institutions of public higher education, who are determined to be qualified by law or by admission standards established by the respective governing boards, should be admitted to either (1) a district of the California Community Colleges, in accordance with Section 76000, (2) the California State University, or (3) the University of California. (CA Education Code § 66011) Also see codes 66201, and 66202.

If you meet the admission requirements and are a resident of California, you will be admitted to one of the three types of public colleges in California.

❖ Community College

Enrolling Part-time While Still in High School

Many homeschooled high school students in California have taken classes at their local community college. What California law says regarding community college admissions for high school students is this:

> *(a) The governing board of any school district may determine which students would benefit from advanced scholastic or vocational work. The intent of this section is to provide educational enrichment opportunities for a limited number of eligible pupils, rather than to reduce current course requirements of elementary and secondary schools. The governing board may authorize those students, upon recommendation of the principal of the school that the pupil attends, and with parental consent, to attend a community college as special part-time or full-time students and to undertake one or more courses of instruction offered at the community college level.*
> *(c) The students shall receive credit for community college courses that they complete at the level determined appropriate by the school district and community college district governing boards.*

(d) (1) The principal of a school may only recommend a pupil for a community college summer session if that pupil meets all of the following criteria:
(A) Demonstrates adequate preparation in the discipline to be studied.
(B) Exhausts all opportunities to enroll in an equivalent course, if any, at his or her school of attendance. (EC § 48800)

(d) For purposes ... (of funding) ... a special part-time student may enroll in up to, and including, 11 units per semester or the equivalent thereof, at the community college. (EC § 76001)

The following **new law** became effective January 1, 2004:

B) The governing board of a community college district may restrict the admission or enrollment of a special part-time or full-time student during any session based on any of the following criteria:
(1) Age.
(2) Completion of a specified grade level.
(3) Demonstrated eligibility for instruction using assessment methods and procedures....
(EC § 76002)

What this all means is that it is possible for a high school student to take classes at the community college, even while the student is still enrolled in high school. However, there is no requirement that the community college *must* enroll your private school student if the college administration decides he does not meet their minimum requirements. Further, the new law shown above (EC § 76002) allows each community college to set minimum standards for enrolling high school students. This means that the standards will likely vary among the community colleges, and it also means that there will be less assessment on an individual basis. For example, if a community college decides to enroll only those high school students who are at least 16 years old, or who are in 11th or 12th grade, then that standard will be applied to all students.

Even with the new rules, most high school students who want to take a class or two at the local community college should find it an easy process. The college will have an application which must be completed. Often, there is a special application for high school students, so be sure to ask and make sure you have the correct application. If there is an application just for high school students wanting to attend part-time, then there is usually a place on it for the school principal to sign, giving his recommendation, and for the parents to sign, giving their consent.

For basic classes which have no prerequisite, the student is often able to simply enroll. For more advanced classes, he may be required to submit a high school transcript showing related courses completed in high school.

Before applying, find out if the community college your student is applying to has set minimum enrollment requirements for high school students. While the new law allowing minimum standards may preclude some of the younger students from attending, the process should actually make it easier for the older high school students who fall within the range of standards. If your student meets the minimum standards and enrollment still becomes a problem, offer to provide letters of recommendation from community members or standardized test results, ask to have the student tested using the college's own placement exams, or ask if he may take just one very basic class on a trial basis to prove his abilities.

Students enrolled as part-time college students will be considered as high school students at college and may be required to give verification that they are continuing their high school studies. In other words, they are not exempt from compulsory attendance laws until they either turn eighteen; pass a high school proficiency exam; get a high school diploma; or enroll in the junior college as a special full-time student, in which case they will have to take all the high school general education requirements at college.

College Credits or High School Credits?

While the college has the final authority to determine whether it will grant high school or college credits, the usual practice is to award college credits for college courses even if the student is still in high school. Occasionally a student will be asked which type of credits he desires. **Always choose college credits.** Getting college credits means the student will have a college transcript and will be able to use the credits toward college graduation. There is nothing to prohibit your own private high school from either awarding duplicate credit on the high school transcript, or from waiving a high school graduation requirement because equivalent work was completed at college.

Enrolling Full-time While Still in High School

Occasionally, a student desires to enter community college as a full-time student *instead* of completing high school first. While this is not as common as taking a class or two while continuing high school, it is a possibility for academically advanced students. Please note that if your student has passed the CHSPE or received a high school diploma, he should apply as a regular incoming college freshman, which is covered on the following page.

> *(c) A parent or guardian of a pupil who is not enrolled in a public school may directly petition the president of any community college to authorize the attendance of the pupil at the community college as a special part-time or full-time student on the ground that the pupil would benefit from advanced scholastic or vocational work that would thereby be available.*
>
> *(d) Any pupil authorized to attend a community college as a special full-time student shall, nevertheless, be required to undertake courses of instruction of a scope and duration sufficient to satisfy the requirements of law.* (parentheses added) (EC § 48800.5)

"Petitioning the governing board" to admit your child sounds a bit intimidating, but usually it simply means filling out the regular application or a special application form for high school students, if the college has one. Each district makes its own forms, so they vary somewhat, but usually all will require three signatures: one indicating a recommendation by the high school principal, one indicating permission from the parent, and one by the student. Some will ask for a transcript, and others will ask for a verification of grade-point average. They may ask for a letter or two of recommendation from someone else in the community. A pastor, employer, businessman, or other responsible adult who knows your child well enough to recommend him as a hard worker and serious-minded, mature student will do fine.

The point of all these requirements is not to scare you away, but to make sure that the college-level courses are filled with college-level students. The colleges want to avoid having students skip high school and enroll as special full-time students if those students would benefit more from continuing their high school education and enrolling in college after graduation.

Skipping high school to enroll full-time in community college is probably not the best option for the majority of students. The California Community College system is a secular institution geared toward offering post-secondary and adult education; it is not intended as a substitute for high school. Many eighteen and nineteen year old students find their faith is challenged at college. Expect this to be more difficult for a sixteen or seventeen year old special full-time student. If you are in doubt, a safer option would be to have the student continue with his high school program and take only a couple of college classes as a part-time student.

Admission to Community College as an Incoming Freshman after Graduating from High School or Passing the CHSPE

The governing board of a community college district shall admit to the community college any California resident, and may admit any nonresident, possessing a high school diploma or the equivalent thereof. (EC § 76000)

If your student has a high school diploma or has passed the CHSPE, there is no question that the community college must admit him. Community colleges are, after all, public schools.

If you meet any <u>one</u> of the following requirements, you are eligible for admission to the community college:

1. You have a high school diploma.
2. You have passed the CHSPE or GED test.
3. You are over eighteen years old.

Community colleges serve various needs of different levels of education. Students may prepare themselves for admission to a four-year institution with junior standing, or they may choose one of many one or two year certificate programs which lead to immediate job placement.

Applications are available at the admissions office on request. Be sure to also get a copy of the school's catalog to check which programs are offered and to find out if there are prerequisites for any of the courses you plan to take.

❖ Accredited High School Courses, California State University, and University of California

While the CSU and UC admissions processes will be discussed separately, it is important to note that new (as of Fall 2004) requirements relating to accreditation of high schools will affect both university systems. Both university systems require that incoming college freshman must have completed certain course requirements during high school. These high school course requirements are commonly called the "a-g" requirements.

The UC system has adopted a program of requiring high school courses which are used to satisfy the a-g requirements to be "pre-approved" by the UC. However, beginning with 2004, the UC will no longer consider courses which are offered in high schools which are not accredited by the Western Association of Schools and Colleges. This means, in essence, that homeschooled students, and students who attend any other school which is not WASC accredited, will not be eligible to enter any UC campus through the a-g requirements. There are a few alternative means of gaining acceptance to the UC, and these will be discussed in the "University of California" section beginning on page 260.

The California State University *system* has not adopted the requirement that high school courses be taken at only WASC-accredited schools. However, two important issues should be noted: first, individual CSU campuses may adopt the accreditation requirements for a-g courses even if the CSU system as a whole does not; second, in the past, CSU has followed the pattern of the UC system, but several years behind. So although many CSU campuses are currently accepting a-g courses from non-accredited high schools, this could change in the future. Bottom line for CSU-bound students: get the catalog from the university you plan to attend and check with the admissions department to find out if any changes are planned which will affect you at the time you plan to attend.

❖ California State University

Much of the information in this section is taken directly from the CSU website: www.csumentor.edu. It is well worth signing up for an account to be able to enter all of the planning sections of the website. Accounts are free and require only minimal information to be given. Even without an account, much valuable information is available on the website.

Requirements for entrance to the California State University are planned to allow admission of the top one third of all high school graduates. The following course pattern is required of incoming freshman students. The requirements listed are subject to change - GET A CATALOG[22] from the university you plan to attend.

> 4 years: English
> 3 years: Mathematics (algebra, geometry, and intermediate algebra)
> 2 years: U.S. history and social science
> 2 years: 1 year biological and 1 year physical
> 2 years: Foreign language (the same language)
> 1 year: Visual and performing arts: art, dance, theater/drama, or music
> 1 year: Elective chosen from the subject areas listed above or other college preparatory course (2 semesters or 1 year-long course)

In addition to the above courses, students must meet the "eligibility index" requirement. The eligibility index is a weighted combination of a student's grade point average during the final three years of high school and a score on either the American College Test (ACT) or Scholastic Aptitude Test (SAT). Calculation of eligibility indices and required minimums for California high school graduates is computed as follows:

total **SAT** score + (800 × high school grade point average) = 2900	**OR**	(10 × total **ACT** score) + (200 × high school grade point average) = 694

For example, a student who scored 1080 on the SAT, and had a 2.85 grade point average would compute his eligibility this way: SAT score of 1080 + (800 × 2.85) = 3360. This student exceeds the minimum score of 2900; thus he meets the minimum eligibility index requirement.

Impacted Majors and Programs

When students apply to a CSU campus, they designate a major area of study. Some campuses receive more applicants for specialized study areas than they can possibly accept. These major programs are designated as "impacted" and have more rigorous admissions criteria than for general eligibility. For example, nursing programs at many CSU campuses are impacted, all programs at CSU San Diego and CSU San Luis Obispo are impacted, and many other programs at various CSU campuses are also impacted. If you apply to an impacted program, be aware that your chances of being accepted are less than if you were to apply to a non-impacted program. Also, applications for impacted programs are usually accepted only during a short period of time each year, usually in the early fall of your senior year of high school. Check the university's website and plan well ahead.

---

[22] College-bound students should check college catalogs at the start of high school to see what courses they need to take during high school in order to meet the college admissions requirements by the time they graduate. At the beginning of 11th grade, they should again check current catalogs of prospective universities. Taking courses which meet the most stringent requirements among the colleges being considered will assure that they meet the minimum requirements. Most lists of admissions requirements and applications are now available on the Internet.

Transferring to CSU from Community College

Students who have taken community college courses during high school, and students who have attended community college *after* high school should be aware that it is usually easier to transfer into CSU after completing one or two years of college work at the community college level. One reason this option is easier for homeschooled students is that once a student has completed two years of transferable credits at the community college, his high school transcript is not so important—the university will be paying more attention to work completed at the community college. Check with your local community college for information about transferring to the CSU after completing community college work.

❖ University of California

The UC has an excellent website which thoroughly explains the admissions process and provides links to the individual UC campuses: www.ucop.edu/pathways/. Much of the information in this book is taken directly from the website, but there is lots more there than space herein allows. This book provides only general information intended to assist you in planning high school with an eye to college admissions. For detailed information, especially as regards a specific UC campus or program, check the website.

While there are minimum admissions requirements for the University of California, meeting these minimum standards is no guarantee of acceptance. Admission to any of the UC campuses is a highly selective process. In addition to meeting the minimum requirements, students should be aware that they will be evaluated by grade point average, performance on the college admissions exams, extracurricular and leadership activities, and special talents. Students seeking admission must be prepared to demonstrate that they have a high level of academic achievements, personal accomplishments and outstanding character qualities that will make them an asset to the university. Students considering applying to the University of California should obtain a current catalog by the end of the 10th grade so they can be sure they have time to complete the required courses during 11th and 12th grades.

There are four different ways to establish eligibility to be admitted to the University of California. Only two of these means can be used by homeschooled students: eligibility by examination alone, and eligibility by exception. Of the remaining two, eligibility in the local context is inapplicable to homeschoolers and not covered in this book, and eligibility in the statewide context will be explained first below because, although it is dependent upon completion of the a-g courses at a WASC accredited school, the overall requirements are also important to those seeking eligibility by exception.

Regardless of which means a student follows to establish eligibility, an application must be submitted between November 1 and December 1 of the senior year of high school.

Eligibility in the Statewide Context

There are three separate requirements to establish eligibility in the statewide context.

1.   A-G Subject Requirements

Although students at non-WASC accredited high schools will not be able to have their a-g courses approved by the UC, understanding the a-g requirements is still important. Most universities have similar course requirements, so the a-g list can be used as a guide to deciding what courses to take at the beginning of high school regardless of which college or university a student ultimately attends. Of course, students will be checking with the catalogs of the potential universities and narrowing their choices later in high school, but these 15 course requirements are typical of what is required by top universities throughout the country. Also, students seeking to establish eligibility by exception will have the best chance of success if they have taken or exceeded these requirements even though the courses used to satisfy them may not be UC approved.

To satisfy the a-g subject requirements, students must complete the following 15 courses. Each course must be one year (two semesters) or the equivalent. At least 7 of the 15 must be taken in the last two years of high school.

a   History/Social Science -- 2 years required. Two years of history/social science, including one year of world history, cultures and geography; and one year of U.S. history or one-half year of U.S. history and one-half year of civics or American government.

b   English -- 4 years required. Four years of college preparatory English that include frequent and regular writing, and reading of classic and modern literature. Not more than two semesters of ninth-grade English can be used to meet this requirement.

c   Mathematics -- 3 years required, 4 years recommended. Three years of college preparatory mathematics that include the topics covered in elementary and advanced algebra and two- and three-dimensional geometry. Approved integrated math courses may be used to fulfill part or all of this requirement, as may math courses taken in the seventh and eighth grades that your high school accepts as equivalent to its own math courses.

d   Laboratory Science -- 2 years required, 3 years recommended. Two years of laboratory science providing fundamental knowledge in two of these three core disciplines: biology (which includes anatomy, physiology, marine biology, aquatic biology, etc.), chemistry and physics. The final two years of an approved three-year integrated science program may be used to fulfill this requirement. Not more than one year of ninth-grade laboratory science can be used to meet this requirement.

e   Language Other than English -- 2 years required, 3 years recommended. Two years of the same language other than English. Courses should emphasize speaking and understanding, and include instruction in grammar, vocabulary, reading, composition and culture. Courses in language other than English taken in the seventh and eighth grade may be used to fulfill part of this requirement if your high school accepts them as equivalent to its own courses.

f   Visual and Performing Arts (VPA) -- 1 year required. One year of visual and performing arts chosen from the following: dance, drama/theater, music or visual art.

g   College Preparatory Electives -- 1 year required. One year (two semesters), in addition to those required in "a-f" above, chosen from the following areas: visual and performing arts (non-introductory level courses), history, social science, English, advanced mathematics, laboratory science and language other than English (a third year in the language used for the "e" requirement or two years of another language).

2.   **Scholarship Requirement**

The Scholarship Requirement defines the grade point average (GPA) students must attain in the "a-g" subjects and the corresponding SAT I (or ACT) and SAT II test scores they must earn. The lower a student's GPA is, the higher his test scores must be. A minimum GPA of 2.8 is required.

Only the grades earned in "a-g" subjects in the 10th, 11th and 12th grades are used to calculate the GPA for UC admissions. Courses taken in ninth grade can be used to meet the Subject Requirement if the student earns a grade of C or better, but they will not be used to calculate the GPA.

To read the chart, first figure the GPA for the a-g courses, as described above and in Chapter 9. Then find the GPA in the chart below. The test score total to the right of the GPA is the minimum required "Total Test Score." To determine the Total Test Score, follow this formula:

[SAT I composite score] + [2 x (SAT II Writing score + SAT II Mathematics score + third required SAT II score)].

SAT I composite is highest combined mathematics and verbal scores from a single sitting. Highest individual SAT II scores, from any sitting, will be considered. An ACT score may substitute for a SAT I composite. An ACT to SAT I conversion table is provided.

Table of Grade-Point Averages & Corresponding Required Test Scores for University of California

"a-g" GPA	Total Test Score	"a-g" GPA	Total Test Score	"a-g" GPA	Total Test Score
2.80 - 2.84	4640	3.05 - 3.09	3720	3.30 - 3.34	3248
2.85 - 2.89	4384	3.10 - 3.14	3616	3.35 - 3.39	3192
2.90 - 2.94	4160	3.15 - 3.19	3512	3.40 - 3.44	3152
2.95 - 2.99	3984	3.20 - 3.24	3408	3.45 - 3.49	3128
3.00 - 3.04	3840	3.25 - 3.29	3320	above 3.50	3120

ACT to SAT I Conversion

ACT Score	Equivalent SAT I Score	ACT Score	Equivalent SAT I Score	ACT Score	Equivalent SAT I Score	ACT Score	Equivalent SAT I Score
36	1600	29	1300	22	1030	16	780
35	1580	28	1260	21	990	15	740
34	1520	27	1220	20	950	14	680
33	1470	26	1180	19	910	13	620
32	1420	25	1140	18	870	12	560
31	1380	24	1110	17	830	11	500
30	1340	23	1070				

3.   **Examination Requirement**

Students must submit scores form the SAT I or ACT, <u>and</u> three scores from the SAT II, as described below:

Either the Scholastic Assessment Test I: Reasoning Test (SAT I) or the ACT. The verbal and mathematics scores on the SAT I must be from the same sitting. The ACT composite score must be submitted.

Three Scholastic Assessment Test II: Subject Tests (SAT II), including Writing, Mathematics Level 1 or Level 2, and one test in one of the following areas: English literature, foreign language, science or social studies.

Eligibility by Examination Alone

Students who do not meet the requirements for Eligibility in the Statewide Context may be able to qualify for admission to the University by examination alone. To satisfy the minimum requirements for Eligibility by

Examination Alone, the student must achieve a composite score of 31 or higher on the ACT or a total score on the SAT I of at least 1400. In addition, he must earn a total score of 1760 or higher on the three SAT II: Subject Tests with a minimum score of 530 on each test.

Students cannot qualify for admission by examination alone if they have completed 12 or more units of transferable coursework at another college or university following high school graduation, or if they have taken transferable college courses in any subject covered by the SAT II: Subject Tests.

Eligibility by Exception

Students who do not meet the Eligibility by Examination Alone criteria in order to become statewide eligible (to all UC campuses), may still apply to an University of California campus and hope to be admitted by exception. To do so, students should do everything possible to demonstrate subject matter competency in each of the a-g subject areas by taking SAT II subject area exams and/or community college courses. They should also take the SAT I or ACT exam. In their applications, students should demonstrate other skills and strengths, whether in leadership, community service, athletics, the arts, or other areas.

The UC has made it clear that their intent is to allow talented students to be admitted to the UC even though the students did not attend a WASC accredited high school. Here, in part, is the UC policy on eligibility by exception:

> *It is the policy of the University of California that:*
> *(1) It is essential that its campuses have the flexibility to admit a small proportion of students by exception to the eligibility requirements.*
> *(2) Students admitted by exception to the eligibility requirements must demonstrate a reasonable potential for success at the University.*
> *(3) The proportion of students admitted by exception shall be up to 6 percent of newly enrolled freshmen and up to 6 percent of newly enrolled advanced standing students at each campus.*
> *(4) Within the 6 percent designations, up to 4 percent may be drawn from disadvantaged students and up to 2 percent from other students.*
> *(5) Disadvantaged students shall be defined as students from low socio-economic backgrounds or students having experienced limited educational opportunities.*
> (Policy on Undergraduate Admissions by Exception. Office of the President, July 1996.)

Admission as a Transfer Student

Top priority for UC admission is given to eligible California community college junior level transfer applicants. Such applicants must demonstrate that they are well prepared for their majors and they must have earned 60 semester units or 90 quarter units of transferable work.

If a student is not accepted to the University of California as a freshman, a common option is to enroll in the community college for the first two years of college work. When he then applies as a transfer student to the UC, his high school work is immaterial. What the university will want to see is his community college transcript.

University of California Independent Study

Although the University of California does not grant degrees based solely on off-campus work, it does offer a good selection of college and continuing education courses by correspondence. Over 200 courses are offered by the

Extension Department of Independent Study, with subjects in business, art, foreign languages, English, math and science.

Independent Study instructors are faculty members of UC or state colleges, or are professionals in technical or business fields. Enrollment is always open and students may take up to one year to complete a course, progressing at their own pace and studying at times and places most convenient to them. Required and recommended textbooks for all courses are kept in stock and may be ordered at the time of enrollment.

For a free catalog write to:
Independent Study UC Extension
Dept. AN
2223 Fulton Street
Berkeley, CA, 94720

❖ Index of California Education Code Excerpts

The California Education Code should be available in the reference section at your local public library.

❖ Index